ANCIENT MEXICAN HISTORY

OLMEC, MAYA, TEOTIHUACAN, ZAPOTEC, TOLTEC, & AZTEC CIVILIZATIONS

6 BOOKS IN 1

BOOK 1
THE ENIGMA OF THE OLMEC: MEXICO'S ANCIENT FOUNDERS (1500 BCE - 400 BCE)

BOOK 2
MAYA MASTERY: UNVEILING THE SECRETS OF A FLOURISHING CIVILIZATION (2000 BCE - 1500 CE)

BOOK 3
TEOTIHUACAN: CITY OF THE GODS (100 BCE - 750 CE)

BOOK 4
ZAPOTEC RESILIENCE: A JOURNEY THROUGH ANCIENT OAXACA (500 BCE - 800 CE)

BOOK 5
TOLTEC WARRIORS: RISE AND FALL OF AN EMPIRE (900 CE - 1200 CE)

BOOK 6
AZTEC ASCENDANCY: FROM HUMBLE BEGINNINGS TO IMPERIAL MIGHT (1325 CE - 1521 CE)

BY A.J. KINGSTON

Published by A. J. Kingston
Library of Congress Cataloging-in-Publication Data
ISBN 978-1-83938-501-8
Cover design by Rizzo

Disclaimer

The contents of this book are based on extensive research and the best available historical sources. However, the author and publisher make no claims, promises, or guarantees about the accuracy, completeness, or adequacy of the information contained herein. The information in this book is provided on an "as is" basis, and the author and publisher disclaim any and all liability for any errors, omissions, or inaccuracies in the information or for any actions taken in reliance on such information.

The opinions and views expressed in this book are those of the author and do not necessarily reflect the official policy or position of any organization or individual mentioned in this book. Any reference to specific people, places, or events is intended only to provide historical context and is not intended to defame or malign any group, individual, or entity.

The information in this book is intended for educational and entertainment purposes only. It is not intended to be a substitute for professional advice or judgment. Readers are encouraged to conduct their own research and to seek professional advice where appropriate.

Every effort has been made to obtain necessary permissions and acknowledgments for all images and other copyrighted material used in this book. Any errors or omissions in this regard are unintentional, and the author and publisher will correct them in future editions.

Join Our Productivity Group and Access your Bonus

If you're passionate about history books and want to connect with others who share your love of the subject, joining our Facebook group (search for "History Books by A.J.Kingston") can be a great way to do so. By joining a group dedicated to history books, you'll have the opportunity to connect with like-minded individuals, share your thoughts and ideas, and even discover new books that you might not have come across otherwise. You can also access your FREE BONUS once you joined our Facebook group called "History Books by A.J.Kingston".

One of the biggest advantages of joining our Facebook group is the sense of community it provides. You'll be able to interact with other history book enthusiasts, ask questions, and share your own knowledge and expertise. This can be especially valuable if you're a student or someone who is just starting to explore the world of history books.

If you love audiobooks, then joining our YouTube channel that offers free audiobooks on a weekly basis can be a great way to stay entertained and engaged. By subscribing to our channel, you'll have access to a range of audiobooks across different genres, all for free. Not only this is a great opportunity to enjoy some new audiobooks, but it's also a chance to discover new authors and titles that you might not have come across otherwise.

Lastly, don't forget to follow us on Facebook and YouTube by searching for A.J. Kingston.

TABLE OF CONTENTS – BOOK 1 - THE ENIGMA OF THE OLMEC: MEXICO'S ANCIENT FOUNDERS (1500 BCE - 400 BCE)

TABLE OF CONTENTS – BOOK 2 - MAYA MASTERY: UNVEILING THE SECRETS OF A FLOURISHING CIVILIZATION (2000 BCE - 1500 CE)

TABLE OF CONTENTS – BOOK 3 - TEOTIHUACAN: CITY OF THE GODS (100 BCE - 750 CE)

TABLE OF CONTENTS – BOOK 4 - ZAPOTEC RESILIENCE: A JOURNEY THROUGH ANCIENT OAXACA (500 BCE - 800 CE)

TABLE OF CONTENTS – BOOK 5 - TOLTEC WARRIORS: RISE AND FALL OF AN EMPIRE (900 CE - 1200 CE)

TABLE OF CONTENTS – BOOK 6 - AZTEC ASCENDANCY: FROM HUMBLE BEGINNINGS TO IMPERIAL MIGHT (1325 CE - 1521 CE)

Introduction

In the heartland of the Americas lies a tapestry of cultures, civilizations, and mysteries that have captivated the imagination of explorers, scholars, and adventurers for centuries. From the enigmatic Olmec to the formidable Aztec, the ancient history of Mexico is a testament to the resilience, creativity, and enduring legacy of its peoples. In this comprehensive book bundle, "Ancient Mexican History: Olmec, Maya, Teotihuacan, Zapotec, Toltec, & Aztec Civilizations," we embark on a remarkable journey through time and across the diverse landscapes of Mexico to uncover the secrets of these fascinating civilizations.

"Book 1 - The Enigma of the Olmec" transports us to the dawn of Mesoamerican history, where the Olmec laid the foundations for the great civilizations that would follow. This volume explores the mysteries surrounding Mexico's ancient founders, from their colossal stone heads to their profound cultural contributions.

In "Book 2 - Maya Mastery," we delve into the thriving Maya civilization that spanned over two millennia. From their celestial observations to the intricate hieroglyphics that adorn their temples, we unveil the secrets of a civilization known for its advanced city-states and rich cultural heritage.

"Book 3 - Teotihuacan: City of the Gods" immerses us in the awe-inspiring world of Teotihuacan, a metropolis of pyramids, murals, and mysteries. We uncover the art, culture, and enigmatic decline of this ancient city that once ruled the Valley of Mexico.

"Book 4 - Zapotec Resilience" takes us on a journey through the rugged landscapes of ancient Oaxaca. Here, we explore the innovative Zapotec civilization, their writing system, and the enduring impact of their culture on the region.

In "Book 5 - Toltec Warriors," we witness the rise and fall of an empire renowned for its military might and religious significance. We delve into the world of Quetzalcoatl, the feathered serpent deity, and the Toltec's profound influence on Mesoamerican history.

Finally, "Book 6 - Aztec Ascendancy" leads us through the epic story of the Aztec Empire, from its humble beginnings on the island of Tenochtitlan to its imperial might that dominated Central Mexico. We witness the conquests of Montezuma and the arrival of the Spanish, which marked a turning point in the region's history.

Throughout this captivating journey, we explore the intricate artistry, architectural wonders, and cultural exchanges that defined these civilizations. We delve into their societies, religious practices, and daily lives, gaining a deep appreciation for the rich tapestry of Mesoamerican history.

Join us as we embark on this extraordinary voyage through time, where ancient pyramids pierce the skies, intricate glyphs tell tales of gods and heroes, and the echoes of these remarkable civilizations continue to resonate in the vibrant cultures of modern Mexico. "Ancient Mexican History" is a celebration of the enduring power of history to inform, inspire, and connect us to the remarkable legacies of the past.

BOOK 1
THE ENIGMA OF THE OLMEC
MEXICO'S ANCIENT FOUNDERS
(1500 BCE - 400 BCE)

BY A.J. KINGSTON

Chapter 1: Mysteries of Mesoamerica

Ancient Mesoamerican cultures are a diverse and fascinating tapestry of civilizations that flourished in the region now known as Mexico and parts of Central America. These cultures developed over thousands of years, leaving behind a rich legacy of art, architecture, language, and complex social structures. They include the Olmec, Maya, Teotihuacan, Zapotec, Toltec, and Aztec civilizations, among others.

The Olmec civilization, one of the earliest Mesoamerican cultures, emerged around 1500 BCE in the tropical lowlands of what is now Mexico's Gulf Coast. They are often considered the "Mother Culture" of Mesoamerica due to their influence on later civilizations. The Olmec are best known for their colossal stone heads, massive stone sculptures that have puzzled researchers for decades. These enigmatic sculptures depict distinctive facial features and may represent important leaders or deities in Olmec society.

Moving forward in time, the Maya civilization arose around 2000 BCE and reached its peak during the Classic period (approximately 250 CE to 900 CE). The Maya are renowned for their advanced writing system, known as hieroglyphs, which allowed them to record their history and religious beliefs on intricate stelae and codices. Additionally, the Maya made significant contributions in mathematics, developing the concept of zero independently from other ancient civilizations.

Teotihuacan, situated near modern-day Mexico City, was a major urban center that thrived between 100 BCE and 750 CE. It is known for its iconic pyramids, the Pyramid of the Sun and the Pyramid of the Moon. Teotihuacan's influence extended far beyond its borders, with evidence of trade networks reaching into Central America. Despite its significance, the identity of the people who built Teotihuacan remains a mystery.

The Zapotec civilization, centered in the Oaxaca Valley, displayed remarkable artistic achievements and an early writing system known as the Zapotec script. Their art and architecture, including intricate pottery and impressive stone carvings, reflect the Zapotecs' cultural sophistication. The Zapotec script is one of the earliest writing systems in Mesoamerica and has contributed to our understanding of ancient Zapotec culture.

The Toltec civilization, located in Tula, was known for its warrior culture and military prowess. They are often associated with the god Quetzalcoatl and were believed to have influenced later civilizations like the Aztecs. The Toltecs built impressive pyramids and temples, demonstrating their architectural skills and religious practices.

The Aztecs, also known as the Mexica, established one of the most powerful empires in Mesoamerica in the 14th and 15th centuries. Their capital city, Tenochtitlan, was situated on an island in the middle of Lake Texcoco, where modern-day Mexico City stands. The Aztecs developed a complex social hierarchy, with a powerful ruler, Montezuma II, at the pinnacle. They practiced a polytheistic religion, featuring deities like Huitzilopochtli and Tlaloc, and conducted elaborate rituals, including human sacrifices.

The diversity of ancient Mesoamerican cultures is reflected not only in their architectural marvels and artistic achievements but also in their agricultural practices, trade networks, and intricate social systems. These civilizations shared common elements such as religious beliefs, a reverence for nature, and a complex calendar system that tracked celestial events, agricultural cycles, and religious ceremonies.

Despite their similarities, each Mesoamerican culture had its own unique characteristics and contributions to the broader tapestry of human history. Their legacies continue to captivate researchers, archaeologists, and enthusiasts, shedding light on the complexity and richness of ancient Mesoamerican civilizations that once thrived in the heart of the Americas.

Archaeological discoveries are windows into the past, offering profound insights into the lives, cultures, and histories of ancient civilizations. These remarkable findings, often unearthed through painstaking excavation and research, provide tangible evidence of human existence and achievements across various epochs and regions.

One of the most iconic archaeological discoveries in history is the tomb of Tutankhamun, an Egyptian pharaoh of the 18th dynasty. British archaeologist Howard Carter's 1922 discovery of this intact tomb in the Valley of the Kings revealed a treasure trove of artifacts, including the famous golden death mask. This find offered a rare glimpse into the opulence and symbolism of ancient Egyptian burial practices.

In 1947, a shepherd stumbled upon the Dead Sea Scrolls in the Qumran Caves near the Dead Sea in Israel. These well-preserved ancient Jewish manuscripts, dating from the 3rd century BCE to the 1st century CE, contain biblical texts, religious writings, and historical documents. The Dead Sea Scrolls have significantly enriched our understanding of Judaism and early Christianity.

The city of Pompeii, buried under volcanic ash and pumice after the eruption of Mount Vesuvius in 79 CE, lay hidden for centuries until its rediscovery in the 18th century. Archaeological excavations at Pompeii have provided a remarkably preserved snapshot of Roman life in the 1st century CE, offering insights into architecture, art, and daily routines.

The Rosetta Stone, discovered by a French soldier in 1799 during Napoleon's campaign in Egypt, became a key to deciphering Egyptian hieroglyphs. This inscribed stone, which contains a decree issued by Ptolemy V in three scripts (hieroglyphic, Demotic, and Greek), enabled scholars like Jean-François Champollion to unlock the secrets of ancient Egyptian writing.

In the 20th century, the discovery of the Terracotta Army in China's Shaanxi province astounded the world. Thousands of life-sized clay soldiers, horses, and chariots were found in the mausoleum of China's first emperor, Qin Shi Huang. This incredible archaeological find, dating back to the 3rd century BCE, showcases the precision and craftsmanship of ancient Chinese artisans.

More recently, in 1974, paleoanthropologist Donald Johanson unearthed the fossilized remains of "Lucy," an early hominid from over 3 million years ago in the Afar Triangle of Ethiopia. This discovery shed light on human evolution, providing valuable information about our distant ancestors.

Archaeological discoveries extend beyond well-known sites and famous artifacts. They encompass countless excavations worldwide, each contributing to our understanding of human history, culture, and the environment. These findings range from ancient settlements and tools to pottery, coins, and human remains, each offering a piece of the puzzle that is our collective past.

Furthermore, advancements in technology, such as ground-penetrating radar, remote sensing, and 3D scanning, have revolutionized archaeological research. These tools help archaeologists uncover buried structures, hidden artifacts, and ancient landscapes with greater accuracy and efficiency.

The importance of archaeological discoveries transcends academic research; it enriches our cultural heritage and fosters a deeper appreciation of the diversity of human experiences throughout history. Archaeology continues to unveil the mysteries of the past, ensuring that the stories of ancient civilizations are preserved and shared with future generations.

"Unraveling the Past" is a phrase that beautifully encapsulates the essence of archaeology and historical research. It signifies the relentless pursuit of understanding the mysteries and complexities of history by peeling back the layers of time, one discovery at a time.

Archaeologists, historians, and researchers are the modern-day detectives of the past, meticulously sifting through the remnants of ancient civilizations to reconstruct their stories. This process involves excavating archaeological sites, deciphering ancient texts and scripts, analyzing artifacts, and piecing together historical narratives.

Through "Unraveling the Past," we gain access to the lives, cultures, and events of bygone eras. We learn about the achievements and innovations of ancient societies, their customs and traditions, and the challenges they faced. It allows us to connect with our ancestors and appreciate the human journey across time and geography.

"Unraveling the Past" also underscores the ongoing nature of historical exploration. As new technologies, methods, and perspectives emerge, our understanding of history deepens and evolves. The past is not a static entity; it is a dynamic field of inquiry that continually reveals fresh insights and perspectives.

Moreover, "Unraveling the Past" reminds us of the intrinsic value of preserving and protecting our archaeological and historical heritage. The artifacts, monuments, and records left behind by past generations are fragile and finite. They hold the key to understanding the human experience, and it is our responsibility to safeguard these treasures for future generations of scholars, researchers, and enthusiasts.

In essence, "Unraveling the Past" encapsulates the spirit of curiosity, discovery, and reverence for history. It is a journey of intellectual and emotional connection with the people and cultures that preceded us, reminding us that the tapestry of human history is woven from countless threads of exploration and understanding.

Chapter 2: The Birth of the Olmec Civilization

Early Olmec settlements are crucial pieces of the puzzle when it comes to understanding the origins and development of the Olmec civilization, often referred to as the "Mother Culture" of Mesoamerica. These settlements, dating back to around 1500 BCE, offer important insights into the early stages of this influential ancient society.

The Olmec civilization is primarily associated with the tropical lowlands of what is now the Mexican states of Veracruz and Tabasco, along the Gulf of Mexico. Early Olmec settlements were situated in this region and played a pivotal role in shaping the cultural and social foundations of the Olmec civilization.

One of the key early Olmec sites is San Lorenzo Tenochtitlán, which was occupied from around 1500 BCE to 900 BCE. San Lorenzo is renowned for its colossal stone sculptures, including the famous "Colossal Heads." These massive stone heads, often weighing several tons, are believed to represent important individuals, possibly rulers or deities. The presence of such monumental sculpture at this early stage indicates the Olmec's advanced artistic and cultural achievements.

Another significant early Olmec site is La Venta, which thrived from approximately 900 BCE to 400 BCE. La Venta is noted for its impressive ceremonial complexes, including earthen pyramids and sunken plazas. The site also yielded artifacts such as stone altars, stelae, and pottery with intricate designs. These findings suggest that La Venta was a center of religious and ceremonial activities, reflecting the spiritual aspects of Olmec culture.

These early Olmec settlements were marked by their innovative land use and hydraulic engineering. The Olmec built extensive drainage systems and canals to manage the region's challenging tropical environment, allowing them to cultivate crops such as maize, beans, and squash. This agricultural expertise was a crucial factor in the Olmec's ability to sustain their society.

Furthermore, the presence of monumental architecture, complex social structures, and the establishment of trade networks with distant regions indicate that the early Olmec settlements were not isolated but engaged in interactions with neighboring cultures. These interactions likely contributed to the cultural exchange and influence that would become a hallmark of the Olmec civilization.

The emergence of these early Olmec settlements was a precursor to the development of more sophisticated Olmec city-states like La Venta and Tres Zapotes, which would come to define the Olmec civilization during its Classic period (approximately 1200 BCE to 400 BCE). As the Olmec civilization evolved, its cultural and artistic achievements continued to influence and inspire subsequent Mesoamerican societies, including the Maya and the Zapotec.

In summary, early Olmec settlements represent the foundation upon which one of the most influential ancient civilizations in Mesoamerica was built. They provide valuable insights into the Olmec's early cultural, artistic, and agricultural achievements and offer a glimpse into the complexities of ancient Mesoamerican societies.

The emergence of complex society is a significant milestone in human history, marked by the transition from small, simple communities to larger, more organized civilizations. This process represents a critical phase of human development characterized by several key factors and transformations.

Agricultural Revolution: The shift from nomadic, hunter-gatherer lifestyles to settled agriculture was a pivotal catalyst for complex society. The ability to cultivate crops and domesticate animals allowed for surplus food production, which, in turn, supported larger populations. This surplus created opportunities for specialized labor, enabling the development of diverse professions and social hierarchies.

Urbanization: The growth of complex societies often led to the establishment of cities. Urban centers served as hubs for economic, political, religious, and cultural activities. The concentration of people in cities fostered interactions, innovation, and the development of advanced infrastructure, such as roads, buildings, and sewage systems.

Social Stratification: Complex societies introduced social hierarchies, with distinct social classes or castes based on factors like wealth, occupation, and birthright. Elites emerged, wielding political and economic power, while the majority of the population engaged in various roles, from farming to craftsmanship.

Governance and Administration: The need to manage larger populations and resources necessitated the creation of governance systems and administrative structures. Complex societies often developed centralized forms of government, ranging from monarchies and city-states to empires. These systems were responsible for law enforcement, tax collection, and defense.

Specialization and Trade: The diversification of labor in complex societies led to the emergence of specialized trades and professions. Craftsmen, merchants, priests, and bureaucrats played essential roles in the economic and cultural life of these civilizations. The exchange of goods and services through trade networks connected regions and facilitated cultural exchange.

Written Language: Many complex societies developed written languages to record information, laws, religious texts, and historical accounts. Writing systems allowed for the codification of knowledge, the spread of information, and the preservation of cultural heritage. Written records contributed to the continuity of complex societies over time.

Religious and Cultural Expression: Complex societies often featured complex belief systems, including organized religions and mythologies. Temples, monuments, and art served as expressions of cultural identity and spirituality. These societies developed sophisticated art forms, architecture, and rituals that reflected their values and beliefs.

Technological Advancements: The advancement of technology was a hallmark of complex societies. Innovations in agriculture, metallurgy, construction, and transportation improved living conditions, increased productivity, and enhanced the overall quality of life.

Examples of complex societies include the ancient civilizations of Mesopotamia, Egypt, the Indus Valley, China, Greece, and Rome. Each of these civilizations exhibited the traits mentioned above and left a lasting legacy in terms of governance, culture, and technology.

The emergence of complex society marked a profound shift in human history, enabling the development of advanced cultures and civilizations that have shaped the world we live in today. It represents a testament to human adaptability, ingenuity, and the ability to create complex, interconnected societies from humble beginnings.

Cultural foundations form the bedrock upon which the identity, values, and traditions of a society are built. These foundations encompass a wide range of elements that shape the cultural fabric of a community, nation, or civilization. They are vital to understanding the beliefs, practices, and social norms of a particular group of people.

Language: Language is a fundamental component of cultural identity. It serves as a means of communication, preserving oral traditions, and transmitting knowledge from one generation to the next. The structure and vocabulary of a language often reflect the worldview, social structure, and historical experiences of a culture.

Religion and Belief Systems: Religion plays a significant role in cultural foundations. It encompasses spiritual beliefs, rituals, and moral values that guide the lives of individuals within a society. Religious practices can shape everything from art and architecture to social customs and laws.

Mythology and Folklore: Mythology and folklore are rich sources of cultural identity and storytelling. They often contain narratives about the creation of the world, heroic figures, and moral lessons. These stories help define a culture's collective memory and provide a sense of continuity.

Cultural Traditions: Cultural traditions encompass a wide array of customs, rituals, and practices that are passed down through generations. These may include ceremonies, festivals, holidays, and rites of passage. These traditions are a source of cultural cohesion and identity.

Arts and Expressive Culture: The arts, including visual arts, music, dance, literature, and theater, are essential aspects of cultural expression. They serve as vehicles for creativity, emotional expression, and storytelling. Artistic forms often reflect cultural values, aesthetics, and historical themes.

Social Norms and Etiquette: Cultural foundations include the unwritten rules and social norms that guide behavior within a society. These norms govern interactions, relationships, and expectations of individuals. They often encompass concepts of politeness, respect, and propriety.

Cuisine and Food Culture: Food is a central element of culture, reflecting local agriculture, climate, and historical influences. Traditional dishes, cooking methods, and culinary customs are integral to cultural identity. Sharing meals is often a way of bringing people together.

Family Structure and Kinship: The organization of families and kinship systems varies widely among cultures. Understanding these structures is essential for comprehending the roles, responsibilities, and relationships of individuals within a society.

Clothing and Dress Codes: Clothing and attire often have cultural significance. Traditional garments, styles, and dress codes can convey information about social status, gender roles, and regional affiliations.

Education and Knowledge Transmission: The methods and systems of education are integral to cultural foundations. These systems determine how knowledge is acquired and passed down. Education often reflects a culture's values, priorities, and approach to learning.

Historical Events and Collective Memory: Historical events and collective memory contribute to a culture's identity. The way a society remembers and commemorates its past, including triumphs and traumas, influences its worldview and sense of self.

Cultural foundations are dynamic and can evolve over time due to factors such as globalization, migration, and technological advancements. They are not static but adapt to changing circumstances while retaining core elements of identity and heritage. Understanding these foundations is essential for appreciating the diversity of human cultures and fostering cross-cultural understanding.

Chapter 3: The Colossal Heads of La Venta

Monumental sculptures represent one of the most captivating and enduring forms of artistic expression throughout human history. These colossal creations, often crafted from stone, bronze, or other durable materials, have left an indelible mark on our cultural landscape. They stand as powerful symbols of human creativity, vision, and the enduring quest to capture the essence of our existence in tangible form.

One of the earliest examples of monumental sculptures can be traced back to ancient civilizations like the Egyptians, who erected imposing statues of their pharaohs and deities. The Great Sphinx of Giza, a colossal limestone statue with the body of a lion and the head of a pharaoh, is an iconic representation of Egyptian art and spirituality. Standing at over 20 meters in height, it guards the Giza Plateau and serves as a testament to the architectural and artistic achievements of the ancient Egyptians.

In the realm of ancient Greece, monumental sculptures achieved unparalleled heights of realism and aesthetic excellence. The Parthenon Marbles, originally part of the Parthenon temple in Athens, exemplify the mastery of Greek sculptors. These exquisite works of art depict gods, heroes, and mythological figures with unparalleled grace and precision. The colossal statue of Zeus at Olympia, created by the sculptor Phidias, was another Greek masterpiece, standing around 13 meters tall and crafted from ivory and gold.

Moving across the globe to the ancient Americas, the Olmec civilization left an enduring legacy with their colossal stone heads. These massive stone sculptures, with distinctive facial features and helmets, have puzzled researchers for centuries. They are believed to represent important individuals or deities and stand as enigmatic symbols of Olmec culture's artistic prowess and cultural significance.

In the heart of Rome, the equestrian statue of Marcus Aurelius captures the power and grandeur of the Roman Empire. This bronze statue, created in the 2nd century CE, portrays the emperor astride a horse in a dynamic and lifelike pose. It serves as a reminder of the strength and authority of Roman rulers during that era.

The colossal Moai statues of Easter Island, carved from compressed volcanic ash, are among the most iconic monumental sculptures in the world. These towering figures, some reaching over 30 feet in height and weighing up to 80 tons, have long fascinated explorers and scholars. They were created by the indigenous Rapa Nui people and remain a testament to their extraordinary craftsmanship and cultural heritage.

In more recent history, the Statue of Liberty stands as a symbol of freedom and democracy in the United States. Designed by Frédéric Auguste Bartholdi and dedicated in 1886, this colossal copper statue represents Libertas, the Roman goddess of freedom. With a height of 151 feet, including its pedestal, it welcomes immigrants to the shores of the United States and has become an enduring emblem of hope and liberty.

Monumental sculptures have also been used to convey political messages and ideologies. The colossal statues of Lenin and Stalin, erected during the Soviet era in various locations across the former USSR, served as propagandistic symbols of communist power and ideology. While some of these statues have been removed or relocated, they remain a testament to the political and cultural impact of monumental sculpture.

The 20th century witnessed the emergence of contemporary monumental sculptures that pushed the boundaries of artistic expression. Alexander Calder's "Flamingo" in Chicago and Richard Serra's "Tilted Arc" in New York City challenged conventional notions of form and space. These sculptures invited viewers to engage with their urban environments in new and thought-provoking ways.

Furthermore, monumental sculptures continue to evolve and adapt to the changing artistic landscape. Contemporary artists like Anish Kapoor, Jeff Koons, and Ai Weiwei have created awe-inspiring works that captivate audiences and challenge our perceptions of scale, materiality, and meaning. These modern sculptures often incorporate cutting-edge technologies and unconventional materials to push the boundaries of artistic expression.

In addition to their artistic and cultural significance, monumental sculptures often serve as landmarks and points of reference within cities and landscapes. They contribute to the identity of a place, drawing tourists and locals alike to appreciate their beauty and the stories they tell. These sculptures can serve as focal points for public gatherings, celebrations, and protests, making them integral to the social fabric of communities.

The creation of monumental sculptures is a complex and labor-intensive process that requires not only artistic talent but also engineering expertise. Sculptors must consider the durability of materials, structural integrity, and environmental factors to ensure the longevity of their works. Additionally, the transportation and installation of these colossal creations can be logistical feats in their own right.

In summary, monumental sculptures represent an enduring and captivating form of artistic expression that spans cultures, centuries, and continents. These colossal creations serve as powerful symbols of human creativity, cultural identity, and the enduring quest to capture the essence of our existence in tangible form. From the majestic Sphinx of Giza to the contemporary masterpieces of today, monumental sculptures continue to captivate and inspire audiences around the world, reminding us of the boundless potential of human imagination and craftsmanship.

The iconic stone heads of the Olmec civilization, ancient inhabitants of what is now Mexico's Gulf Coast, stand as enigmatic and awe-inspiring monuments that have fascinated researchers and visitors alike for generations. These colossal stone sculptures, created over 3,000 years ago, are among the earliest known examples of monumental art in the Americas and are recognized as some of the most distinctive and mysterious relics of Mesoamerican culture.

Carved from large basalt boulders, these stone heads are massive in scale, with some towering over nine feet in height and weighing up to 40 tons. Their imposing size and intricate details, including unique facial features, headdresses, and elaborate ear ornaments, have left an indelible mark on the archaeological and artistic landscape of the region.

The origins of these iconic stone heads remain shrouded in mystery, with numerous questions surrounding their purpose, symbolism, and the identity of the individuals they represent. Scholars believe that they may depict rulers, deities, or other significant figures in Olmec society, but the exact identities and meanings remain subjects of debate and speculation.

The stone heads are often referred to as the "Olmec Colossal Heads" due to their sheer size and the civilization that created them. The Olmec civilization, often considered the "Mother Culture" of Mesoamerica, thrived between 1400 BCE and 400 BCE in the tropical lowlands of present-day Mexico's Veracruz and Tabasco states. The heads were carved during the Middle Formative period of Olmec civilization, which is roughly dated from 900 BCE to 400 BCE.

One of the most intriguing aspects of the stone heads is the meticulous craftsmanship displayed in their creation. The Olmec artisans demonstrated exceptional skill in carving these massive stone sculptures with primitive tools made from hard materials like jade and basalt. Their ability to transform colossal boulders into detailed human faces reflects their artistic prowess and dedication.

The facial features of the stone heads are distinct and individualized, suggesting that they may represent specific individuals rather than generic portraits. Some of the stone heads exhibit features such as prominent lips, broad noses, and distinctive facial expressions, further emphasizing the idea that they may depict actual rulers or important leaders from Olmec society.

The stone heads also feature elaborate headdresses and headgear, which are thought to be significant symbols of authority and power. These headdresses often include intricate designs, such as feathers and other symbolic elements, which may provide clues about the social or religious significance of the individuals portrayed.

The Olmec stone heads are a testament to the cultural and artistic achievements of this ancient civilization. They reflect not only the skill and creativity of Olmec artisans but also the societal structures and values of the time. While the true purpose and meaning of these sculptures remain enigmatic, they are believed to have played a role in religious rituals, civic ceremonies, or as markers of important sites.

Furthermore, the transportation and placement of these colossal stone heads have been subjects of intrigue and debate. The boulders from which they were carved are not native to the regions where they were found, raising questions about how the Olmec transported such massive stones over considerable distances and then erected them with precision.

The discovery of the stone heads in the mid-20th century marked a significant breakthrough in the study of Olmec civilization and its artistic legacy. Archaeologists, anthropologists, and historians have tirelessly worked to uncover the secrets of these iconic sculptures, shedding light on the Olmec's contributions to Mesoamerican culture.

Beyond their archaeological significance, the Olmec stone heads have also become symbols of cultural pride and identity for modern-day Mexicans and people of Mesoamerican heritage. They are emblematic of the rich and diverse cultural tapestry of the region and serve as a reminder of the enduring legacy of the Olmec civilization.

Today, many of these iconic stone heads are on display in museums and archaeological sites throughout Mexico and the world. These sculptures continue to captivate the imaginations of visitors, offering a glimpse into the artistic achievements and cultural complexity of the Olmec civilization.

In summary, the iconic stone heads of the Olmec civilization represent a remarkable chapter in the history of Mesoamerican art and culture. These colossal sculptures, carved with precision and skill, remain a source of fascination and wonder, inspiring both scholarly inquiry and a sense of cultural identity among modern-day audiences. While many questions surrounding their origins and meanings persist, their enduring presence serves as a testament to the enduring legacy of the Olmec civilization and its contributions to the cultural heritage of the Americas.

Artistic expression is a fundamental facet of human creativity, allowing individuals and communities to convey emotions, ideas, and experiences through a wide array of visual, auditory, and performance-based mediums. It serves as a powerful means of communication and a reflection of cultural, social, and personal perspectives.

Artistic expression is a universal phenomenon that spans across time and geography, encompassing various forms and styles that have evolved and diversified throughout history. From prehistoric cave paintings to contemporary digital art, the human impulse to create and communicate through art remains a driving force of cultural and intellectual exploration.

Visual art, including painting, sculpture, drawing, and photography, provides a canvas for artists to translate their thoughts and feelings into tangible forms. Throughout history, visual art has been a vehicle for conveying the human experience, often capturing moments of joy, sorrow, beauty, and introspection. The mastery of techniques, such as perspective, color theory, and composition, has allowed artists to explore and innovate in ways that challenge perceptions and provoke thought.

Sculpture, both traditional and contemporary, adds a three-dimensional dimension to artistic expression. Sculptors manipulate materials like stone, wood, metal, and clay to create tangible representations of their visions. The tactile nature of sculpture allows viewers to interact with art on a physical level, often inviting them to touch, feel, and experience the artwork in a deeply sensory way.

Drawing, with its simplicity and immediacy, has served as a fundamental form of artistic expression for centuries. From the exquisite detail of a Renaissance sketch to the bold lines of a contemporary comic book, drawing allows artists to capture moments of inspiration, observation, and imagination with relative ease. Sketches and illustrations often serve as the initial stages of a more extensive artistic process, providing the foundation for more elaborate works.

Photography, a relatively recent addition to the artistic repertoire, revolutionized the way we perceive and record the world. Through the lens of a camera, photographers freeze moments in time, preserving fleeting emotions, landscapes, and events. Photography is a powerful medium for documenting reality and telling stories, whether through photojournalism, portraiture, or fine art photography.

Moving beyond the visual arts, music is a profound form of artistic expression that transcends language barriers and speaks directly to the human soul. Musicians harness the power of sound, rhythm, melody, and harmony to convey emotions, provoke thought, and inspire action. Music spans a vast spectrum of genres and styles, each with its own unique cultural and emotional resonance.

Classical music, with its intricate compositions and orchestral arrangements, has produced timeless masterpieces that continue to captivate audiences worldwide. The symphonies of Mozart, the concertos of Beethoven, and the operas of Verdi are just a few examples of how classical music has left an indelible mark on the world of artistic expression.

Popular music, from rock 'n' roll to hip-hop, reflects the evolving tastes and cultural shifts of society. Musicians like Elvis Presley, The Beatles, Bob Dylan, and Beyoncé have not only shaped the musical landscape but have also influenced social and political movements through their lyrics and performances. The power of popular music lies in its ability to connect with diverse audiences on a personal and emotional level.

Dance is another dynamic form of artistic expression that marries movement, rhythm, and physicality. Dancers use their bodies as instruments to convey stories, emotions, and ideas. From classical ballet to contemporary dance forms like hip-hop and contemporary, dance transcends boundaries and engages the senses in a visceral way. It is a language of the body, capable of communicating the inexpressible.

Literature, encompassing novels, poetry, essays, and plays, invites readers to explore the depths of human thought and imagination. Authors craft words and narratives to weave stories that resonate with readers on intellectual and emotional levels. Literary works have the power to provoke introspection, empathy, and social change, making them a cornerstone of artistic expression.

Novels, with their immersive narratives and complex characters, allow readers to step into different worlds and perspectives. Authors like Leo Tolstoy, Jane Austen, Gabriel García Márquez, and Toni Morrison have crafted literary masterpieces that continue to shape our understanding of human nature and society.

Poetry distills language to its most essential and evocative form, using rhythm, rhyme, and metaphor to convey complex emotions and ideas. Poets like William Shakespeare, Emily Dickinson, Langston Hughes, and Maya Angelou have crafted verses that resonate with readers across generations.

Essays and non-fiction works provide a platform for critical thinking and discourse. Essayists like Ralph Waldo Emerson, Virginia Woolf, James Baldwin, and Susan Sontag have explored a wide range of topics, from philosophy and politics to personal reflections on the human condition.

Plays, as a form of dramatic literature, bring stories to life on the stage. Playwrights like William Shakespeare, Anton Chekhov, Tennessee Williams, and August Wilson have created enduring works that challenge, entertain, and provoke thought through live performances.

Performance art pushes the boundaries of traditional artistic expression by blurring the lines between visual art, theater, and physicality. Performance artists use their bodies and actions to convey concepts and emotions, often challenging societal norms and conventions.

Artistic expression is not confined to traditional mediums but extends into digital and multimedia forms. Digital art, video installations, virtual reality experiences, and interactive media are examples of how technology has expanded the possibilities of artistic creation and engagement.

Street art, characterized by its public and often unauthorized nature, brings art to the streets, allowing artists to engage with a broader audience. Graffiti, murals, and public installations serve as visual statements, expressions of dissent, or celebrations of local culture.

The power of artistic expression lies in its ability to inspire, challenge, and transform individuals and society. It provides a means of connecting with our shared humanity, transcending language and cultural barriers. Art allows us to explore the depths of our emotions, contemplate the mysteries of existence, and envision a world that is both familiar and extraordinary.

Artistic expression is not limited to professional artists but is a fundamental aspect of the human experience. Whether through a doodle in a notebook, a heartfelt song sung in the shower, or a spontaneous dance in the living room, we all have the capacity to create and connect through art. In this way, artistic expression is a universal language that speaks to the innate creativity and imagination that resides within each of us.

In summary, artistic expression encompasses a vast and diverse spectrum of forms and mediums, each offering a unique lens through which to explore the human experience. It is a reflection of our collective creativity, diversity, and capacity for innovation. Artistic expression transcends boundaries and enriches our lives by inviting us to engage with the world in new and meaningful ways. It serves as a testament to the enduring power of the human spirit to create, communicate, and inspire.

Chapter 4: Olmec Art and Symbolism

Visual language is a complex and multifaceted means of communication that transcends spoken or written words, allowing individuals and cultures to convey ideas, emotions, and narratives through images, symbols, and visual elements. It is a universal form of expression that speaks directly to our senses, emotions, and intellect, making it a powerful tool for both artistic creativity and effective communication.

From ancient cave paintings to modern graphic design, visual language has evolved and adapted to various contexts, technologies, and cultural influences. It encompasses a wide range of visual mediums, including painting, drawing, photography, film, graphic design, and more, each with its own unique vocabulary and grammar.

At its core, visual language relies on the principles of composition, color theory, perspective, and symbolism to convey meaning and evoke emotional responses. Artists, designers, and communicators use these principles to create visual narratives that engage, inform, and inspire.

One of the most iconic examples of visual language can be found in the ancient cave paintings of prehistoric humans. These intricate and often beautifully executed artworks, dating back thousands of years, depict scenes from daily life, hunting, and spiritual beliefs. While these paintings lack written language, they communicate a wealth of information about the cultures and societies of the past, providing insights into their beliefs, practices, and way of life.

In the realm of fine art, visual language serves as a means of self-expression and exploration of the human experience. Painters like Leonardo da Vinci, Vincent van Gogh, and Frida Kahlo used their canvases to convey complex emotions, ideas, and observations about the world around them. Their brushstrokes, use of color, and composition became a visual language that spoke directly to viewers, inviting them to interpret and connect with the art on a personal level.

Visual language also plays a pivotal role in shaping our perceptions of the world. Photography, for example, captures moments in time and provides a visual record of historical events, cultures, and individuals. Documentary photographers like Dorothea Lange, Ansel Adams, and James Nachtwey have used their cameras to tell powerful stories and advocate for social change, demonstrating the ability of visual language to inform and engage the public.

The language of cinema, a visual medium that combines moving images, sound, and narrative, has a profound impact on our culture and society. Filmmakers like Alfred Hitchcock, Akira Kurosawa, and Martin Scorsese have mastered the art of visual storytelling, using cinematography, editing, and mise-en-scène to immerse audiences in their narratives. Film's ability to evoke emotions, transport viewers to different worlds, and explore complex themes makes it a rich and dynamic form of visual language.

Graphic design is another form of visual language that plays a crucial role in contemporary communication. Graphic designers use elements like typography, color, imagery, and layout to convey messages, whether in advertising, branding, editorial design, or web design. The design choices they make have a significant impact on how information is perceived and understood, making visual language an essential tool for marketing, advocacy, and storytelling.

Symbols and icons are fundamental components of visual language, serving as concise and universally recognizable means of communication. From traffic signs to corporate logos, symbols convey information quickly and efficiently, transcending language barriers. The power of symbols lies in their ability to convey complex concepts and ideas with a single visual element.

Visual language is not confined to the realm of art and design; it also influences our daily lives in subtle and profound ways. The design of our environments, architecture, and urban planning all rely on visual language to create functional and aesthetically pleasing spaces. Whether it's the layout of a city street or the interior of a home, visual elements influence how we interact with and experience our surroundings.

In the digital age, the internet and social media have transformed the landscape of visual language. Images, videos, infographics, and memes have become dominant forms of online communication, shaping public discourse and culture. The rise of platforms like Instagram, YouTube, and TikTok underscores the importance of visual content in today's digital communication.

Visual language also plays a role in cultural identity and heritage. Traditional art forms, such as indigenous paintings, textiles, and sculptures, convey the histories, beliefs, and values of specific cultures. These visual expressions serve as a means of preserving and celebrating cultural traditions, fostering a sense of belonging and continuity among communities.

Moreover, visual language is a dynamic and evolving field that continues to adapt to technological advancements and cultural shifts. Virtual reality (VR), augmented reality (AR), and interactive media are expanding the possibilities of visual storytelling and communication, offering immersive and interactive experiences that engage multiple senses.

In summary, visual language is a rich and versatile mode of communication that encompasses a wide range of artistic and practical applications. It is a universal and timeless means of expression that speaks to our senses, emotions, and intellect. From ancient cave paintings to contemporary digital media, visual language has the power to inform, engage, and inspire, making it an integral part of human culture and communication. Whether as a tool for artistic expression, a medium for social change, or a means of conveying information, visual language continues to shape our understanding of the world and our place in it.

Spiritual significance is a deeply personal and cultural concept that encompasses the spiritual and religious meanings, beliefs, and practices that hold significance for individuals and communities. It plays a profound role in shaping human identity, providing a sense of purpose, and guiding ethical and moral frameworks. Spiritual significance is not limited to any particular religion or belief system; rather, it is a universal and multifaceted aspect of human existence that manifests in diverse ways across cultures and traditions.

At its core, spiritual significance is a reflection of the human desire to seek meaning and connection beyond the material and physical realms. It addresses questions about the purpose of life, the nature of existence, and the relationship between individuals, the cosmos, and the divine. For many, spirituality is an integral part of their identity and a source of guidance, comfort, and inspiration.

Religion is one of the most prominent expressions of spiritual significance, providing structured belief systems, rituals, and practices that guide the spiritual journey of adherents. Major world religions such as Christianity, Islam, Judaism, Hinduism, Buddhism, and Sikhism offer a framework for understanding the divine, moral values, and the afterlife. These religions have deep spiritual significance for billions of people around the world, shaping their worldviews, ethics, and daily lives.

In Christianity, for example, spiritual significance is grounded in the belief in Jesus Christ as the Savior and the teachings of the Bible. The Christian faith provides a sense of spiritual purpose, salvation, and the hope of eternal life. It also emphasizes the importance of love, compassion, and forgiveness as central values.

Islam centers on the spiritual significance of submission to the will of Allah (God) as revealed in the Quran. It offers a path to spiritual fulfillment through prayer, fasting during Ramadan, acts of charity (zakat), and the pilgrimage to Mecca (Hajj). These practices are deeply meaningful to Muslims, fostering a sense of devotion and closeness to the divine.

Hinduism, one of the world's oldest religions, encompasses a diverse array of beliefs, deities, and practices. Spiritual significance in Hinduism is found in concepts like dharma (duty), karma (the law of cause and effect), and moksha (liberation from the cycle of rebirth). Hindu rituals, temples, and festivals offer opportunities for spiritual growth and connection with the divine.

Buddhism, founded by Siddhartha Gautama (Buddha), focuses on the pursuit of enlightenment and the alleviation of suffering. Spiritual significance in Buddhism centers on the Four Noble

Truths, the Eightfold Path, and meditation practices. Buddhists seek inner peace, wisdom, and liberation from the cycle of suffering.

Sikhism, originating in the Punjab region of India, emphasizes the oneness of God (Waheguru) and the importance of selfless service and equality. Sikh spiritual significance is found in daily prayer, meditation on the Guru Granth Sahib (the holy scripture), and acts of seva (selfless service).

Indigenous spiritual traditions around the world offer unique perspectives on spiritual significance, often rooted in a deep connection to nature, ancestors, and the land. These traditions may include rituals, ceremonies, and storytelling that pass down cultural and spiritual wisdom from generation to generation.

For many people, spirituality extends beyond organized religion and is a deeply personal and introspective journey. It may involve practices such as meditation, mindfulness, yoga, and seeking a direct connection with the divine or the transcendent. Spirituality can provide a sense of inner peace, purpose, and personal growth, regardless of religious affiliation.

Spiritual significance also plays a role in ethical and moral frameworks. Many belief systems, religious or not, offer guidelines for ethical behavior and moral decision-making. These principles often reflect core values such as compassion, justice, honesty, and respect for others. Spiritual significance can guide individuals in making ethical choices and navigating the complexities of life.

Cultural traditions and rituals are integral to the expression of spiritual significance. These traditions may include ceremonies, festivals, and rites of passage that mark significant moments in an individual's or community's spiritual journey. For example, weddings, funerals, coming-of-age ceremonies, and harvest festivals are occasions that hold deep spiritual meaning and connect people to their cultural and religious heritage.

Art and creativity also play a role in expressing spiritual significance. Throughout history, art forms such as music, visual arts, dance, and literature have been used to convey spiritual and religious themes. Religious music, sacred art, dance rituals, and sacred texts are examples of how creative expression serves as a vehicle for spiritual exploration and communication with the divine.

The natural world often holds profound spiritual significance for many individuals and cultures. Nature-based spirituality, often referred to as animism or earth-centered spirituality, views the natural world as sacred and interconnected. Mountains, rivers, forests, and animals may be considered spiritual entities or symbols that inspire reverence and respect.

In summary, spiritual significance is a deeply ingrained and multifaceted aspect of the human experience that transcends cultural, religious, and individual boundaries. It addresses fundamental questions about the nature of existence, purpose, and the divine. Whether expressed through organized religion, personal spirituality, cultural traditions, or creative expression, spiritual significance provides a source of meaning, connection, and guidance for individuals and communities around the world. It serves as a testament to the enduring quest for spiritual fulfillment and understanding that is inherent to the human condition.

Chapter 5: Trade and Influence: Olmec's Reach Beyond

Olmec trade networks were a crucial aspect of the Olmec civilization, one of the earliest and most influential Mesoamerican cultures. These trade networks facilitated the exchange of goods, materials, and cultural influences among Olmec communities and with neighboring regions. While the Olmec civilization is often associated with the Gulf Coast of Mexico, their trade connections extended far beyond their heartland.

Regional Trade: Within the Olmec heartland, which encompassed present-day states of Veracruz and Tabasco, regional trade was significant. Olmec communities engaged in the exchange of resources such as jade, obsidian, and ceramics. These materials were used for crafting tools, jewelry, and pottery, and their distribution indicates the existence of specialized production centers.

Long-Distance Trade: The Olmecs were known to have engaged in long-distance trade with regions as distant as the Valley of Mexico and Oaxaca. This trade involved the movement of prized goods like greenstone, a type of jade, which was highly valued for its aesthetic and symbolic qualities. The presence of Olmec-style artifacts in these distant regions suggests that they played a key role in the broader Mesoamerican trade networks.

Maritime Trade: Given the Olmec heartland's location along the Gulf Coast, maritime trade was an essential component of their network. The use of river systems and coastal access facilitated the movement of goods both within the heartland and along the coast. Evidence of Olmec-style pottery and artifacts found in coastal regions attests to their involvement in maritime trade.

Cultural Exchange: Trade networks were not limited to the exchange of physical goods but also allowed for the flow of cultural influences. The Olmecs are credited with the spread of iconographic symbols and artistic styles that influenced subsequent Mesoamerican civilizations. The distinctive Olmec "colossal heads" have been found far from the heartland, suggesting the dissemination of their cultural and artistic achievements.

Religious and Ritual Exchange: Along with material goods and cultural symbols, Olmec trade networks likely facilitated the exchange of religious and ritual practices. The spread of religious iconography and practices, including the veneration of certain deities, may have contributed to the development of shared religious traditions in Mesoamerica.

Economic Significance: Olmec trade networks played a pivotal role in the economic life of their civilization. Specialized production of goods and the exchange of surplus resources helped sustain Olmec society and likely contributed to its prosperity. The ability to access valuable resources from distant regions enhanced the Olmec's economic strength.

Legacy: The Olmec trade networks left a lasting legacy in Mesoamerican history. They set the stage for the emergence of subsequent civilizations, such as the Maya and the Aztecs, who continued and expanded upon the trade traditions established by the Olmecs. The exchange of ideas, goods, and cultural elements laid the foundation for the rich tapestry of Mesoamerican civilizations that followed.

In summary, Olmec trade networks were a vital component of their civilization, enabling the movement of goods, ideas, and cultural influences across the ancient Mesoamerican landscape. These networks not only contributed to the economic prosperity of the Olmec society but also played a pivotal role in shaping the cultural and religious landscape of Mesoamerica, leaving a lasting impact on the civilizations that succeeded them.

Cultural diffusion is a process through which cultural traits, ideas, beliefs, practices, technologies, and customs spread from one culture or society to another. It is a fundamental aspect of human interaction and has been occurring for millennia, leading to the enrichment and diversification of cultures around the world. Cultural diffusion can take various forms and occurs through mechanisms such as trade, migration, conquest, and communication.

Trade and Economic Exchange: Trade has historically been one of the most significant drivers of cultural diffusion. When different cultures engage in trade, they exchange not only goods and resources but also cultural elements. For example, the Silk Road, a network of trade routes that connected East and West, facilitated the exchange of not only silk and spices but also ideas, art, and religious beliefs between Asia and Europe.

Migration and Diaspora: Human migration, whether voluntary or forced, has played a crucial role in cultural diffusion. When people move to new regions or countries, they bring their culture with them. Over time, this blending of cultures can lead to the emergence of hybrid or multicultural societies. For instance, the African diaspora resulted in the spread of African cultural elements, including music, cuisine, and religious practices, to the Americas.

Conquest and Imperialism: Conquests and imperial expansions throughout history have often led to the diffusion of the conqueror's culture to the conquered. The spread of Roman culture throughout Europe, the dissemination of Spanish culture in Latin America, and the British Empire's influence on its colonies are examples of how political and military power can facilitate cultural diffusion.

Communication and Media: Advances in communication technologies, such as the printing press, radio, television, and the internet, have greatly accelerated the process of cultural diffusion. These technologies enable the rapid dissemination of information, ideas, and cultural products worldwide. For instance, the global popularity of American movies, music, and fast food is a result of the widespread reach of mass media.

Religion and Missionary Activity: Religious beliefs and practices have often been diffused through missionary activities. Missionaries travel to new regions to spread their faith, leading to the adoption of new religious beliefs and practices. For example, the spread of Buddhism from India to East Asia was facilitated by the efforts of missionaries and scholars.

Colonization and Hybridization: Colonial encounters frequently resulted in the blending of cultures. Colonizers and indigenous populations exchanged not only goods but also ideas, languages, and social practices. This hybridization of cultures can lead to the emergence of unique cultural expressions and traditions.

Cultural Borrowing and Syncretism: Cultural diffusion often involves the borrowing and adaptation of elements from one culture into another. This process can result in the creation of new cultural expressions or syncretic beliefs. For example, the blending of indigenous traditions with Catholicism in many Latin American countries led to the development of unique religious practices and festivals.

Language and Linguistic Borrowing: Language is a significant aspect of culture, and linguistic diffusion occurs when languages influence each other. For instance, the English language has borrowed words and phrases from various languages, including Latin, French, and Spanish, due to historical interactions and cultural exchange.

Cultural Exchange and Globalization: In the modern era, globalization has accelerated cultural diffusion on a global scale. Increased travel, international trade, and the interconnectedness of economies and societies have led to the widespread sharing of cultural elements. Globalization has given rise to a global culture characterized by the fusion of diverse cultural elements.

Challenges and Controversies: While cultural diffusion can lead to enrichment and diversity, it can also raise challenges and controversies. Cultural imperialism, cultural appropriation, and the erosion of indigenous cultures are some of the concerns associated with the rapid diffusion of dominant cultures and global consumerism.

In summary, cultural diffusion is a dynamic and ongoing process that has shaped the course of human history. It reflects the interconnectedness of human societies and the capacity of cultures to evolve, adapt, and enrich one another through contact and exchange. While it has its benefits and challenges, cultural diffusion is a testament to the resilience and adaptability of cultures in an ever-changing world.

Legacy beyond borders is a concept that encapsulates the

enduring impact and influence of individuals, ideas, cultures, and civilizations beyond the boundaries of their place and time. It reflects the capacity of human achievements and contributions to transcend geographic, cultural, and temporal limits, leaving a lasting imprint on the world and future generations.

Throughout history, individuals and cultures have left legacies that extend far beyond the borders of their origins. These legacies encompass a wide range of domains, including art, science, philosophy, religion, politics, and technology. They serve as a testament to the enduring power of human creativity, innovation, and the human spirit.

One of the most notable examples of legacy beyond borders is the Renaissance, a cultural and intellectual movement that originated in 14th-century Italy but had far-reaching effects across Europe and beyond. The Renaissance's emphasis on humanism, art, and learning sparked a period of profound transformation in various fields, from the arts and sciences to politics and philosophy. The works of Renaissance artists like Leonardo da Vinci and Michelangelo continue to inspire and influence artists and thinkers worldwide.

Scientific discoveries and innovations have also left legacies that transcend borders. The contributions of scientists such as Isaac Newton, Albert Einstein, and Marie Curie have had a global impact on our understanding of the natural world and technological advancements. Their work laid the foundation for countless scientific breakthroughs and technological applications that continue to shape our lives today.

In the realm of literature, the works of authors like William Shakespeare, Leo Tolstoy, and Gabriel García Márquez have been translated into numerous languages and are celebrated worldwide. These literary giants have left a legacy of storytelling, exploration of human nature, and social commentary that resonates with readers across cultures and generations.

Philosophical ideas have also crossed borders, challenging conventional wisdom and inspiring new ways of thinking. The Enlightenment, with its emphasis on reason, individual rights, and the separation of church and state, had a profound impact on political and philosophical thought, influencing the development of modern democratic societies and human rights.

Religion, too, has left legacies that extend beyond borders. The teachings of figures like Jesus, Buddha, and Muhammad have shaped the beliefs and practices of billions of people around the world. The spread of Christianity, Buddhism, and Islam has transcended cultural and geographical boundaries, leaving a lasting spiritual and cultural legacy.

Technological innovations have revolutionized the way we live and connect with one another. The invention of the internet, for instance, has transformed communication, commerce, and access to information on a global scale. The legacy of pioneers like Tim Berners-Lee, who created the World Wide Web, continues to reshape the world's social, economic, and cultural landscape.

Artistic expressions and movements have often transcended borders, enriching global culture. The influence of movements like Cubism, Surrealism, and Pop Art can be seen in art and design around the world. The legacy of artists like Frida Kahlo, Pablo Picasso, and Jackson Pollock extends far beyond their home countries, inspiring artists and enthusiasts worldwide.

Humanitarian efforts and social movements have also left legacies that cross borders. Figures like Mahatma Gandhi and Nelson Mandela, known for their struggles against injustice and colonialism, have become symbols of resilience and peaceful resistance. Their legacies continue to inspire social and political movements advocating for equality, justice, and human rights.

In the realm of sports, athletes like Muhammad Ali, Pelé, and Serena Williams have transcended borders and become global icons. Their achievements in boxing, soccer, and tennis have not only inspired athletes but also broken down barriers and promoted social change.

Scientific collaborations and international cooperation have allowed us to address global challenges collectively. The legacy of initiatives like the International Space Station (ISS) demonstrates how nations can come together to advance scientific knowledge and space exploration, transcending geopolitical boundaries.

Education and the dissemination of knowledge play a vital role in creating legacies beyond borders. Universities and institutions of learning serve as hubs of knowledge production and dissemination, attracting students and scholars from around the world. The legacies of educational institutions like Harvard, Oxford, and the Sorbonne extend beyond their respective countries, fostering a global community of scholars and innovators.

Humanitarian organizations and initiatives, such as the Red Cross and Médecins Sans Frontières (Doctors Without Borders), exemplify the spirit of global collaboration and solidarity. These organizations provide assistance and relief in crisis-stricken regions, transcending borders to alleviate suffering and save lives.

In summary, legacy beyond borders is a testament to the enduring impact of human endeavors, ideas, and achievements. It underscores the interconnectedness of our world and the capacity of individuals, cultures, and civilizations to shape the course of history and inspire future generations. Whether through art, science, philosophy, literature, technology, or social change, legacies that transcend borders remind us of the universality of human aspiration and the potential for positive change on a global scale.

Chapter 6: The Decline and Disappearance of the Olmec

Theories of decline have long been a subject of interest and debate in various fields, including history, sociology, political science, and economics. These theories seek to explain the reasons and underlying factors that contribute to the decline or deterioration of individuals, societies, civilizations, or institutions. While the specifics may vary, theories of decline often share common themes and perspectives.

One prominent theory of decline is the cyclical theory of history, which suggests that civilizations and societies go through predictable cycles of growth, maturity, decline, and ultimately, collapse. This theory draws inspiration from historical examples such as the rise and fall of the Roman Empire. According to this view, societies and civilizations experience periods of expansion and prosperity, followed by internal decay, external pressures, and eventual decline.

Historical examples of the cyclical theory of decline often point to common factors that contribute to downfall. These include political corruption, economic instability, social inequality, military overextension, and moral decay. The idea is that these internal and external pressures gradually erode the foundations of a society or civilization, leading to its eventual decline.

Another theory of decline centers on economic factors. Economic theories of decline emphasize the role of economic mismanagement, resource depletion, financial crises, and unsustainable economic practices in the decline of nations and civilizations. Scholars such as Jared Diamond, in his book "Collapse: How Societies Choose to Fail or Succeed," explore the impact of environmental degradation and resource exhaustion on the decline of past civilizations.

Furthermore, some theories of decline focus on the role of political institutions and leadership. Political decay and institutional decline theories argue that the deterioration of political systems, the rise of authoritarianism, and the failure of institutions to adapt to changing circumstances can lead to societal decline. The work of scholars like Francis Fukuyama, in "Political Order and Political Decay," delves into these concepts.

Social and cultural factors also play a significant role in theories of decline. Cultural decline theories posit that shifts in values, norms, and cultural practices can contribute to societal decline. Factors such as a decline in social cohesion, loss of cultural vitality, and erosion of shared values are seen as potential indicators of decline.

Moreover, demographic theories of decline explore the impact of population dynamics on societal and institutional health. Population decline, aging populations, and declining birth rates can have significant consequences for economies, social welfare systems, and the overall vitality of a society.

Technological and innovation theories of decline focus on the role of technological stagnation or the inability to adapt to technological change as contributing factors to decline. The failure to innovate and keep pace with technological advancements can render industries obsolete, affect economic competitiveness, and have broader societal implications.

Globalization and external pressures theories argue that the interconnectedness of the modern world can expose societies and civilizations to external shocks and vulnerabilities. Economic interdependence, international conflicts, environmental challenges, and pandemics are seen as potential threats that can accelerate decline.

In addition to these theories, some scholars and thinkers have proposed theories of cultural decline that emphasize the erosion of intellectual and artistic achievements, the decline of educational systems, and a perceived coarsening of cultural values and discourse. These theories often reflect concerns about the state of culture and the potential consequences for society.

It is important to note that theories of decline are not deterministic, and historical examples of decline often involve complex interplay among multiple factors. Additionally, societies and civilizations can experience periods of decline followed by renewal and resurgence.

For example, the decline of the Roman Empire was followed by the emergence of the Byzantine Empire and the early Islamic civilization, demonstrating the potential for regeneration and adaptation in the face of decline.

Moreover, theories of decline can sometimes be subjective, influenced by the values and perspectives of the era in which they are proposed. What one generation perceives as a decline may be seen differently by future generations.

In summary, theories of decline offer valuable insights into the complex dynamics that can contribute to the decline of individuals, societies, civilizations, or institutions. These theories draw from a range of disciplines and perspectives, including history, economics, politics, culture, and technology. While they often highlight common themes such as economic mismanagement, political decay, and cultural erosion, it is essential to recognize that decline is not a predetermined outcome, and societies have the capacity to adapt, renew, and transform even in the face of significant challenges. Understanding the factors and theories of decline can inform efforts to mitigate decline and promote resilience and renewal.

Environmental factors refer to the conditions and elements in the natural world that can influence and impact living organisms, ecosystems, and human societies. These factors encompass a wide range of elements, including the physical, biological, and chemical components of the environment. Understanding these factors is crucial for addressing environmental issues, ecological balance, and human well-being.

Climate: Climate is one of the most significant environmental factors. It includes long-term weather patterns, such as temperature, precipitation, humidity, wind patterns, and climate zones. Climate has a profound impact on the distribution of ecosystems, the types of flora and fauna that can thrive in a region, and human activities such as agriculture and urban planning.

Weather: Weather refers to the short-term atmospheric conditions in a specific location. Factors such as temperature fluctuations, precipitation, storms, and seasonal variations can impact daily life, agriculture, transportation, and emergency preparedness.

Geography: The physical geography of an area, including its topography, landforms, and proximity to bodies of water, influences local climates, habitats, and ecosystems. Mountains, valleys, plains, deserts, and coastlines all have unique environmental characteristics.

Ecosystems: Ecosystems consist of living organisms (biotic factors) and their physical surroundings (abiotic factors). These include forests, wetlands, grasslands, coral reefs, and freshwater bodies. Ecosystems provide essential services such as food production, water purification, and climate regulation.

Biodiversity: Biodiversity encompasses the variety of living species on Earth. High biodiversity is essential for ecosystem stability, resilience, and adaptability. Environmental factors, such as habitat destruction, pollution, and climate change, can threaten biodiversity and lead to species extinction.

Air Quality: Air quality is determined by the presence of pollutants and the composition of the atmosphere. Environmental factors like emissions from vehicles, industry, and natural sources can impact air quality, affecting human health and ecosystems.

Water Quality: The quality of freshwater bodies, including rivers, lakes, and groundwater, is vital for human consumption, agriculture, and aquatic life. Pollution, sedimentation, and contamination can degrade water quality.

Soil Quality: Soil quality is influenced by factors like soil composition, nutrient content, pH levels, and organic matter. Healthy soils are essential for agriculture, plant growth, and ecosystem services.

Natural Disasters: Environmental factors can lead to natural disasters such as earthquakes, hurricanes, floods, wildfires, and volcanic eruptions. These events can have devastating impacts on human communities and ecosystems.

Oceans and Seas: Oceans and seas cover a significant portion of the Earth's surface and play a crucial role in regulating climate, providing food, and supporting biodiversity. Ocean acidification, overfishing, and plastic pollution are environmental concerns in these regions.

Solar Radiation: Solar radiation from the sun drives Earth's climate and weather patterns. Variations in solar radiation, such as sunspots and solar cycles, can influence long-term climate changes.

Pollution: Pollution from human activities, including air pollution, water pollution, soil contamination, and noise pollution, can have detrimental effects on the environment and human health.

Climate Change: Climate change, driven by factors such as greenhouse gas emissions and deforestation, is altering global climate patterns, leading to rising temperatures, sea-level rise, and extreme weather events. It has far-reaching implications for ecosystems, economies, and human societies.

Natural Resources: Environmental factors also include the availability and distribution of natural resources like minerals, fossil fuels, freshwater, and arable land. Sustainable management of these resources is essential for future generations.

Human Impact: Human activities, including deforestation, urbanization, agriculture, and industrialization, significantly influence environmental factors. Understanding the human impact on the environment is crucial for addressing environmental challenges.

Erosion and Sedimentation: Erosion, the process of soil and rock removal, and sedimentation, the deposition of eroded materials, can alter landscapes and impact water quality in rivers and streams.

Land Use and Land Cover: Land use patterns, including urbanization, agriculture, and deforestation, can change the land cover and contribute to habitat loss, biodiversity decline, and altered hydrology.

Natural Cycles: Environmental factors also include natural cycles and phenomena such as the water cycle, carbon cycle, nitrogen cycle, and ecological succession. These processes play a fundamental role in maintaining the Earth's ecosystems.

Understanding and monitoring environmental factors are essential for making informed decisions about conservation, resource management, climate mitigation, disaster preparedness, and sustainable development. Addressing environmental challenges requires a holistic approach that considers the complex interplay of these factors and their impacts on the planet and its inhabitants.

Enduring mysteries are captivating and enigmatic phenomena, events, or questions that have puzzled humanity for generations or even centuries. These mysteries span a wide range of subjects, from the natural world and ancient history to the realms of science, the paranormal, and the unexplained. Despite advances in knowledge and technology, these mysteries continue to spark fascination and debate among scholars, scientists, and the general public.

Bermuda Triangle: The Bermuda Triangle, located in the western part of the North Atlantic Ocean, has been the subject of numerous legends and theories. It is known for the alleged disappearance of ships and aircraft under mysterious circumstances. While many incidents can be explained by natural phenomena and human error, the Bermuda Triangle remains a popular mystery.

The Voynich Manuscript: The Voynich Manuscript is an ancient book filled with strange illustrations and undecipherable text. It has confounded linguists and cryptographers for centuries, as no one has been able to decode its meaning or identify its origin.

Stonehenge: Stonehenge, the prehistoric monument in England, continues to baffle researchers with questions about its purpose, construction, and the culture that built it. The arrangement of massive stones and their astronomical alignments remain subjects of study and speculation.

The Great Pyramids: The construction methods and purpose of the Great Pyramids of Giza in Egypt are enduring mysteries. How the ancient Egyptians achieved such precise engineering and the significance of the pyramids in their culture continue to be topics of debate.

The Roanoke Colony: The fate of the Roanoke Colony, a group of early English settlers in what is now North Carolina, remains unknown. The word "CROATOAN" carved into a tree and the disappearance of the colony without a trace have fueled speculation and legends.

Crop Circles: Intricate crop circle formations that appear in fields overnight have puzzled researchers and the public. While many crop circles are hoaxes, some remain unexplained, leading to theories about their origin, such as natural phenomena or extraterrestrial involvement.

The Taos Hum: Residents of Taos, New Mexico, have reported hearing a low-frequency hum or noise, known as the "Taos Hum," for decades. The source of this phenomenon remains a mystery, with theories ranging from geological processes to psychological causes.

Dark Matter and Dark Energy: In astrophysics, dark matter and dark energy are mysterious substances that make up a significant portion of the universe's mass-energy content. Yet, scientists have not directly observed or identified them, leading to ongoing research and debate.

Fermi Paradox: The Fermi Paradox raises the question of why, given the vast number of potentially habitable planets in the universe, we have not detected any signs of extraterrestrial life or received any communication from advanced civilizations. This paradox continues to perplex astronomers and astrobiologists.

The Wow! Signal: The Wow! Signal, a strong radio signal detected in 1977, remains unexplained. While it lasted for only 72 seconds, its origin and cause have not been definitively identified, leading to speculation about its potential extraterrestrial origin.

The Tunguska Event: The Tunguska event was a massive explosion that occurred in Siberia in 1908, leveling trees over a vast area. The cause, likely a meteoroid or comet fragment, left no crater, leading to ongoing research on its details.

The Nazca Lines: The Nazca Lines in Peru consist of massive geoglyphs etched into the desert floor, depicting various animals and geometric shapes. The purpose and methods of creating these enormous designs remain a mystery.

The Oak Island Money Pit: The Oak Island Money Pit, located in Nova Scotia, Canada, has attracted treasure hunters for centuries.

The pit is said to contain a valuable treasure, but despite numerous attempts to excavate it, the mystery remains unsolved.

The Mary Celeste: The Mary Celeste was a ship found adrift in the Atlantic Ocean in 1872 with its crew missing. The ship's intact condition, fully loaded cargo, and the absence of a distress call have led to speculations about what happened to the crew.

The Dyatlov Pass Incident: In 1959, a group of hikers in the Ural Mountains of Russia died under mysterious circumstances. The tent they had been using was found torn from the inside, and the hikers' bodies showed signs of unusual injuries. The exact cause of their deaths remains unknown.

These enduring mysteries continue to capture the imagination and curiosity of people around the world. While some may eventually be explained through scientific advancements or further research, others may continue to defy our understanding, adding to the enduring allure of the unexplained.

Chapter 7: Legacy of the Olmec: Impact on Later Mesoamerican Civilizations

The influence on successor cultures is a fascinating aspect of human history, illustrating how the legacies of past civilizations, societies, and cultures continue to shape the development and identity of subsequent generations. The interplay between the old and the new, the transfer of knowledge, traditions, technologies, and ideas, has played a pivotal role in the evolution of human societies across time and geography.

When we explore the influence of predecessor cultures on their successors, we uncover a tapestry of interconnectedness and cross-pollination that has shaped the course of human civilization. This dynamic process can be observed across various domains:

1. Art and Architecture: Artistic and architectural styles often carry the imprint of earlier cultures. For example, the classical architecture of ancient Greece significantly influenced Roman architecture, which, in turn, left a profound mark on European architectural traditions for centuries. The echoes of these ancient styles can still be seen in modern buildings and monuments.

2. Language and Literature: Language is a carrier of culture, and the development of languages is deeply intertwined with the history of their speakers. Latin, for instance, served as the lingua franca of the Roman Empire, and its legacy persists in the Romance languages such as Italian, Spanish, and French. Similarly, the influence of classical literature, like the works of Homer and Virgil, continues to resonate in contemporary literature and storytelling.

3. Religion and Spirituality: Religious beliefs and practices often transcend time and geography. Ancient religions like Buddhism, Hinduism, and Judaism have left indelible marks on the spiritual traditions of their regions and beyond. Missionary activities and the spread of faiths have resulted in the syncretism of religious practices in successor cultures.

4. Scientific Knowledge and Innovation: Scientific discoveries and innovations build upon the work of earlier cultures. The foundations of modern mathematics, astronomy, and medicine can be traced back to ancient civilizations like the Greeks, Babylonians, and Egyptians. Successor cultures have expanded and refined this knowledge, contributing to the advancement of human understanding.

5. Political and Governance Systems: Political structures and governance systems are often influenced by the precedents set by earlier societies. Concepts such as democracy, federalism, and monarchy have historical roots and continue to evolve in contemporary political landscapes.

6. Legal Systems and Justice: Legal systems and principles of justice are shaped by the legal traditions of the past. The Roman legal system, with its emphasis on codification and jurisprudence, has had a lasting impact on the legal frameworks of many modern countries.

7. Cultural Practices and Traditions: Cultural practices, rituals, and traditions are passed down through generations and evolve over time. Many festivals, ceremonies, and customs celebrated today have ancient origins and have been adapted and integrated into successor cultures.

8. Technology and Innovation: Technological advancements are often built on the foundations laid by earlier societies. The wheel, for example, was a fundamental invention that revolutionized transportation and machinery and continues to be a crucial element of modern technology.

9. Ethical and Philosophical Frameworks: Philosophical and ethical ideas from earlier cultures continue to inform contemporary thought. Concepts of ethics, morality, and social justice are shaped by the philosophical traditions of the past.

10. Culinary Traditions: Food is a reflection of cultural identity, and culinary traditions are often influenced by the ingredients, techniques, and recipes passed down through generations. Spices, cooking methods, and dishes from ancient cultures have left a rich culinary legacy in successor societies.

In examining the influence of predecessor cultures on their successors, it becomes evident that the transmission of knowledge, traditions, and innovations is a dynamic and ongoing process. Cultures do not exist in isolation; they are interconnected and continually adapt to changing circumstances and influences from the past and present.

Furthermore, the exchange and fusion of ideas and practices between cultures have led to the emergence of hybrid cultures and the enrichment of global diversity. The interconnectedness of human societies, facilitated by trade, migration, communication, and cultural exchange, has accelerated the pace of cross-cultural influence and adaptation.

In essence, the influence of predecessor cultures on successor cultures underscores the continuity of human civilization and the enduring legacy of those who came before. It reminds us that our contemporary identities, knowledge, and traditions are shaped by the collective wisdom and creativity of countless generations that have contributed to the tapestry of human history. Understanding this influence allows us to appreciate the richness of our shared heritage and the ongoing evolution of cultures across time and borders.

The Olmec civilization, one of the earliest complex societies in Mesoamerica, left a profound and enduring legacy through its cultural contributions. Emerging around 1500 BCE in what is now modern-day Mexico, the Olmec people laid the foundations for many aspects of Mesoamerican culture and influenced successor civilizations, including the Maya, Zapotec, and Aztec. Their cultural contributions spanned a wide range of domains, leaving a lasting imprint on the rich tapestry of Mesoamerican history.

Art and Iconography: The Olmec are renowned for their distinctive artistic style, characterized by colossal stone heads, intricate pottery, and finely crafted figurines. The colossal stone heads, carved from massive basalt boulders, are among their most iconic creations. These heads, with distinct facial features and headgear, are believed to represent Olmec rulers or deities and have become emblematic of Olmec art. The Olmec's artistic expressions influenced the artistic traditions of subsequent Mesoamerican civilizations.

Religion and Mythology: The Olmec's religious beliefs and mythological narratives laid the groundwork for Mesoamerican spirituality. Their pantheon included deities associated with nature, agriculture, and fertility. The Olmec's veneration of the jaguar, a powerful and revered animal, is evident in their art and symbolism. This reverence for the jaguar continued to be a prominent motif in later Mesoamerican cultures, such as the Maya and Aztec.

Calendar and Astronomical Knowledge: The Olmec developed a calendar system that served as a precursor to the complex calendrical systems of later Mesoamerican civilizations. Their calendar included a 260-day ritual calendar, known as the "Tzolk'in," and a 365-day solar calendar, known as the "Haab." These calendars played a significant role in religious rituals, agriculture, and societal organization. Additionally, the Olmec's astronomical observations and knowledge of celestial events influenced later Mesoamerican cultures' astronomical pursuits.

Agriculture and Food Production: The Olmec were skilled farmers who developed advanced agricultural practices. They cultivated maize (corn), beans, squash, and other crops that formed the basis of Mesoamerican diets for centuries to come. The domestication and cultivation of maize were particularly significant, as it became a staple crop in Mesoamerica and held deep cultural and symbolic importance.

Trade and Exchange: The Olmec established extensive trade networks that extended far beyond their immediate region. They engaged in long-distance trade, exchanging goods such as jade, obsidian, and other valuable resources with distant regions. This trade facilitated the flow of ideas, materials, and cultural influences between the Olmec and neighboring societies, contributing to the cultural diversity of Mesoamerica.

Writing and Glyphs: While the Olmec did not develop a fully developed writing system like the Maya, they left behind some of the earliest examples of Mesoamerican glyphs and symbols. These symbols, found on artifacts and stelae, are believed to convey important information, including names, titles, and perhaps calendrical notations. The Olmec's use of glyphs laid the groundwork for the development of more elaborate writing systems in later Mesoamerican cultures.

Urban Planning and Ceremonial Centers: The Olmec established complex urban centers, such as La Venta and San Lorenzo, characterized by impressive ceremonial architecture, plazas, and ball courts. These centers served as hubs for religious ceremonies, trade, and community gatherings. The layout and design of these centers influenced the planning and construction of later Mesoamerican cities and ceremonial complexes.

Social Hierarchy and Leadership: The Olmec society was characterized by social hierarchy, with distinct classes and rulers who held both political and religious authority. This hierarchical structure set a precedent for the governance systems of later Mesoamerican civilizations, which also featured ruling elites with religious and political roles.

Legacy on Successor Cultures: The Olmec cultural contributions had a profound and enduring impact on successor cultures. The Maya, for example, adopted elements of Olmec art, religion, and calendrical systems into their own culture. The Olmec influence can also be seen in the religious practices, artistic motifs, and architectural styles of later Mesoamerican civilizations, including the Zapotec and Aztec.

In summary, the Olmec civilization's cultural contributions were instrumental in shaping the mosaic of Mesoamerican history. Their artistic achievements, religious beliefs, agricultural practices, and knowledge systems laid the groundwork for the development of subsequent Mesoamerican cultures. The enduring legacy of the Olmec can be seen in the rich tapestry of Mesoamerican civilizations that followed, each building upon the cultural foundations established by this early and influential society.

The concept of enduring influence refers to the lasting impact that individuals, cultures, ideas, and innovations have on the course of human history and the development of societies. Throughout the annals of time, certain individuals and cultures have left an indelible mark on the world, shaping the way people think, live, and interact for generations to come. This enduring influence can be observed across various domains, including culture, science, philosophy, religion, technology, and governance.

Cultural Influence: Perhaps one of the most tangible forms of enduring influence is seen in the realm of culture. Great civilizations such as ancient Greece, Rome, and China have bequeathed to the world a rich legacy of art, literature, architecture, and traditions. The enduring influence of Greek philosophy, Roman engineering, and Chinese calligraphy can still be witnessed in contemporary society. For example, the architectural principles of the ancient Greeks continue to inform modern building design, and the works of Greek philosophers like Plato and Aristotle remain foundational texts in the study of ethics and logic.

Scientific and Technological Advancements: Scientific discoveries and technological innovations have a profound and enduring influence on human progress. The work of visionaries like Isaac Newton, Albert Einstein, and Marie Curie revolutionized our understanding of the natural world. Their contributions to physics, mathematics, and chemistry continue to shape scientific inquiry and technological development. Similarly, ancient inventions such as the wheel, the printing press, and the compass have had a lasting impact on human civilization and continue to be integral to modern life.

Philosophical Ideas: Philosophical ideas and systems of thought have guided human intellectual and moral inquiry for centuries. Thinkers like Confucius, Socrates, and Immanuel Kant have left a legacy of philosophical inquiry that transcends time and borders. Their ideas about ethics, justice, and the nature of reality continue to be studied and debated by scholars and individuals seeking to navigate the complexities of human existence. These enduring philosophies provide a foundation for ethical decision-making, political theory, and personal reflection.

Religious and Spiritual Traditions: Religious and spiritual beliefs have shaped the moral and spiritual fabric of societies for millennia. The enduring influence of religious figures like Jesus,

Buddha, and Muhammad extends far beyond the time and place of their lives. Christianity, Buddhism, and Islam, the religions founded by these figures, respectively, have millions of adherents worldwide and have influenced cultures, art, literature, and social structures. The ethical teachings and spiritual insights contained in religious texts and traditions continue to provide guidance and meaning to countless individuals.

Political Ideals and Governance: Political ideals and systems of governance have a profound impact on the organization of societies. The enduring influence of political philosophers like John Locke, Thomas Jefferson, and Karl Marx can be seen in the formation of governments and the development of political thought. Concepts of democracy, individual rights, and social justice have been central to political movements and revolutions across the globe. These enduring ideals shape the principles and institutions of modern governance.

Literary and Artistic Achievements: Literary works and artistic achievements have the power to transcend time and culture, resonating with audiences across generations. The enduring influence of literary giants such as William Shakespeare, Leo Tolstoy, and Jane Austen is evident in the continued popularity and relevance of their works. Their novels, plays, and poems explore timeless themes of love, power, and human nature. Similarly, the art of renowned painters like Leonardo da Vinci, Vincent van Gogh, and Pablo Picasso continues to inspire and captivate audiences, influencing contemporary artists and cultural expression.

Technological Advancements: The impact of technological advancements on daily life is undeniable. Innovations in fields such as information technology, medicine, and transportation have transformed the way people live, work, and communicate. The enduring influence of inventors like Thomas Edison, Alexander Graham Bell, and Steve Jobs is evident in the devices and technologies that have become essential to modern existence. These innovators have shaped the trajectory of human progress and continue to influence the development of new technologies.

Social Movements and Activism: Social movements and activism have been instrumental in advocating for social change and justice. The enduring influence of figures like Mahatma Gandhi, Martin Luther King Jr., and Nelson Mandela is seen in the ongoing struggle for civil rights and equality. Their commitment to nonviolence, justice, and human rights continues to inspire individuals and movements worldwide, promoting social progress and equality.

In summary, enduring influence is a testament to the enduring power of human thought, creativity, and innovation. It is a reminder that the legacies of individuals, cultures, and ideas can transcend time and leave an indelible mark on the course of human history. These enduring influences continue to shape the way people live, think, and interact, serving as a source of inspiration and guidance for generations to come.

BOOK 2
MAYA MASTERY
UNVEILING THE SECRETS OF A
FLOURISHING CIVILIZATION (2000
BCE - 1500 CE)

BY A.J. KINGSTON

Chapter 1: The Birth of the Maya: Origins and Early Developments (2000 BCE - 1000 BCE)

The ancient Mesoamerican landscape is a mosaic of diverse and dynamic environments that encompassed the territories of civilizations such as the Olmec, Maya, Teotihuacan, Zapotec, Toltec, and Aztec. This rich and varied landscape played a crucial role in shaping the development, culture, and livelihoods of these ancient peoples. From lush rainforests to arid deserts, from fertile lowlands to rugged mountains, the Mesoamerican landscape offered a complex tapestry of ecological niches and resources that sustained thriving societies for millennia.

Lush Rainforests: The dense rainforests of Mesoamerica, particularly in regions such as the Yucatán Peninsula and parts of Guatemala, were characterized by towering trees, lush vegetation, and abundant wildlife. These rainforests provided the Maya civilization with essential resources such as timber for construction, medicinal plants, and a rich variety of food sources, including fruits, nuts, and game animals. However, the thick vegetation also presented challenges in terms of agriculture and transportation.

Arid Deserts: In contrast to the rainforests, arid deserts and semi-arid regions were found in parts of northern Mexico and the southwestern United States. These areas, marked by limited rainfall and harsh conditions, were inhabited by cultures like the Hohokam and the Ancestral Puebloans. Despite the aridity, these ancient societies developed innovative techniques for harnessing water through complex irrigation systems, allowing for the cultivation of crops like maize, beans, and squash.

Fertile Lowlands: Fertile lowlands, including the basin of Mexico, the coastal plains, and river valleys, were home to some of the most influential Mesoamerican civilizations. The availability of arable land, water sources, and temperate climates made these regions highly conducive to agriculture. The Aztecs, for example, established their capital city, Tenochtitlan, on an island in Lake

Texcoco, where they practiced sophisticated agricultural techniques like chinampas, or "floating gardens," to sustain their population.

Rugged Mountains: Mesoamerica's mountainous terrain, which includes the Sierra Madre Occidental and Sierra Madre Oriental in Mexico, presented both challenges and opportunities for ancient societies. These mountain ranges were rich in mineral resources such as precious metals and gemstones, making mining an important economic activity. Additionally, the mountains offered strategic defensive advantages, leading to the establishment of fortified cities in elevated regions.

Volcanic Highlands: The highlands of Mesoamerica, including the Valley of Mexico, were characterized by volcanic activity and fertile volcanic soils. These highland areas were centers of civilization, including Teotihuacan and the later Aztec Empire. The volcanic soils were ideal for agriculture, allowing the cultivation of staple crops like maize, beans, and chili peppers. The availability of freshwater sources in the highlands was crucial for sustaining large urban populations.

Coastlines and Wetlands: The coastal regions and wetlands of Mesoamerica provided a wealth of resources and ecological diversity. Coastal communities, such as those of the Olmec and the Maya, relied on fishing, shellfish gathering, and maritime trade for sustenance and economic exchange. Mangrove swamps and estuaries were important ecosystems that supported a variety of flora and fauna.

River Systems: Mesoamerica boasted several significant river systems, including the Usumacinta River and the Grijalva River in the Maya lowlands. These rivers played a vital role in transportation, trade, and agriculture. The fertile floodplains along these rivers were well-suited for farming, and ancient Mesoamerican societies developed intricate irrigation systems to harness the water's potential.

Cave Systems: The limestone-rich landscape of Mesoamerica gave rise to extensive cave systems, many of which held cultural and religious significance. Caves were viewed as portals to the underworld in Mesoamerican cosmology and were used for rituals, ceremonies, and burials. The Maya, in particular, left behind intricate cave paintings and inscriptions that offer insights into their beliefs and practices.

Biodiversity: The Mesoamerican landscape teemed with biodiversity, featuring a remarkable array of plant and animal species. These natural resources were essential for sustenance, trade, and cultural practices. The rich biodiversity of Mesoamerica included species like jaguars, howler monkeys, cacao trees, and quetzal birds, all of which held cultural and symbolic significance in various Mesoamerican societies.

Environmental Diversity and Adaptation: The diverse Mesoamerican landscape necessitated adaptation strategies by its inhabitants. Ancient peoples developed an intimate understanding of their environments, crafting specialized agricultural techniques, constructing terraced fields, and implementing water management systems to thrive in varied landscapes. The ability to adapt to different ecological niches was a hallmark of Mesoamerican societies.

In summary, the ancient Mesoamerican landscape was a tapestry of ecological diversity that influenced the development and cultural expressions of its inhabitants. It provided the raw materials, agricultural opportunities, and geographical features that shaped the rise and fall of great civilizations. The enduring legacy of these landscapes can still be seen today in the traditions, art, and ecological practices of modern Mesoamerican peoples.

The emergence of Maya culture is a remarkable chapter in the history of Mesoamerica, marked by the growth of one of the most sophisticated and enduring civilizations in the region. The Maya civilization, known for its advanced knowledge, intricate art, complex calendar systems, and monumental architecture, emerged in the heartland of what is now southern Mexico, Guatemala, Belize, Honduras, and El Salvador. This emergence was a gradual and dynamic process that unfolded over millennia, and it left an indelible mark on the cultural tapestry of Mesoamerica.

Early Formative Period: The roots of Maya culture can be traced back to the Early Formative Period, beginning around 2000 BCE. During this time, agricultural practices, pottery-making, and village life began to develop in the Maya lowlands. The cultivation of maize (corn), beans, and squash became the foundation of Maya agriculture, allowing for population growth and the establishment of settled communities.

Preclassic Period: The Preclassic Period, roughly spanning from 2000 BCE to 250 CE, witnessed the rise of complex societies and the emergence of distinct Maya cultural traits. Notable settlements, such as Nakbé, El Mirador, and Kaminaljuyu, began to take shape, featuring monumental architecture and ceremonial plazas. This period saw the construction of the earliest known Maya pyramids and temples, reflecting the religious and societal importance of these structures.

Development of Writing and Glyphs: One of the hallmarks of Maya culture is their hieroglyphic writing system, which began to develop during the Preclassic Period. The Maya script, comprised of intricate symbols and glyphs, was used to record historical events, religious rituals, and astronomical observations. The decipherment of Maya glyphs has provided invaluable insights into their history and beliefs.

Urban Centers and Polities: By the Middle Preclassic Period (1000 BCE - 250 CE), the Maya civilization saw the emergence of powerful city-states and polities. Notable among these was the city of Mirador, characterized by its massive structures, including El Tigre pyramid. These urban centers served as political, religious, and economic hubs, where complex societies thrived.

Long-Distance Trade: The Maya engaged in extensive long-distance trade networks during the Preclassic Period, exchanging valuable resources such as obsidian, jade, cacao, and marine shells with neighboring regions. This trade not only facilitated the exchange of goods but also the spread of cultural influences.

Ceramic Traditions: The Preclassic Period also witnessed the development of distinct Maya ceramic traditions. Maya pottery featured intricate designs and iconography that conveyed their cultural narratives and artistic expressions. These ceramics played a crucial role in rituals and daily life.

Classic Period: The Classic Period (250 CE - 900 CE) is often regarded as the zenith of Maya culture. During this era, Maya city-states like Tikal, Calakmul, Caracol, Copán, and Palenque reached their zenith in terms of political power, artistic achievements, and architectural grandeur. These city-states engaged in political alliances, rivalries, and warfare, leading to the construction of impressive fortifications and defensive structures.

Artistic Achievements: Maya art flourished during the Classic Period, with monumental stelae, elaborately decorated temples, and intricate murals adorning city centers. The stelae were inscribed with hieroglyphs, recounting the histories and achievements of rulers and dynasties. The Maya's artistic endeavors, including pottery, sculpture, and mural paintings, showcased their deep religious and mythological beliefs.

Calendrical Systems: The Classic Period also marked the refinement of Maya calendrical systems, including the Tzolk'in (260-day ritual calendar) and the Haab' (365-day solar calendar). These calendars played a crucial role in religious rituals, agricultural planning, and governance. The Maya's advanced understanding of astronomy enabled them to make precise astronomical observations and calculations.

Decline and Collapse: Despite their cultural achievements, the Classic Period also witnessed the gradual decline and collapse of many Maya city-states. Factors contributing to this decline are complex and include environmental stressors, warfare, resource depletion, and political unrest. Many city-states were abandoned or depopulated during this time.

Postclassic Period: Following the collapse of many Classic Period city-states, the Maya civilization entered the Postclassic Period (900 CE - 1500 CE). During this time, new centers of power emerged, including Chichen Itza and Mayapan in the northern Yucatán Peninsula. The Postclassic Period saw the continued development of Maya culture, including the introduction of new architectural styles and religious practices influenced by external factors.

Spanish Conquest and Colonial Era: The arrival of Spanish conquistadors in the 16th century marked a pivotal and devastating chapter in Maya history. Spanish colonization, accompanied by violence, disease, and forced labor, led to the decline of indigenous populations and the suppression of traditional Maya practices. However, elements of Maya culture and identity persevered, blending with Spanish influences to create a unique mestizo culture.

Contemporary Maya Culture: Today, Maya culture endures in the descendants of the ancient Maya. Many Maya communities in Mesoamerica maintain their traditional languages, rituals, and agricultural practices. The Maya calendar system and hieroglyphic writing, once thought lost, have been partially deciphered and continue to be studied. Maya cultural traditions, including textiles, music, dance, and cuisine, remain vibrant and are celebrated as part of their cultural heritage.

In summary, the emergence of Maya culture was a complex and multifaceted process that spanned millennia, characterized by periods of growth, artistic achievement, political complexity, and eventual decline. Despite the challenges and changes brought by Spanish colonization, elements of Maya culture have persisted and continue to thrive in contemporary Mesoamerica, a testament to the enduring legacy of this remarkable civilization.

The story of early Maya settlements is a fascinating journey through time, revealing the origins of one of the most renowned civilizations in Mesoamerica. The Maya civilization, known for its sophisticated culture, intricate art, and advanced understanding of astronomy and mathematics, had its humble beginnings in the lowland regions of what is now modern-day Mexico, Guatemala, Belize, Honduras, and El Salvador. The emergence of early Maya settlements unfolded over thousands of years and provides insights into the foundations of Maya society.

Archaic Period (7000 BCE - 2000 BCE): The earliest evidence of human habitation in the Maya lowlands dates back to the Archaic Period, a time when hunter-gatherer societies thrived. During this period, small groups of people roamed the lush forests and river valleys, relying on hunting, fishing, and foraging for sustenance. The Archaic Maya developed a deep connection with their natural surroundings and had a basic understanding of plant cultivation.

Formative Period (2000 BCE - 250 CE): The Formative Period marked the transition from mobile, foraging lifestyles to settled agriculture and the establishment of early Maya settlements. Around 2000 BCE, communities began to cultivate maize (corn), beans, and squash, which became the staples of their diet. Agriculture allowed for more permanent settlements to develop, as people could now rely on a stable food supply.

Early Agricultural Villages: Early Maya settlements during the Formative Period were characterized by small agricultural villages. These villages featured simple thatched huts, basic pottery, and agricultural fields. The development of pottery during this time allowed for better food storage and processing.

Rise of Ceramics: Pottery played a pivotal role in the evolution of early Maya settlements. The Formative Period saw the emergence of distinctive Maya ceramic traditions. Early Maya pottery was often plain and utilitarian, but over time, it evolved to include intricate designs and later became a canvas for artistic expression.

Ceremonial Centers and Public Spaces: As Maya communities grew, they began to develop ceremonial centers and public spaces. These centers often included simple pyramidal structures and open plazas. These early architectural features laid the groundwork for the monumental structures and city-states that would arise in later periods.

Emergence of Social Hierarchy: With the transition to settled agriculture and the establishment of permanent settlements, social hierarchies began to develop. Some individuals in early Maya communities likely held positions of leadership or authority, overseeing agricultural activities and communal efforts.

Cultural Developments: Early Maya settlements were not only centers of subsistence but also hubs of cultural development. The Maya people began to create symbolic art, such as figurines and small sculptures, that reflected their growing understanding of the natural world and spirituality. These early cultural expressions laid the foundation for the intricate art and iconography that would later define Maya culture.

Long-Distance Trade: Early Maya settlements engaged in long-distance trade networks, exchanging goods such as obsidian, jade, and marine shells with neighboring regions. This trade facilitated the exchange of ideas, resources, and cultural influences, contributing to the diversity of early Maya society.

Formative Period City-States: By the later stages of the Formative Period, some early Maya settlements had evolved into more complex entities resembling city-states. Notable examples include Nakbé, a large ceremonial center in present-day Guatemala, and El Mirador, known for its massive architectural structures.

Early Maya Script: The Formative Period also saw the emergence of early Maya script and glyphic writing. Although not as sophisticated as the hieroglyphic writing of later periods, these early inscriptions represented a significant step in the development of Maya writing systems.

Decline of Early Settlements: Toward the end of the Formative Period, many early Maya settlements experienced a decline, with some being abandoned. The reasons for this decline are complex and include environmental factors, resource depletion, and potential social upheaval.

In summary, the early Maya settlements represent the foundational stages of a civilization that would go on to achieve great heights in art, science, and culture. These humble beginnings, marked by the transition from nomadic hunting and gathering to settled agriculture, set the stage for the rise of iconic Maya city-states and the development of one of the most enduring and influential civilizations in Mesoamerican history. The cultural innovations, agricultural practices, and social dynamics of these early Maya settlements laid the groundwork for the rich tapestry of Maya culture that would emerge in subsequent centuries.

Chapter 2: Maya City-States: Politics, Society, and Governance (1000 BCE - 500 CE)

The rise of Maya city-states is a pivotal chapter in the history of Mesoamerica, marking the transition from scattered settlements to complex urban centers characterized by advanced architecture, monumental pyramids, intricate hieroglyphic writing, and intricate political structures. The Maya civilization, with its roots in the Preclassic Period (2000 BCE - 250 CE), saw the emergence of powerful city-states across the lowlands of present-day Mexico, Guatemala, Belize, Honduras, and El Salvador. This transformation was a gradual process shaped by political, social, cultural, and environmental factors.

Formative Period (2000 BCE - 250 CE): The Formative Period laid the foundation for the eventual rise of Maya city-states. During this era, the Maya transitioned from nomadic hunter-gatherer societies to settled agricultural communities. Maize, beans, squash, and other crops became staples of their diet, allowing for population growth and the establishment of more permanent settlements.

Early Agricultural Villages: Early Maya settlements during the Formative Period were primarily agricultural villages characterized by simple thatched huts, basic pottery, and agricultural fields. These communities cultivated crops and practiced resource management techniques to ensure their survival in a challenging environment.

Emergence of Social Hierarchy: With the shift to settled agriculture, social hierarchies began to develop within early Maya communities. Some individuals held positions of leadership or authority, overseeing agricultural activities, communal efforts, and potentially religious ceremonies.

Ceremonial Centers and Public Spaces: During the Formative Period, Maya communities began to create ceremonial centers and public spaces. These centers often included simple pyramidal structures and open plazas. They served as focal points for communal activities and rituals, foreshadowing the grander city centers of later periods.

Cultural Developments: Cultural developments also played a significant role in the early stages of Maya city-state emergence. Early Maya communities created symbolic art, such as figurines and small sculptures, reflecting their growing understanding of the natural world and spirituality. These cultural expressions laid the foundation for the intricate art and iconography that would later define Maya culture.

Trade Networks and Influence: Early Maya settlements engaged in long-distance trade networks, exchanging goods such as obsidian, jade, and marine shells with neighboring regions. This trade facilitated the exchange of ideas, resources, and cultural influences, contributing to the diversity of early Maya society.

Late Preclassic Period (250 BCE - 250 CE): The Late Preclassic Period marked a significant transition in the Maya lowlands. During this time, city-states began to emerge as dominant centers of power and influence. Examples include Nakbé, a large ceremonial center in present-day Guatemala, and El Mirador, known for its massive architectural structures.

Rise of Monumental Architecture: One of the defining features of the Maya city-states was their monumental architecture. The Late Preclassic Period saw the construction of the earliest known Maya pyramids and temples, often accompanied by intricate stelae inscribed with hieroglyphs. These structures served religious and political purposes and showcased the power and authority of rulers.

Political Complexity: As city-states developed, they became increasingly politically complex. Each city-state had its own ruling elite, often led by a k'uhul ajaw (divine lord) or ajaw (lord). The political landscape was marked by competition and rivalries among city-states for resources, territory, and influence.

Hieroglyphic Writing and Record-Keeping: The Maya continued to develop their hieroglyphic writing system during the Late Preclassic Period. Hieroglyphic inscriptions, often found on stelae and monuments, recorded historical events, religious rituals, and the genealogy of rulers. These inscriptions provided valuable insights into Maya history and culture.

Classic Period (250 CE - 900 CE): The Classic Period is often regarded as the zenith of Maya civilization. During this era, city-states like Tikal, Calakmul, Caracol, Copán, and Palenque reached their peak in terms of political power, artistic achievements, and architectural grandeur. These city-states engaged in political alliances, rivalries, and warfare, resulting in the construction of impressive fortifications and defensive structures.

Artistic Flourish: Classic Maya art flourished, with monumental stelae, elaborately decorated temples, and intricate murals adorning city centers. The stelae were inscribed with hieroglyphs, recounting the histories and achievements of rulers and dynasties. The artistic endeavors, including pottery, sculpture, and mural paintings, reflected deep religious and mythological beliefs.

Calendrical Systems: The Classic Period saw the refinement of Maya calendrical systems, including the Tzolk'in (260-day ritual calendar) and the Haab' (365-day solar calendar). These calendars played a crucial role in religious rituals, agricultural planning, and governance. The Maya's advanced understanding of astronomy enabled them to make precise astronomical observations and calculations.

Decline and Collapse: Despite their cultural achievements, the Classic Period also witnessed the gradual decline and collapse of many Maya city-states. Factors contributing to this decline are complex and include environmental stressors, warfare, resource depletion, and political unrest. Many city-states were abandoned or depopulated during this time.

Postclassic Period (900 CE - 1500 CE): Following the collapse of many Classic Period city-states, the Maya civilization entered the Postclassic Period. During this time, new centers of power emerged, including Chichen Itza and Mayapan in the northern Yucatán Peninsula. The Postclassic Period saw the continued development of Maya culture, including the introduction of new architectural styles and religious practices influenced by external factors.

In summary, the rise of Maya city-states represents a complex and dynamic process that unfolded over centuries, marked by periods of growth, artistic achievement, political complexity, and eventual decline. These city-states, with their monumental architecture and sophisticated hieroglyphic writing, were the epicenters of Maya culture and politics, and their legacies continue to captivate the world today, offering valuable insights into the rich and multifaceted history of Mesoamerica.

The Maya social hierarchy was a complex and stratified structure that played a crucial role in shaping the civilization's political, religious, and cultural dynamics. Within Maya society, individuals held distinct roles and responsibilities based on their social status, and this hierarchy was central to the functioning of Maya city-states. The Maya civilization, which thrived in the lowlands of Mesoamerica from the Preclassic Period (2000 BCE - 250 CE) to the Postclassic Period (900 CE - 1500 CE), exhibited a diverse range of social classes, each with its own privileges and obligations.

K'uhul Ajaw (Divine Lord) or Ajaw (Lord): At the pinnacle of Maya society were the k'uhul ajaw or ajaw, also known as the divine lords or lords. These rulers were the political and religious leaders of Maya city-states. They claimed divine authority and were believed to have direct connections with the gods. Ruling from elaborate palace complexes, they governed their territories, conducted religious ceremonies, and were responsible for the well-being of their subjects. The title of ruler was hereditary, often passed down within a royal dynasty.

Nobility: Below the rulers, the nobility comprised a privileged class of individuals who held high-ranking positions in Maya society. They included members of the ruling family, nobles, and officials who served the rulers in various administrative and religious capacities. The nobility enjoyed access to luxury goods, elaborate feasts, and prestigious marriages, and they played a crucial role in maintaining the power and stability of city-states.

Elites and Officials: Beneath the nobility were the elites and officials who served as advisors, administrators, and military commanders. These individuals were responsible for the governance of city-states, managing tribute and taxation, overseeing public works projects, and maintaining order. They often held titles that reflected their roles, such as chak'an (governor) or batab (local ruler).

Artisans and Craftsmen: Artisans and craftsmen constituted a skilled and valued segment of Maya society. They were responsible for creating intricate works of art, pottery, textiles, and other valuable goods. Skilled craftsmen were highly respected and contributed to the artistic and cultural richness of the Maya civilization.

Merchants and Traders: Merchants and traders played a crucial role in facilitating long-distance trade networks that connected Maya city-states with neighboring regions. They transported goods such as obsidian, jade, cacao, and marine shells, contributing to the economic prosperity of Maya society. While they did not hold high social status compared to rulers and nobility, successful merchants could amass wealth and influence.

Commoners: The majority of Maya society consisted of commoners who engaged in various occupations, including farming, fishing, and laboring in construction and public projects. Commoners provided the agricultural surplus that sustained city-states and formed the backbone of the labor force. They were subject to taxation and tribute demands from the ruling elite.

Slaves and Captives: Slaves and captives occupied the lowest rung of the Maya social hierarchy. They were individuals who had been captured in warfare or born into slavery. Slaves were used for various tasks, including agricultural labor, construction work, and serving the ruling elite. While they lacked freedom, some were able to gain their freedom through acts of valor or service.

Hierarchy Within Maya City-States: Maya city-states had their own hierarchical structures. At the center of each city-state was the royal palace complex, which included the ruler's residence, temples, and administrative buildings. Surrounding the central core were residential areas where the nobility and elites lived. Beyond this, there were commoner neighborhoods and agricultural fields. The arrangement reflected the hierarchical organization of society, with the ruler and nobility residing in the most prominent locations.

Religious Roles: Maya religion played a significant role in social hierarchy. Priests and priestesses held important positions within the religious structure and conducted ceremonies, rituals, and offerings to appease the gods. Maya rulers often had dual roles as political leaders and high priests, further emphasizing their divine connections.

Gender Roles: Gender roles also played a part in the Maya social hierarchy. While men and women had distinct roles, both genders could achieve prominence and respect within their respective spheres. Men typically held political and religious leadership positions, while women were responsible for domestic duties and child-rearing. Some women, particularly noble women, held positions of authority and influence.

In summary, the Maya social hierarchy was a multifaceted system that defined the roles and responsibilities of individuals within Maya society. It was characterized by distinct classes, with rulers and nobility at the top, followed by elites, commoners, and slaves. This hierarchy was closely intertwined with political, religious, and economic aspects of Maya civilization and contributed to its complexity and stability. Understanding the intricacies of the Maya social hierarchy is essential for comprehending the dynamics of this remarkable Mesoamerican civilization and its enduring legacy.

Governance and leadership were fundamental aspects of the Maya civilization, and they played a central role in shaping the political, social, and religious dynamics of Maya city-states. The Maya, who thrived in the lowlands of Mesoamerica from the Preclassic Period (2000 BCE - 250 CE) to the Postclassic Period (900 CE - 1500 CE), developed a complex system of governance characterized by hereditary rulership, divine authority, and elaborate political hierarchies.

Divine Authority and Rulership: At the heart of Maya governance was the belief in divine authority vested in rulers. Maya rulers, often referred to as k'uhul ajaw (divine lords) or ajaw (lords), were believed to have direct connections with the gods. This divine aspect of rulership was a cornerstone of Maya political ideology and was essential for maintaining order and legitimacy in society. Rulers were seen as intermediaries between the human world and the divine realm.

Hereditary Rulership: Maya rulership was typically hereditary, passed down within royal dynasties. The position of ruler was not open to commoners or outsiders but was confined to the ruling elite and nobility. Inheritance of the throne was based on royal lineage and often followed strict rules of primogeniture, where the eldest son would succeed the current ruler.

City-States and Local Governance: Maya civilization was composed of numerous city-states, each with its own ruler and political structure. These city-states were often autonomous entities with their own administrative systems, territories, and allegiances. Governance at the local level was conducted by rulers, governors (chak'an), and officials who oversaw the affairs of the city-state, including taxation, public works, and defense.

Political Alliances and Conflicts: Maya city-states frequently engaged in political alliances, rivalries, and conflicts. These alliances were forged through marriage alliances, trade agreements, and shared military objectives. City-states formed powerful alliances to strengthen their positions and to counter external threats. Conflicts between city-states were not uncommon and often revolved around territorial disputes, resource competition, or attempts to assert dominance.

Hieroglyphic Inscriptions: Maya rulers recorded their political achievements, genealogies, and historical events on monumental stelae, altars, and other inscriptions using hieroglyphic writing. These inscriptions provided a record of the ruler's reign, important events, and the lineage of rulers in a particular city-state. They were used to legitimize the ruler's authority and to commemorate important ceremonies and conquests.

Religious Leadership: Maya rulers often held dual roles as political leaders and high priests. Religion played a central role in Maya society, and rulers were responsible for conducting religious ceremonies, offering sacrifices, and appeasing the gods. This dual role reinforced the ruler's divine authority and emphasized the interconnection between religion and governance.

Councils and Advisors: Maya rulers were advised by councils and a network of advisors who played crucial roles in decision-making. These advisors included priests, nobles, military commanders, and administrative officials. Rulers often sought their counsel on matters of governance, including trade, warfare, taxation, and alliances.

Tribute and Taxation: City-states relied on tribute and taxation to sustain their political and economic stability. Commoners and subject communities were required to provide tribute in the form of agricultural produce, labor, and valuable goods. This tribute supported the ruling elite and the maintenance of city-state infrastructure.

Enduring Legacies: The governance and leadership structures of the Maya civilization have left enduring legacies in contemporary Maya communities. While the political landscape has evolved over the centuries, some elements of traditional Maya governance, such as local councils and community leadership, persist in modern Maya society. Additionally, the Maya hieroglyphic writing system and inscriptions continue to provide valuable insights into the political history and governance of the ancient Maya.

In summary, governance and leadership were integral components of Maya civilization, marked by hereditary rulership, divine authority, and complex political hierarchies. The Maya city-states were dynamic entities with distinct political structures, alliances, and conflicts. Maya rulers played pivotal roles as political leaders and religious figures, reinforcing the interconnectedness of governance and spirituality. Understanding the intricacies of Maya governance is essential for comprehending the political and cultural dynamics of this remarkable Mesoamerican civilization.

Chapter 3: Writing and Glyphs: Decoding the Maya Script (500 CE - 1000 CE)

The Maya writing system, also known as Maya hieroglyphics, is one of the most complex and sophisticated writing systems of the ancient world. Developed by the Maya civilization, which thrived in the lowlands of Mesoamerica from the Preclassic Period (2000 BCE - 250 CE) to the Postclassic Period (900 CE - 1500 CE), this script was used for a wide range of purposes, including recording historical events, religious rituals, astronomical observations, and genealogies. The Maya writing system is characterized by its intricate glyphs and its ability to convey both phonetic and logographic meanings.

Hieroglyphic Writing: The Maya writing system is often referred to as "hieroglyphic" due to its use of intricate symbols or glyphs to represent words, syllables, or concepts. These glyphs were meticulously carved or painted onto various surfaces, including stelae, codices (books made of bark paper), pottery, and architecture. The Maya hieroglyphic script is distinct from the cuneiform script of Mesopotamia or the hieroglyphs of ancient Egypt.

Phonetic and Logographic Elements: One of the remarkable features of the Maya script is its combination of phonetic and logographic elements. While some glyphs represent whole words or concepts (logograms), others represent syllables (syllabic signs). This duality allows for a flexible and nuanced expression of the Maya language. The Maya script is, therefore, a logosyllabic system.

Syllabic Signs: The Maya writing system contains approximately 800 distinct syllabic signs, each representing a combination of a consonant and a vowel sound. These syllabic signs allowed scribes to write any word in the Maya language by combining the appropriate syllables. Syllabic signs are typically composed of one to three components and can be arranged in various ways to form complex words.

Logograms: In addition to syllabic signs, the Maya script also features logograms, which represent entire words or concepts. Logograms are often accompanied by phonetic complement signs that clarify the pronunciation of the word. Logograms were used for important names, places, and deities, among other things.

Complexity and Precision: Maya hieroglyphics are known for their complexity and precision. Some glyphs are highly detailed and intricate, making them visually stunning. Scribes underwent extensive training to master the script, and their expertise allowed them to create inscriptions that conveyed detailed historical narratives, astronomical calculations, and religious texts.

Hieroglyphic Blocks: Maya inscriptions are typically organized into hieroglyphic blocks, which consist of a central glyph surrounded by additional glyphs that provide context and meaning. These blocks are read in a sequence that conveys the intended message or narrative. Reading Maya hieroglyphs involves deciphering the relationships between glyphs within a block and understanding their chronological order.

Codices and Books: The Maya also created codices, which were books made of bark paper. These codices contained hieroglyphic writing and illustrated scenes. While many Maya codices were destroyed during the Spanish conquest, a few have survived, such as the Dresden Codex and the Madrid Codex. These codices provide valuable insights into Maya calendrical systems, astronomy, and religious beliefs.

Decipherment: The decipherment of the Maya writing system was a significant achievement in the field of Mesoamerican archaeology and linguistics. Scholars such as David Stuart and Michael D. Coe made breakthroughs in understanding the script's phonetic and logographic elements. The decipherment revealed insights into Maya history, culture, and society, including the names of rulers, historical events, and religious rituals.

Continued Study: Maya hieroglyphs continue to be the subject of ongoing research and study. Scholars are working to decipher remaining inscriptions and expand our understanding of Maya history and culture. The script's intricate nature and the vast quantity of surviving inscriptions ensure that there is much still to be learned from this remarkable writing system.

In summary, the Maya writing system, characterized by its hieroglyphic script, phonetic and logographic elements, and complexity, is a testament to the intellectual achievements of the Maya civilization. It served as a means of recording history, expressing religious beliefs, and communicating complex ideas. The decipherment of Maya hieroglyphs has opened new doors to understanding the rich and multifaceted culture of the ancient Maya, providing valuable insights into their language, society, and worldview.

Maya glyphs and hieroglyphics are the written symbols and script of the Maya civilization, representing a remarkable system of communication that played a vital role in recording their history, culture, and beliefs. The Maya script, known for its complexity and sophistication, is both logographic and syllabic, allowing scribes to convey meaning through a combination of symbols that represented whole words, syllables, or concepts. This system of writing, created by the Maya people, remains a testament to their intellectual achievements and serves as a key to unlocking the secrets of their civilization.

Logograms and Syllabic Signs: Maya glyphs are divided into two main categories: logograms and syllabic signs. Logograms are symbols that represent entire words or concepts, while syllabic signs represent syllables composed of consonant-vowel combinations. The combination of these two types of glyphs allowed Maya scribes to convey a wide range of information in their inscriptions.

Hieroglyphic Blocks: Maya hieroglyphics are typically organized into hieroglyphic blocks. These blocks consist of a central glyph that serves as the main element of the inscription, surrounded by additional glyphs that provide context, modifiers, or additional information. Reading Maya hieroglyphs involves deciphering the relationships between glyphs within a block and understanding their chronological order.

Detailed and Intricate Glyphs: Maya glyphs are known for their intricate and detailed designs. Some glyphs are highly artistic, incorporating elements of nature, culture, and mythology. The visual complexity of the glyphs adds an aesthetic dimension to Maya inscriptions, making them not only functional but also visually captivating.

Phonetic Complement Signs: To aid in the pronunciation of logograms, Maya scribes often included phonetic complement signs. These signs indicated the syllabic sounds that accompanied the logogram. This allowed readers to understand how to pronounce the word represented by the logogram, as the Maya script did not record vowels explicitly.

Hieroglyphic Inscriptions: Hieroglyphic inscriptions were created using various materials, including stone, pottery, stucco, and bark paper. They were carved, painted, or incised onto these surfaces, preserving a wealth of information about Maya history, politics, religion, and daily life. Inscriptions were commonly found on stelae (stone monuments), temple facades, altars, and ceramic vessels.

Codices and Books: The Maya also created codices, which were books made of bark paper. These codices contained hieroglyphic writing and illustrated scenes that provided information about the Maya calendar, astronomy, mythology, and rituals. While many Maya codices were destroyed during the Spanish conquest, a few have survived, offering valuable insights into Maya knowledge and traditions.

Decipherment: The decipherment of Maya hieroglyphs was a significant breakthrough in the study of Mesoamerican archaeology and linguistics. Scholars such as David Stuart and Michael D. Coe made substantial contributions to understanding the script's phonetic and logographic elements. Their work led to the decoding of Maya inscriptions, allowing researchers to read and interpret the texts.

Historical Records: Maya hieroglyphs served as historical records, documenting events such as royal successions, battles, and important ceremonies. These inscriptions provided valuable information about Maya rulers, their achievements, and the dynastic history of city-states. They also shed light on political alliances, conflicts, and territorial boundaries.

Religious and Ritual Texts: Maya hieroglyphics played a central role in religious and ritual contexts. Inscriptions recorded religious ceremonies, offerings to deities, and the movement of celestial bodies. This information was crucial for the Maya in conducting their religious practices and understanding the cosmos.

Continued Research: The study of Maya glyphs and hieroglyphics continues to be an active area of research. Ongoing efforts focus on deciphering remaining inscriptions and expanding our understanding of Maya culture, history, and language. New discoveries and insights into the script's nuances continue to emerge, enriching our knowledge of the ancient Maya civilization.

Legacy and Cultural Significance: Maya hieroglyphs are a testament to the intellectual and artistic achievements of the Maya civilization. They underscore the importance of writing and literacy in Maya society and reveal the depth of their knowledge in various fields. The preservation of Maya hieroglyphs in inscriptions and codices has allowed contemporary scholars to piece together the story of the Maya people and appreciate their contributions to the world of written language and culture.

In summary, Maya glyphs and hieroglyphics represent an extraordinary system of writing that played a pivotal role in documenting the history, beliefs, and culture of the Maya civilization. Their combination of logograms and syllabic signs, along with intricate visual design, allowed Maya scribes to create rich and multifaceted inscriptions. The decipherment of Maya hieroglyphs has opened doors to understanding the Maya world, and ongoing research continues to unveil the secrets encoded in these remarkable symbols.

Unlocking Maya history is a fascinating journey that involves decoding the mysteries of one of the most remarkable civilizations of the ancient world. The Maya civilization, which thrived in the lowlands of Mesoamerica from approximately 2000 BCE to 1500 CE, left behind a legacy of sophisticated cities, intricate hieroglyphic writing, complex calendars, and a rich cultural heritage. Unlocking the history of the Maya involves piecing together the puzzle of their past through archaeological discoveries, deciphering hieroglyphics, and exploring the remnants of their culture that endure to this day.

Archaeological Discoveries: The foundation of unlocking Maya history lies in the excavation and study of archaeological sites. Over the years, archaeologists have unearthed ancient Maya cities, temples, pyramids, palaces, and artifacts that offer insights into their daily lives, architecture, and technological achievements. Sites such as Tikal, Palenque, Caracol, and Copán have revealed the grandeur of Maya civilization.

Hieroglyphic Decipherment: One of the most significant breakthroughs in understanding Maya history was the decipherment of Maya hieroglyphs. Initially considered undecipherable, the work of scholars like David Stuart and Michael D. Coe led to the unlocking of this intricate script. Deciphered hieroglyphs provide a wealth of information about Maya rulers, dynasties, historical events, and religious rituals.

Calendar Systems: The Maya are renowned for their intricate calendar systems, including the Tzolk'in (260-day sacred calendar) and the Haab' (365-day solar calendar). Understanding and decoding these calendars is essential for unraveling Maya history. The calendars allowed the Maya to track celestial events, predict agricultural cycles, and plan religious ceremonies.

Historical Inscriptions: Maya cities are adorned with hieroglyphic inscriptions on stelae, monuments, and temple facades. These inscriptions record historical events, including royal successions, battles, and ceremonies. They provide invaluable historical records that help piece together the chronology of Maya civilization.

Codices and Books: Despite the destruction of many Maya codices during the Spanish conquest, a few have survived and offer essential insights into Maya history. These bark-paper books contain hieroglyphic writing and illustrations that convey information about astronomy, religious rituals, and mythology. The Dresden Codex and the Madrid Codex are among the most famous surviving examples.

Trade and Economy: The study of trade networks and economic systems is another key to unlocking Maya history. The Maya engaged in extensive trade, exchanging goods such as obsidian, jade, cacao, and textiles with neighboring regions. Understanding trade routes and economic practices provides a glimpse into Maya society and its interactions with other cultures.

Religion and Cosmology: Maya religion was deeply intertwined with their daily lives and history. Temples, pyramids, and other structures served as centers for religious ceremonies and astronomical observations. Hieroglyphic inscriptions reveal details about the worship of deities, rituals, and the Maya understanding of the cosmos.

Settlement Patterns: Analyzing settlement patterns, urban planning, and the layout of Maya cities is crucial for understanding their societal organization and history. The design of Maya cities, with plazas, ball courts, and monumental architecture, reflects their social and political structure.

Legacy and Continuity: The Maya civilization did not vanish entirely but transformed into modern Maya communities that continue to preserve elements of their ancestral culture. Exploring the contemporary Maya way of life and traditions provides valuable insights into the enduring legacy of Maya history.

Environmental Factors: Understanding the environmental factors that influenced Maya history is also essential. The Maya adapted to a diverse range of ecosystems, from tropical rainforests to arid lowlands, and their agricultural practices, such as terracing and raised fields, played a significant role in sustaining their civilization. In summary, unlocking Maya history is a multidisciplinary endeavor that combines archaeology, decipherment, anthropology, and the study of culture and society. It is a journey that involves piecing together fragments of the past to create a comprehensive picture of this extraordinary civilization. The Maya's achievements in art, science, architecture, and governance continue to captivate researchers and enthusiasts, shedding light on a civilization that thrived for millennia and left an indelible mark on the history of Mesoamerica.

Maya celestial observations represent a profound aspect of the ancient Maya civilization's knowledge and culture. The Maya, who inhabited the lush rainforests and fertile lowlands of Mesoamerica for thousands of years, developed a keen understanding of the cosmos. Their celestial observations were not only instrumental for practical purposes, such as agriculture and timekeeping, but they also held deep religious and cultural significance. Through the study of celestial phenomena, the Maya created complex calendrical systems, constructed architectural marvels aligned with celestial events, and established a profound connection between the earthly realm and the celestial heavens.

Astronomy and Cosmology: At the heart of Maya celestial observations was the understanding of astronomy and cosmology. The Maya observed and recorded celestial events, such as the movements of the sun, moon, planets, and stars, with great precision. Their celestial knowledge was intertwined with their religious beliefs and mythology, shaping their worldview and guiding their actions.

Solar Observations: The Maya carefully tracked the movements of the sun, recognizing its vital role in agriculture and daily life. They developed a solar calendar known as the Haab', which consisted of 365 days. This calendar allowed them to predict solstices and equinoxes, crucial events for agricultural planning.

Lunar Observations: The moon also played a significant role in Maya celestial observations. The Maya had a lunar calendar called the Tzolk'in, consisting of 260 days. This calendar was used for religious and ritual purposes, as well as for tracking the moon's phases, which were essential for determining planting and harvesting times.

Venus and Planetary Observations: Venus, often referred to as the "Morning Star" and the "Evening Star," held special significance for the Maya. They carefully observed Venus's appearances and disappearances on the horizon, which had both astronomical and religious meanings. Venus observations were incorporated into the Maya calendar and played a role in determining auspicious times for various activities.

Stellar Observations: The Maya had a deep knowledge of the stars and constellations. They used stars as navigational aids and integrated stellar alignments into the layout of their cities and ceremonial centers. Notable examples include the alignment of certain buildings with specific stars during solstices.

Architectural Alignments: Maya architectural achievements often displayed a profound understanding of celestial phenomena. Many temples and pyramids were oriented to align with the sun or stars during significant events like solstices or equinoxes. These alignments highlight the Maya's reverence for the cosmos and their belief in the interconnectedness of the earthly and celestial realms.

Eclipses: The Maya possessed the ability to predict solar and lunar eclipses with remarkable accuracy. Eclipses were seen as significant celestial events, and the Maya associated them with portents, omens, and religious ceremonies. Their ability to predict eclipses was a testament to their advanced astronomical knowledge.

Mythology and Religion: Maya celestial observations were deeply intertwined with their mythology and religion. Deities and celestial bodies were closely linked in their belief system. For instance, the sun god Kinich Ahau and the moon goddess Ix Chel were central figures in Maya mythology, and their movements were observed and celebrated.

Calendrical Systems: The Maya developed several intricate calendrical systems, including the Long Count calendar, which tracked longer periods of time, and the Tzolk'in and Haab', which governed daily life and agriculture. These calendars were used for a wide range of purposes, from marking historical events to scheduling religious ceremonies.

Rituals and Ceremonies: Celestial observations played a vital role in Maya rituals and ceremonies. Important events in the celestial calendar, such as solstices and equinoxes, were marked by elaborate ceremonies conducted by priests and rulers. These rituals often involved offerings, sacrifices, and prayers to appease celestial deities.

Continued Cultural Significance: Today, the Maya's celestial observations continue to hold cultural significance among contemporary Maya communities. Traditional practices and ceremonies, rooted in celestial knowledge, are still observed by some Maya groups, preserving the ancient connection between the people and the cosmos.

In summary, Maya celestial observations reflect the profound relationship between the Maya civilization and the cosmos. Their advanced knowledge of astronomy, calendrical systems, and architectural alignments demonstrated their deep reverence for celestial phenomena. Celestial events served as markers of time, guided agricultural practices, and provided a framework for religious beliefs and rituals. Maya celestial observations remain a testament to their intellectual achievements and continue to inspire awe and fascination in the modern world, offering insights into the rich cultural tapestry of this ancient civilization.

Sacred Maya calendars are at the heart of the ancient Maya civilization's intricate system of timekeeping and cosmology. These calendars were not merely tools for tracking days and years; they held profound religious and cultural significance, shaping every aspect of Maya life, from agriculture to rituals and governance. The Maya developed multiple calendars, each serving a specific purpose, and their intricate understanding of celestial phenomena allowed them to create calendars that continue to captivate scholars and enthusiasts alike.

The Tzolk'in Calendar: The Tzolk'in, also known as the "sacred calendar" or the "divinatory calendar," was central to Maya religious and ritual life. It consists of 260 days, with each day represented by a combination of a number and a glyph. The Tzolk'in was used for divination, determining auspicious times for ceremonies, and guiding personal and communal activities.

The Haab' Calendar: The Haab' calendar, sometimes called the "civil calendar" or the "solar calendar," consisted of 365 days divided into 18 months of 20 days each, with a final five-day month known as the "wayeb." This calendar governed agriculture, allowing the Maya to schedule planting and harvesting based on the changing seasons and solar events.

The Long Count Calendar: The Long Count calendar was a remarkable creation that allowed the Maya to track longer periods of time. It used a base-20 counting system, combining various units to measure time in terms of "k'ins" (days), "winals" (20 days), "tuns" (360 days), "k'atuns" (7,200 days), and "b'aktuns" (144,000 days). The Long Count was instrumental for recording historical events and marking the passage of centuries.

The Calendar Round: The Calendar Round was a 52-year cycle that resulted from the simultaneous interplay of the Tzolk'in and Haab' calendars. It allowed the Maya to synchronize these calendars, creating a repeating cycle of dates. After 52 years, the same Tzolk'in date would align with the same Haab' date, but it would be in a different Calendar Round.

Astronomical Alignments: The Maya were skilled astronomers who observed celestial phenomena with great precision. They used their knowledge of celestial events, such as solstices, equinoxes, and the movements of Venus, to align their calendars and temples with the heavens. These alignments played a crucial role in religious rituals and architectural design.

Religious Significance: Sacred Maya calendars were deeply intertwined with religious beliefs and practices. The Tzolk'in, in particular, played a central role in divination and rituals. Each day had specific attributes and meanings associated with it, and priests would consult the Tzolk'in to determine the most propitious times for various activities, including ceremonies, sacrifices, and important decisions.

Ceremonial Cycles: The Maya conducted elaborate ceremonies and rituals throughout the year, guided by the sacred calendars. These ceremonies often corresponded to celestial events, such as solar and lunar eclipses, equinoxes, and the heliacal rising of Venus. Rituals were performed to honor deities, seek divine guidance, and maintain the balance of the cosmos.

Agricultural Practices: The Haab' calendar was instrumental for Maya agriculture. It allowed them to schedule planting and harvesting based on the changing seasons and solar positions. The five-day month of "wayeb" was considered a time of transition and potential danger, during which rituals were performed to protect crops and communities.

Political and Dynastic Significance: The Long Count calendar played a significant role in recording historical events and dynastic histories. Maya rulers used it to inscribe stelae and monuments with their achievements and reigns. These inscriptions provided a chronological record of rulers and events, contributing to the understanding of Maya political history.

Modern Interpretations: Maya calendars continue to hold fascination in the modern world. While the ancient Maya civilization declined, their calendar systems and cosmological beliefs persist among contemporary Maya communities. Scholars, archaeologists, and enthusiasts continue to study and interpret the Maya calendars, uncovering new insights into their complexity and cultural significance.

Misconceptions and the 2012 Phenomenon: The Maya calendars garnered widespread attention in the lead-up to December 21, 2012, which marked the end of a b'aktun in the Long Count calendar. Many misconceptions and sensationalized interpretations arose, suggesting that this date signified the end of the world. However, scholars clarified that it marked the end of one cycle and the beginning of another, similar to the changing of a calendar year.

In summary, sacred Maya calendars represent a remarkable achievement of timekeeping and cosmology in the ancient world. The Maya's intricate understanding of celestial phenomena allowed them to create calendars that not only served practical purposes but also held deep religious, cultural, and political significance. These calendars provided a framework for Maya life, from guiding agricultural practices to shaping religious rituals, and their legacy endures in the study of Mesoamerican culture and the fascination with ancient civilizations.

Astronomy and rituals in various cultures have long been intertwined, reflecting the profound connection between humanity and the cosmos. Throughout history, people have looked to the skies with wonder, seeking to understand the celestial bodies that adorn the night and day. This fascination with the heavens has given rise to rituals, ceremonies, and belief systems that incorporate celestial events and cosmic symbolism. The intricate relationship between astronomy and rituals has been a defining feature of numerous civilizations and cultures, from the ancient Egyptians and Maya to modern-day observances.

Ancient Egyptian Astronomy and Rituals: In ancient Egypt, astronomy played a significant role in religious and funerary practices. The alignment of temples and pyramids with celestial events, such as the rising of specific stars like Sirius, demonstrated the Egyptians' reverence for the heavens. The annual flooding of the Nile, essential for agriculture, was closely linked to the heliacal rising of the star Sirius, signaling the start of the flood season. This celestial event was marked by rituals and festivals.

Maya Astronomy and Rituals: The ancient Maya civilization of Mesoamerica was renowned for its advanced understanding of astronomy, particularly the movements of celestial bodies like the sun, moon, and Venus. Maya astronomers meticulously observed these phenomena and incorporated their observations into religious ceremonies and rituals. Temples and pyramids were often aligned with astronomical events, serving as instruments for marking important dates and conducting rituals associated with the celestial cycles.

Solstices and Equinoxes: Solstices and equinoxes, which mark the changing seasons and the sun's apparent movement in the sky, have held immense significance in various cultures. Many rituals and festivals coincide with these celestial events. For example, the summer and winter solstices are celebrated in cultures around the world with ceremonies, gatherings, and the construction of ancient structures aligned with these solar milestones.

Eclipses: Solar and lunar eclipses, which have been viewed with awe and sometimes fear throughout history, have often prompted rituals and ceremonies. In some cultures, eclipses were seen as omens or portents, and rituals were performed to appease the celestial forces responsible for these phenomena. Eclipse observations also contributed to the development of early astronomy.

Star Worship: The worship of specific stars or constellations is a recurring theme in the history of astronomy and rituals. In ancient Mesopotamia, the Babylonians associated certain deities with celestial bodies and conducted rituals to honor them. Similarly, in Hinduism, the star Sirius (known as Nakshatra) is revered, and its position in the night sky is considered auspicious for various rituals and ceremonies.

Cosmic Creation Myths: Many cultures have creation myths that involve celestial events and deities. These myths often serve as the foundation for religious rituals and beliefs. For example, the Greek myth of the Titan Atlas holding up the heavens is tied to the naming of the Atlas Mountains, and the story of creation in the Bible's book of Genesis includes the creation of the sun, moon, and stars.

Lunar Calendars: Lunar calendars, based on the phases of the moon, have been widely used for religious and cultural purposes. In Islamic culture, the lunar calendar determines the timing of religious observances, including Ramadan. Similarly, the Jewish calendar is lunar-based and plays a central role in determining the timing of religious holidays such as Passover and Rosh Hashanah.

Modern Astronomy and Rituals: In the modern era, the connection between astronomy and rituals continues to be observed. Astronomy enthusiasts and amateur astronomers often gather for stargazing events, astronomical observations, and celestial celebrations. The annual Perseid meteor shower, for example, draws people around the world to witness the "shooting stars" and engage in celestial rituals.

Astrology: While not a scientific discipline, astrology is deeply rooted in the belief that celestial bodies influence human behavior and destiny. Astrology has its own set of rituals and practices, such as chart readings, horoscope consultations, and the casting of astrological charts for significant life events.

New Year Celebrations: New Year celebrations in various cultures are often tied to astronomical events. For instance, the Western New Year coincides with the first day of the Gregorian calendar, which is based on the Earth's orbit around the sun. In Chinese culture, the Lunar New Year aligns with the second new moon after the winter solstice, marking the beginning of the lunar calendar.

Modern Observatories: Modern astronomical observatories and research facilities contribute to the understanding of the cosmos and serve as centers for scientific study. While not religious in nature, these observatories conduct rituals of a different kind — the systematic observation and study of the universe to expand our knowledge of the cosmos.

In summary, the interplay between astronomy and rituals has been a consistent and profound aspect of human culture and history. From ancient civilizations that aligned their structures with celestial events to modern celebrations of cosmic phenomena, the connection between the earthly and the celestial realms has been a source of wonder, inspiration, and spiritual significance for people throughout time. Astronomy and rituals continue to shape our understanding of the cosmos and our place within it, reflecting the enduring human quest to connect with the mysteries of the universe.

Chapter 5: Artistic Brilliance: Maya Architecture and Visual Arts (200 BCE - 1000 CE)

Maya architectural marvels stand as enduring testaments to the sophistication and ingenuity of the ancient Maya civilization. Spanning thousands of years, from the Preclassic to the Postclassic period (approximately 2000 BCE to 1500 CE), the Maya constructed awe-inspiring cities and monumental structures that continue to captivate archaeologists, historians, and travelers alike. These architectural wonders not only showcase the Maya's engineering prowess but also offer insights into their complex societal organization, religious beliefs, and cultural achievements.

Tikal: Among the most iconic of Maya cities, Tikal is a UNESCO World Heritage Site located in modern-day Guatemala. Tikal's pyramids, temples, and plazas rise above the dense jungle canopy, creating a breathtaking skyline. The towering Temple IV, also known as the "Double-Headed Serpent," is one of the tallest pre-Columbian structures in the Americas, offering panoramic views of the surrounding landscape. Tikal's architecture reflects the Maya's deep connection to the cosmos, with temples aligned to astronomical events.

Palenque: Nestled in the Chiapas region of Mexico, Palenque is renowned for its exquisite architecture and sculptures. The Temple of the Inscriptions houses the tomb of the renowned Maya ruler Pakal the Great, discovered in 1952. The temple's intricate hieroglyphic inscriptions provide valuable historical records. Palenque's Palace is a marvel of Maya architecture, adorned with ornate stucco friezes and intricate carvings, depicting various scenes from Maya mythology and history.

Copán: Situated in present-day Honduras, Copán is known for its intricately carved stelae and altars. The Hieroglyphic Stairway, a monumental staircase adorned with hieroglyphs detailing the dynastic history of Copán, is a prime example of Maya architectural and artistic achievement. The Copán Acropolis features temples, plazas, and the Ball Court, reflecting the Maya's religious and ritualistic practices.

Chichen Itza: Located in Mexico's Yucatán Peninsula, Chichen Itza is one of the most famous Maya archaeological sites. The Kukulkan Pyramid, also known as El Castillo, is an architectural marvel with its precise alignment to the equinoxes, resulting in the famous "serpent" shadow that appears to descend the pyramid's steps during the equinoxes. The Great Ball Court at Chichen Itza is the largest known ball court in Mesoamerica, showcasing the importance of the ball game in Maya culture.

Uxmal: Uxmal, another UNESCO World Heritage Site in the Yucatán Peninsula, boasts a distinctive architectural style characterized by elaborate geometric patterns and Puuc-style architecture. The Pyramid of the Magician, a step pyramid with an elliptical base, is a remarkable feat of engineering and design. Uxmal's Nunnery Quadrangle is adorned with intricately carved facades featuring Maya glyphs and mythological scenes.

Caracol: Situated in Belize, Caracol was one of the largest Maya cities during its heyday. The massive Caana (Sky Palace) pyramid stands as one of the largest man-made structures in Belize. Caracol's complex network of causeways and roads showcases the city's urban planning and infrastructure.

Calakmul: Located deep within the Calakmul Biosphere Reserve in Mexico, Calakmul was a powerful Maya city-state. The city is known for its massive pyramids, including Structure II, which is one of the tallest Maya pyramids ever discovered. Calakmul's architecture reflects the rivalry and competition between Maya city-states in the Classic period.

El Mirador: Located in the remote Petén region of Guatemala, El Mirador is one of the earliest and largest Maya cities. Its massive structures, including the La Danta pyramid, are some of the oldest known Maya architectural marvels. El Mirador's architectural layout and construction techniques reveal the early stages of Maya urban development.

These Maya architectural marvels not only serve as windows into the past but also highlight the Maya's intricate understanding of mathematics, engineering, and astronomy. The precise alignments of temples with celestial events, intricate stucco and stone carvings, hieroglyphic inscriptions, and the grandeur of the pyramids all reflect the Maya's cultural achievements and their deep connection to the cosmos. As these ancient cities continue to be explored and studied, they unveil more secrets of the Maya civilization and inspire wonder at the enduring legacy of their architectural genius.

Visual arts and sculptures have played a central role in human culture and expression throughout history, transcending time, place, and culture. These artistic forms are a testament to the creativity, imagination, and skill of artists who have sought to capture the beauty, emotions, and ideas of their respective eras. From ancient cave paintings to contemporary installations, visual arts and sculptures have been vehicles for storytelling, symbolism, and communication, reflecting the values, beliefs, and experiences of diverse societies.

Ancient Cave Paintings: Some of the earliest known examples of visual arts can be found in ancient cave paintings, dating back tens of thousands of years. These prehistoric artworks, such as those in the Lascaux Caves in France or the Altamira Cave in Spain, depict animals, hunting scenes, and symbolic representations. These early artists used natural pigments and their surroundings to create captivating imagery that provides insights into the lives and cultures of ancient peoples.

Egyptian Art: Ancient Egypt is renowned for its iconic visual arts and sculptures. The pyramids, temples, and tombs are adorned with hieroglyphics, paintings, and sculptures that convey the stories of pharaohs, gods, and daily life in the Nile Valley. The grandeur and precision of Egyptian art, seen in colossal statues like the Great Sphinx and the bust of Nefertiti, continue to awe and inspire.

Classical Greek Sculpture: The ancient Greeks made enduring contributions to the world of visual arts and sculpture. Their mastery of the human form, seen in sculptures like the Venus de Milo and the Discus Thrower (Discobolus), celebrated the idealized beauty of the human body. These sculptures, often made of marble, exemplify the Greek reverence for aesthetics and harmony.

Renaissance Art: The Renaissance marked a revival of interest in classical art and humanism. Artists like Leonardo da Vinci, Michelangelo, and Raphael produced masterpieces that are celebrated for their technical virtuosity and thematic depth. The Mona Lisa's enigmatic smile, Michelangelo's David, and the Sistine Chapel's ceiling are iconic examples of Renaissance visual arts and sculpture.

Impressionism: The Impressionist movement, led by artists like Claude Monet, Edgar Degas, and Pierre-Auguste Renoir, challenged traditional artistic conventions. Their works captured fleeting moments, the play of light, and the impermanence of scenes. Impressionist paintings, such as Water Lilies and Dancers at the Bar, sought to evoke emotions and sensations rather than provide a strict representation of reality.

Modern and Contemporary Art: The 20th and 21st centuries have witnessed diverse and innovative movements in visual arts and sculpture. Cubism, surrealism, abstract expressionism, pop art, and installation art are just a few of the movements that have pushed the boundaries of artistic expression. Artists like Pablo Picasso, Salvador Dalí, Jackson Pollock, Andy Warhol, and Ai Weiwei have challenged conventional notions of art.

Sculptures of Ancient Mesoamerica: In ancient Mesoamerica, civilizations like the Maya and Aztec created intricate sculptures that often served religious and ritualistic purposes. These sculptures depicted deities, rulers, and mythological narratives. The colossal Olmec stone heads, for example, remain enigmatic symbols of ancient Mesoamerican culture, while Aztec sculptures like the Coatlicue statue are striking examples of their religious art.

African Sculpture: The visual arts and sculptures of Africa are rich and diverse, with each region and culture contributing unique artistic traditions. African sculptures are known for their abstraction, symbolism, and use of materials like wood, metal, and ivory. Masks, figurative sculptures, and ceremonial objects are integral to African art, representing spiritual, social, and cultural values.

Asian Art: Asia boasts a wide range of visual arts and sculptures reflecting its diverse cultures and traditions. Chinese bronzes, Japanese woodblock prints, Indian temple sculptures, and Islamic calligraphy all offer unique perspectives on art and spirituality. The Terracotta Army in China, a vast collection of sculpted soldiers, horses, and chariots, is a testament to the artistic achievements of the Qin Dynasty.

Indigenous Art: Indigenous cultures worldwide have a rich tradition of visual arts and sculptures that are deeply connected to their spiritual beliefs, traditions, and landscapes. Native American totem poles, Australian Aboriginal dot paintings, and Inuit stone carvings are examples of indigenous art forms that celebrate heritage and spirituality.

Environmental Art: In recent decades, artists have explored the concept of art as a way to interact with and reshape the environment. Environmental art, also known as land art or earthworks, involves creating installations and sculptures in natural landscapes. Artists like Robert Smithson, Andy Goldsworthy, and Maya Lin use natural materials and settings to create thought-provoking and often temporary works of art.

Digital and New Media Art: The digital age has ushered in new forms of visual arts and sculptures. Digital art, virtual reality installations, and interactive media have expanded the possibilities for artistic expression and audience engagement. Artists like Nam June Paik, Jenny Holzer, and Olafur Eliasson explore the intersection of technology and art.

In summary, visual arts and sculptures are a testament to the human capacity for creativity, expression, and storytelling. From the earliest cave paintings to the cutting-edge digital art of the present day, these artistic forms continue to evolve, challenge conventions, and provide insight into the diverse cultures and perspectives that shape our world. Visual arts and sculptures transcend language and time, serving as powerful vehicles for communication, reflection, and connection across the boundaries of culture and history.

Maya artistic innovations represent a remarkable chapter in the history of Mesoamerican culture and artistry. The ancient Maya civilization, known for its advanced understanding of mathematics, astronomy, and architecture, also demonstrated profound creativity and innovation in the realm of visual arts. Their artistic achievements, characterized by intricate designs, intricate details, and symbolism, continue to captivate scholars and art enthusiasts. Here, we explore some of the key Maya artistic innovations that left an enduring mark on the art world.

Hieroglyphic Writing and Glyphs: One of the most distinctive Maya artistic innovations was the development of a complex writing system composed of hieroglyphic glyphs. Unlike the alphabetic scripts of many other civilizations, Maya hieroglyphs incorporated both logograms (representing entire words or concepts) and syllabic symbols. This script was used to inscribe historical events, religious texts, and the narratives of rulers and gods on various surfaces, including stelae, pottery, and codices. The Dresden Codex, one of the few surviving Maya books, is a prime example of this writing system. The artistic combination of glyphs with intricate drawings created visually striking texts that conveyed both information and aesthetics.

Ceramic Art: Maya ceramic art was distinguished by its exceptional craftsmanship and intricate decorative motifs. Ceramics were not merely functional; they were also pieces of art. Maya potters utilized various techniques, including slip painting, incision, and modeling, to create vessels adorned with elaborate scenes, symbols, and hieroglyphic inscriptions. These ceramics provided valuable insights into Maya daily life, mythology, and history. The polychrome pottery of the Late Classic period, characterized by intricate detailing and vivid colors, remains highly regarded for its artistic sophistication.

Stelae and Monuments: The Maya created monumental stone stelae and monuments that were intricately carved with hieroglyphs and imagery. These massive stone structures served as commemorative markers for important events, including royal accessions, military victories, and ritual ceremonies. Maya stelae often depicted rulers, gods, and historical scenes in intricate detail. The artistic innovation lay in their ability to convey not only historical information but also artistic beauty and cultural symbolism through stone carving.

Relief Sculpture and Stucco: Maya architecture often featured intricate relief sculptures and stucco decorations. Facades of temples and palaces were adorned with scenes of gods, rulers, and mythical creatures. These intricate carvings displayed a mastery of proportion, perspective, and symbolism. The use of stucco allowed for even more elaborate and delicate designs. The Temple of the Cross at Palenque and the Temple of the Inscriptions at Copán are notable examples of this artistic innovation.

Codices and Manuscripts: The Maya created intricate codices, or manuscript books, that were made of bark paper. These codices contained hieroglyphic texts and detailed illustrations of religious rituals, calendrical information, and historical events. While only a few Maya codices have survived, their artistic and cultural significance is immense. The Grolier Codex, for instance, is celebrated for its vivid paintings and hieroglyphs that offer insights into Maya cosmology and rituals.

Textile Art: Maya textile art displayed an exceptional level of craftsmanship and artistic innovation. Intricately woven and embroidered textiles were adorned with intricate patterns, symbols, and colors that conveyed cultural and religious significance. Textiles were used for clothing, ceremonial garments, and as offerings in rituals. The skillful use of natural dyes and weaving techniques allowed the Maya to create textiles of exceptional beauty and complexity.

Iconography and Symbolism: Maya artists developed a rich system of symbolism and iconography that conveyed complex religious, cosmological, and cultural concepts. Symbols such as the ceiba tree, the maize god, the jaguar, and the quetzal bird carried deep cultural meaning and were used in artistic representations to convey spiritual ideas. The use of these symbols contributed to the creation of a visual language that communicated the Maya worldview.

Murals and Frescoes: Some Maya cities featured murals and frescoes on the interior walls of temples and palaces. These large-scale paintings depicted scenes of daily life, religious ceremonies, and mythological narratives. The murals showcased the Maya's mastery of color, composition, and storytelling through visual art. The Bonampak Murals, discovered in a remote Maya site, are renowned for their vivid depictions of court life and warfare.

In summary, Maya artistic innovations were characterized by a deep connection between art, culture, and symbolism. Their contributions to hieroglyphic writing, ceramic art, stelae carving, codices, textile art, iconography, and mural painting continue to be celebrated for their creativity, complexity, and cultural significance. Maya artists left an enduring legacy that not only reveals their remarkable artistic skills but also offers a window into the rich and multifaceted world of Maya civilization.

Chapter 6: Trade Networks and Interactions: Maya Influence on Mesoamerica (1000 CE - 1500 CE)

Maya trade routes were the arteries through which goods, ideas, and culture flowed within the expansive Maya civilization, creating a network that connected diverse regions and played a pivotal role in shaping their society. Stretching across Mesoamerica, from modern-day Mexico to Central America, these trade routes facilitated the exchange of a wide array of commodities, including agricultural products, luxury items, and artistic creations. The intricate web of Maya trade routes not only contributed to economic prosperity but also fostered cultural exchange and societal development.

Geographical Diversity: The Maya civilization was geographically diverse, with distinct ecological zones that ranged from tropical rainforests to highland plateaus. This diversity of environments allowed for the cultivation of a wide variety of crops, such as maize, cacao, cotton, and vanilla, each adapted to specific climate zones. The geographical variation created a natural incentive for trade as Maya city-states sought to acquire resources that were not readily available in their own regions.

Maritime Trade: The Maya civilization bordered both the Pacific Ocean and the Caribbean Sea, providing ample opportunities for maritime trade. Coastal cities and ports, such as Tulum on the Yucatán Peninsula, served as hubs for trade along the coasts and facilitated interactions with other Mesoamerican cultures, including the Olmec and later, the Aztec.

Overland Trade Routes: Overland trade routes were crucial for connecting the highland and lowland regions of the Maya civilization. The highlands produced valuable resources like obsidian, jade, and quetzal feathers, while the lowlands were known for their agricultural output. Well-established paths and roads, often maintained by city-states or alliances, allowed for the movement of goods between these regions. The Classic Maya city of Calakmul, located deep within the rainforest, controlled important trade routes that passed through its territory.

Interregional Trade: The Maya were active participants in broader Mesoamerican trade networks. They engaged in trade with neighboring cultures, such as the Teotihuacan civilization in central Mexico, which was a major trade partner. Obsidian, a volcanic glass used for tools and weapons, was a valuable commodity traded extensively. The Maya also exchanged textiles, pottery, and luxury goods like cacao, which was used as currency and for making chocolate.

Cacao as Currency: Cacao beans held a special place in Maya trade, serving not only as a valuable commodity but also as a form of currency. The Maya used cacao to facilitate trade and engage in economic transactions. Cacao-based drinks were highly prized in Maya society and were used in rituals and ceremonies. Cacao beans were so important that they were sometimes used in place of more traditional forms of currency.

Long-Distance Trade: The Maya engaged in long-distance trade that extended beyond their immediate neighbors. Evidence suggests that they traded with regions as far away as modern-day Honduras, Belize, Guatemala, and even as far south as El Salvador and Nicaragua. This long-distance trade required intricate organization and the establishment of trusted trade relationships.

Impact on Maya Society: Maya trade routes had a profound impact on their society. Trade brought valuable resources to different regions, enhancing the quality of life for Maya people. It allowed for the acquisition of exotic items and promoted the spread of artistic and cultural influences. Through trade, the Maya gained access to materials like jade and obsidian, which were highly prized for their craftsmanship. The exchange of ideas and religious practices also occurred along trade routes, contributing to the cultural diversity within the Maya world.

City-State Rivalry: Competition over control of trade routes often led to conflicts and rivalries among Maya city-states. Dominance of key trade routes was a source of political power and economic influence. City-states like Tikal and Calakmul vied for control of critical trade paths, and conflicts over trade played a role in shaping the political landscape of the Maya civilization.

Decline and Shifts in Trade: The decline of the Classic Maya civilization around the 9th century CE was accompanied by changes in trade patterns. While some trade continued, the vast Maya city-states of the southern lowlands experienced a decline in population and economic activity. The reasons for this decline remain a subject of debate among scholars, but factors such as environmental stress, warfare, and political instability likely played a role.

In summary, Maya trade routes were the lifeblood of their civilization, enabling the movement of goods, ideas, and culture throughout their expansive territory. These trade networks not only facilitated economic exchange but also contributed to the richness and diversity of Maya society. Through overland routes, maritime trade, and long-distance connections, the Maya engaged with neighboring cultures, established economic alliances, and played an active role in the broader Mesoamerican trade networks. The legacy of their trade routes endures as a testament to the Maya's economic prowess and their ability to thrive in a geographically diverse and interconnected world.

Cultural exchanges have played a pivotal role in shaping the development of societies throughout history, facilitating the flow of ideas, customs, beliefs, art, and technology across regions and civilizations. These exchanges have been driven by various factors, including trade, conquest, migration, diplomacy, and intellectual curiosity. As cultures interacted and intersected, they enriched each other and contributed to the dynamic tapestry of human civilization.

Trade and Economic Exchanges: Trade has been one of the primary drivers of cultural exchanges throughout history. As goods moved along trade routes, merchants and traders carried not only commodities but also cultural elements with them. The Silk Road, for example, connected East and West, facilitating the exchange of silk, spices, precious metals, and ideas between Europe and Asia. Along these trade routes, cultures encountered one another, leading to the diffusion of art, cuisine, religions, and technologies.

Spices like pepper, cinnamon, and cloves became prized in medieval Europe after trade with Asia.

Conquest and Imperialism: Conquests and the spread of empires have often resulted in the forcible exchange of cultures. The Roman Empire, at its height, spanned three continents and absorbed elements of Greek, Egyptian, and other regional cultures. Similarly, the Mongol Empire under Genghis Khan and his successors facilitated cultural exchange between East and West, as they united vast territories through conquest. Conquering empires often imposed their language, religion, and governance on subject peoples, creating a fusion of cultures.

Diplomacy and Political Exchanges: Diplomacy and political relations between states have also played a significant role in cultural exchanges. Royal marriages, alliances, and treaties often led to the exchange of artists, scholars, and cultural artifacts between courts. Renaissance Italy, for instance, benefited from diplomatic relations with the Byzantine Empire, leading to the migration of Greek scholars and manuscripts to the Italian peninsula, which played a pivotal role in the revival of classical learning.

Religious and Missionary Exchanges: Religion has been a powerful force in cultural exchanges. Missionaries and religious pilgrims have traveled across continents to spread their faith and convert others. The spread of Christianity, Buddhism, Islam, and other religions led to cultural encounters that influenced art, architecture, language, and belief systems. For example, the spread of Buddhism from India to East Asia resulted in the adaptation of Buddhist art and iconography in China, Japan, and Korea.

Intellectual and Scientific Exchanges: Intellectual and scientific exchanges have been instrumental in the advancement of human knowledge. The Islamic Golden Age, for example, saw scholars from different cultures, including Persians, Arabs, and Greeks, contributing to fields like mathematics, astronomy, medicine, and philosophy. The House of Wisdom in Baghdad served as a hub for translating and disseminating Greek, Indian, and Persian works, which eventually influenced European scholarship during the Renaissance.

Migration and Diaspora: Human migration has led to the establishment of diasporic communities that preserve and transmit their cultural heritage. Chinese communities in Southeast Asia, Jewish diaspora communities, and the African diaspora in the Americas are examples of how migration has enriched global cultural diversity. Migrant communities often maintain connections with their ancestral cultures and contribute to the cultural fabric of their host societies.

Artistic and Cultural Exchanges: Artistic and cultural exchanges have resulted in the blending of styles, techniques, and aesthetics. The fusion of African, European, and Indigenous American artistic traditions in the Americas, particularly during the colonial period, gave rise to unique art forms, such as Afro-Caribbean and Latin American art. The European Renaissance was influenced by the rediscovery of classical Greek and Roman art and literature, which had been preserved and transmitted by Islamic scholars.

Language and Linguistic Exchanges: Language is a fundamental aspect of culture, and linguistic exchanges have been instrumental in shaping languages and dialects. The English language, for instance, has absorbed words and phrases from Latin, French, Dutch, and many other languages due to historical interactions and conquests. Multilingualism is often a reflection of cultural exchanges, where languages evolve through contact and mutual influence.

Cultural Diplomacy: In the modern era, cultural diplomacy has become a deliberate strategy for promoting understanding and goodwill between nations. Cultural exchange programs, international festivals, and exhibitions facilitate the sharing of arts, music, literature, and cuisine. Organizations like UNESCO promote the preservation and exchange of cultural heritage as a means of fostering peace and mutual respect among nations.

In summary, cultural exchanges have been a driving force in human history, fostering cross-cultural interactions that have enriched societies and contributed to the development of human civilization. These exchanges have transcended geographical, linguistic, and ideological boundaries, resulting in a complex interplay of ideas, traditions, and innovations. While they have sometimes been driven by trade or conquest, they have also been the result of intellectual curiosity, diplomacy, and the shared human desire to connect and learn from one another. As we navigate an increasingly interconnected world, understanding the historical significance and ongoing impact of cultural exchanges is essential for fostering global harmony and cooperation.

The influence of the ancient Maya civilization extended far beyond the borders of their city-states and territories, leaving an indelible mark on the cultural, scientific, and artistic landscape of Mesoamerica and even beyond. The Maya civilization, known for its advanced knowledge of astronomy, mathematics, and hieroglyphic writing, played a pivotal role in shaping the development of neighboring cultures and making enduring contributions to the wider world.

Scientific and Mathematical Legacy: The Maya's sophisticated understanding of astronomy and mathematics had a profound influence on the scientific traditions of Mesoamerica. Their precise calendar systems, including the 260-day Tzolk'in calendar and the 365-day Haab' calendar, were used for agricultural and ceremonial purposes. These calendars served as the basis for many Mesoamerican cultures, including the Aztec and Zapotec civilizations, who adopted and adapted them. The Maya also developed the concept of zero independently, a mathematical breakthrough that significantly impacted the field of mathematics.

Astronomy and Cosmology: Maya astronomy and cosmology influenced not only their immediate neighbors but also cultures further afield. The Maya's ability to accurately predict celestial events, such as solar and lunar eclipses, planetary movements, and the Venus cycle, was highly regarded. Their astronomical knowledge was sought after by other Mesoamerican cultures and contributed to the development of astronomical traditions in the region. The Maya's understanding of celestial phenomena had a lasting impact on the way subsequent civilizations interpreted the heavens.

Hieroglyphic Writing and Codices: Maya hieroglyphic writing, one of the most complex and expressive writing systems of the ancient world, influenced the development of writing systems in Mesoamerica. The Maya created a substantial body of written texts, known as codices, which contained historical records, religious texts, and astronomical information. Although many of these codices were destroyed during the Spanish conquest, a few survived and continue to be studied. The Aztecs, for example, developed their own pictorial writing system, influenced in part by Maya hieroglyphs.

Artistic Traditions: Maya artistic traditions, characterized by intricate sculptures, murals, and ceramics, left a significant imprint on the artistic expressions of neighboring cultures. The Zapotec civilization, based in the Oaxaca Valley, adopted Maya stylistic elements in their art and architecture. The Zapotecs' use of hieroglyphic writing, albeit with modifications, was influenced by Maya writing conventions. The influence of Maya art and symbolism can also be seen in the iconography of the Mixtec civilization, particularly in their codices and jewelry.

Religious Influence: Maya religious beliefs and practices had a substantial influence on the spiritual traditions of Mesoamerica. The Maya pantheon of gods and goddesses, including deities like Itzamná, Kukulkan (the feathered serpent), and the Maize God, were often incorporated into the belief systems of neighboring cultures. The worship of these deities and the ritualistic practices associated with them, such as bloodletting and human sacrifice, were adopted by other Mesoamerican civilizations like the Aztecs.

Trade and Cultural Exchange: The extensive trade networks established by the Maya facilitated the exchange of goods, ideas, and cultural practices with neighboring regions. Valuable commodities like cacao, obsidian, and precious stones were traded across Mesoamerica. The cultural diffusion that occurred along these trade routes contributed to the spread of Maya customs, cuisine, and religious rituals. The Maya's use of cacao as currency, for example, influenced the economic systems of other Mesoamerican cultures.

Urban Planning and Architecture: Maya urban planning and architectural innovations had a lasting impact on the design of Mesoamerican cities. The layout of Maya cities, characterized by plazas, temples, ball courts, and palaces, influenced the architectural design of subsequent civilizations. The Aztec capital of Tenochtitlan, with its grid-like layout and monumental architecture, showed the influence of Maya urban planning principles. Additionally, the use of pyramids and temples in Mesoamerican architecture can be traced back to Maya architectural traditions.

Legacy in Modern Mesoamerica: Today, the Maya legacy endures in the modern countries of Mexico, Guatemala, Belize, Honduras, and El Salvador, where descendants of the ancient Maya continue to preserve their cultural heritage. Maya languages, including K'iche', Kaqchikel, and Yucatec, are still spoken by millions of people in the region. Traditional Maya clothing, weaving techniques, and artistic traditions are proudly maintained and celebrated. Furthermore, the Maya's knowledge of medicinal plants and healing practices continues to influence traditional medicine in Mesoamerica.

In summary, the influence of the ancient Maya civilization transcended geographical borders and time, leaving an enduring mark on the cultural, scientific, and artistic heritage of Mesoamerica and beyond. Their achievements in astronomy, mathematics, hieroglyphic writing, art, and urban planning continue to be a source of fascination and admiration. The Maya's contributions to the world's cultural diversity and intellectual achievements serve as a testament to the enduring legacy of this remarkable civilization.

Chapter 7: The Maya's Enigmatic Decline: Unraveling the Mystery (1400 CE - 1500 CE)

Challenges and internal factors are essential components of any civilization's history and development. They shape a society's trajectory and influence its ability to thrive or face difficulties. The ancient Maya civilization, renowned for its achievements, also grappled with various challenges and internal factors that contributed to its complex history. Here, we explore some of these challenges and internal factors that affected the Maya civilization.

Environmental Factors: The Maya civilization inhabited diverse ecological regions, including tropical rainforests and highland plateaus. While these environments offered opportunities for agriculture and resource extraction, they also presented challenges. Deforestation, soil erosion, and water management were persistent issues in the lowland rainforests. Unsustainable agricultural practices, such as slash-and-burn farming, contributed to environmental degradation. Over time, these factors may have strained resources and impacted the Maya's ability to sustain their population.

Climate Change: Climate variability and droughts played a significant role in the Maya civilization's history. Periodic droughts in the Yucatán Peninsula and the southern lowlands disrupted agricultural cycles and water supply. These climate fluctuations may have led to food shortages, social unrest, and the abandonment of some urban centers. The Classic Maya collapse around the 9th century CE is associated with a series of prolonged droughts that put pressure on resources and contributed to political and social upheaval.

Resource Depletion: The Maya relied on various resources, including agricultural land, forests, freshwater sources, and minerals like jade and obsidian. The exploitation of these resources, particularly in the lowland regions, led to their depletion over time. The loss of fertile soil, deforestation, and overharvesting of natural resources may have undermined the Maya's ability to sustain their civilization and contributed to societal stress.

Political Fragmentation: The Maya civilization was not a monolithic entity but consisted of numerous city-states that often engaged in rivalries and conflicts. Political fragmentation and competition for resources led to localized conflicts and warfare among city-states. While competition can drive innovation, prolonged conflicts could also divert resources away from societal development and stability.

Social Inequality: Like many ancient civilizations, the Maya society exhibited social hierarchies, with rulers, nobility, and commoners occupying different strata. The elite class enjoyed privileges, while commoners and laborers may have faced hardships and limited access to resources. Social inequality can lead to tensions within a society, and disparities in resource distribution may have contributed to societal challenges.

Economic Factors: The Maya economy was based on agriculture, trade, and craft production. Economic success was closely tied to agricultural productivity, which could be impacted by factors like climate, resource depletion, and agricultural practices. Economic instability or declines in trade networks could affect the Maya civilization's prosperity and resilience.

Religious and Ritual Practices: The Maya's religious beliefs and rituals played a central role in their society, influencing political decisions and societal organization. However, the practice of human sacrifice, bloodletting, and other rituals may have contributed to social stress and conflict, especially when resources were strained. Religious leaders and rulers held significant power, which could lead to political and social tensions.

Foreign Influences: The Maya civilization was not isolated, and it engaged in trade and cultural exchanges with neighboring civilizations like the Teotihuacan and later, the Aztecs. While such exchanges enriched Maya culture, they also exposed the civilization to foreign influences, which could have both positive and negative effects on societal stability.

Demographic Pressures: The Maya civilization experienced population growth over time, leading to increased competition for resources. Demographic pressures, combined with other factors like environmental stress, could have strained the capacity of urban centers to support their populations.

In summary, the Maya civilization faced a complex interplay of challenges and internal factors that influenced its development and eventual decline. Environmental factors, climate change, resource depletion, political fragmentation, social inequality, economic factors, religious practices, foreign influences, and demographic pressures all contributed to the Maya civilization's complex history. Understanding these challenges and internal dynamics is essential for gaining insights into the rise, achievements, and eventual transformations of this remarkable ancient civilization.

The end of the Classic Maya civilization is a subject of considerable historical intrigue and debate among scholars. This enigmatic and complex period marks the decline of one of the most advanced and sophisticated civilizations in Mesoamerica. The Classic Maya era, characterized by monumental architecture, complex hieroglyphic writing, and advanced knowledge of mathematics and astronomy, came to an end during a series of transformations and upheavals that continue to captivate historians and archaeologists.

One of the central questions surrounding the decline of the Classic Maya civilization is what led to its eventual collapse. Numerous theories have been proposed, but it's important to recognize that the decline was a multifaceted process influenced by a combination of internal and external factors.

Environmental Challenges: The Maya civilization was closely tied to its environment, and environmental factors played a significant role in its decline. Deforestation, soil erosion, and unsustainable agricultural practices, such as slash-and-burn farming, led to environmental degradation over centuries. The dense populations of the Maya cities put immense pressure on resources, particularly in the lowland rainforests, leading to resource depletion and food shortages. Additionally, the Maya faced periodic droughts, some of which were particularly severe, which disrupted agricultural cycles and water supply. Climate change and environmental stress may have contributed to the Maya's struggles.

Demographic Pressures: The Maya civilization experienced population growth over time, leading to increased competition for resources. The dense urban centers of the Maya civilization required a constant influx of resources, including food, water, and building materials. As the population grew, so did the pressure on the environment to sustain these urban centers. The inability to meet the demands of a growing population could have contributed to social unrest and instability.

Political Fragmentation: The Maya civilization was not a unified empire but a collection of city-states, each with its own ruler and elite class. Political fragmentation and rivalries among these city-states were a recurring theme in Maya history. Localized conflicts and warfare among city-states were common, diverting resources and potentially contributing to political and social instability. The competition for resources and power may have weakened the Maya civilization internally.

Social Inequality: Like many ancient societies, the Maya exhibited social hierarchies, with rulers, nobility, and commoners occupying different strata. Social inequality could lead to tensions within society, especially if disparities in resource distribution were perceived as unjust. The elite class enjoyed privileges, while commoners and laborers may have faced hardships. Social tensions and discontent could have strained the social fabric of Maya cities.

Economic Factors: The Maya economy was based on agriculture, trade, and craft production. Economic success was closely tied to agricultural productivity, which, as mentioned earlier, could be affected by environmental stress and resource depletion. Declines in trade networks or economic instability could impact the Maya civilization's prosperity and resilience.

Religious and Ritual Practices: The Maya's religious beliefs and rituals played a central role in their society, influencing political decisions and societal organization. While these practices were integral to Maya culture, some rituals, such as human sacrifice and bloodletting, may have contributed to social stress and conflict, particularly during times of resource scarcity.

Foreign Influences: The Maya civilization was not isolated and engaged in trade and cultural exchanges with neighboring civilizations, including the Teotihuacan and later, the Aztecs. These exchanges enriched Maya culture but also exposed it to foreign influences, which could have both positive and negative effects on societal stability.

Complex Interplay of Factors: It's crucial to emphasize that the decline of the Classic Maya civilization likely resulted from the complex interplay of these factors rather than a single cause. Different regions and city-states may have experienced the decline differently, and the timing and severity of the decline were not uniform across the Maya world.

The "Maya Collapse": The decline of the Classic Maya civilization is often referred to as the "Maya collapse." While it is indeed a decline in the sense of a significant societal transformation, the term "collapse" can be misleading. Instead of a sudden, cataclysmic event, the decline of the Maya civilization occurred over several centuries, with different city-states experiencing varying degrees of decline and transformation. Some city-states, like Tikal and Calakmul, saw a decline in monumental construction and population, while others, such as the northern Yucatán city of Chichen Itza, continued to thrive for some time.

The Role of Resilience: It's important to recognize that the Maya civilization exhibited a degree of resilience during this period. Despite the challenges and transformations, elements of Maya culture and society persisted. Maya communities adapted to changing circumstances, and some even continued to engage in trade and cultural exchange.

In summary, the end of the Classic Maya civilization represents a complex and multifaceted historical puzzle. While environmental factors, political fragmentation, social inequality, and other internal factors contributed to the decline, the precise sequence of events and their interactions remain subjects of ongoing research and debate. The Maya civilization's legacy endures in the modern-day Maya communities of Mexico, Guatemala, Belize, and

Honduras, as well as in the fascination and admiration of scholars and enthusiasts who seek to understand this remarkable ancient civilization's history and achievements.

The Post-Classic period of Maya civilization is a fascinating and often overlooked chapter in the history of Mesoamerica. While the Classic Maya civilization, characterized by grand city-states and monumental architecture, experienced a decline, the Post-Classic era witnessed the survival and transformation of Maya culture in the face of new challenges and opportunities. This period, spanning from approximately the 10th century CE to the Spanish conquest in the 16th century CE, is marked by a resilient Maya civilization that continued to thrive, adapt, and make significant contributions to the region's history.

Continuation of Maya Urban Centers: Despite the decline of many Classic Maya city-states during the Terminal Classic period (roughly 800 CE to 1000 CE), several urban centers persisted and even flourished during the Post-Classic era. Cities like Chichen Itza in the Yucatán Peninsula and Mayapan in the northern Yucatán maintained their prominence. These cities, while influenced by Toltec and other external elements, retained distinct Maya architectural styles and cultural traditions.

Maya-Toltec Syncretism: The Post-Classic period witnessed the arrival of external influences, notably from the Toltec civilization, which originated in central Mexico. Toltec-inspired elements, such as the feathered serpent god Quetzalcoatl, made their way into Maya iconography and religious practices. The fusion of Maya and Toltec cultural elements, often referred to as "Maya-Toltec syncretism," resulted in unique artistic expressions, religious beliefs, and architectural innovations.

Trade and Commerce: Trade continued to be a vital aspect of Maya civilization during the Post-Classic period. The Maya maintained extensive trade networks, exchanging goods such as cacao, salt, obsidian, jade, textiles, and ceramics. These networks facilitated cultural exchanges and the flow of commodities throughout Mesoamerica. The Yucatán Peninsula served as a key hub for regional trade, connecting the Maya lowlands with other Mesoamerican cultures.

Maya Maritime Trade: One of the remarkable aspects of Maya survival during the Post-Classic period was their ability to engage in maritime trade. The Maya were skilled seafarers who navigated the waters of the Caribbean Sea and the Gulf of Mexico. They traded along coastal routes and established contact with distant cultures, including the Maya of the Yucatán, the Totonac civilization of Veracruz, and even the powerful city of Tulum on the east coast of the Yucatán Peninsula. This maritime trade allowed for the exchange of exotic goods and cultural influences.

Maya Warfare and Conflict: The Post-Classic period also saw significant conflict among Maya city-states. While some regions enjoyed relative stability, others experienced warfare and political rivalries. These conflicts were driven by a variety of factors, including competition for resources, power struggles, and the desire to control trade routes. Maya city-states like Mayapan were known for their fortifications, reflecting the importance of defense during this era.

Maya Hieroglyphic Writing and Codices: The Maya's sophisticated hieroglyphic writing system continued to be used during the Post-Classic period. Although many of the Classic period codices were destroyed during the Spanish conquest, a few survived, providing valuable insights into Maya history, calendrical systems, and cosmology. The study of these codices has allowed scholars to decipher Maya hieroglyphs and gain a deeper understanding of their culture.

Religious Continuity: Maya religious practices persisted during the Post-Classic period, with some adaptations and syncretism with external influences. Rituals, including bloodletting ceremonies and human sacrifice, continued to be significant components of Maya spirituality. The worship of deities like Chaac, the rain god, and the feathered serpent god Quetzalcoatl reflected the Maya's reverence for the natural world and their cosmological beliefs.

Maya Ballgame: The ancient Maya ballgame, known as "pok-ta-pok" in some Maya languages, remained an important cultural and religious activity during the Post-Classic era. This sport, played in ball courts with a rubber ball, had ritualistic and ceremonial significance. Ballgame courts were prominent features in Maya cities, and the sport served as a way to maintain social cohesion and religious connections.

Arrival of the Spanish: The arrival of Spanish conquistadors, led by Hernán Cortés, in the early 16th century marked a pivotal moment in Maya history. The Spanish conquest resulted in significant changes, including the introduction of Christianity, the imposition of Spanish authority, and the disruption of traditional Maya lifeways. Many Maya city-states fell under Spanish control, leading to a decline in indigenous autonomy and cultural practices.

Legacy and Cultural Resilience: Despite the profound changes brought by the Spanish conquest, the Maya people and their culture endured. Elements of Maya culture, such as language, spirituality, agricultural practices, and artistic traditions, persisted. Today, Maya communities in Mexico, Guatemala, Belize, and Honduras continue to celebrate and preserve their cultural heritage, maintaining a connection to their ancient past while adapting to the challenges of the modern world.

In summary, the Post-Classic Maya period is a testament to the resilience and adaptability of this remarkable civilization. While it faced challenges, including external influences and internal conflicts, the Maya civilization continued to thrive, innovate, and contribute to the rich tapestry of Mesoamerican history. The enduring legacy of the Maya people is evident in their cultural traditions, language, and the fascination they continue to inspire in scholars and enthusiasts worldwide.

BOOK 3
TEOTIHUACAN
CITY OF THE GODS (100 BCE - 750 CE)

BY A.J. KINGSTON

Chapter 1: The Rise of Teotihuacan: Origins and Early Development (100 BCE - 100 CE)

The history of Mesoamerica is a tapestry woven from the threads of countless cultures that flourished before the rise of Teotihuacan. These pre-Teotihuacan cultures, each with its own unique characteristics and contributions, laid the foundation for the magnificent civilization that would later emerge at Teotihuacan itself. In this narrative, we embark on a journey through time to explore some of these remarkable cultures that thrived in the region we now know as central Mexico.

The Olmec Civilization: Often regarded as the "Mother Culture" of Mesoamerica, the Olmec civilization emerged around 1500 BCE and is one of the earliest known complex societies in the region. The Olmec heartland, located in the tropical lowlands of what is now the Mexican states of Veracruz and Tabasco, was characterized by impressive ceremonial centers, massive stone sculptures, and intricate jade artifacts. The Olmec are credited with many cultural innovations, including the first known writing system in the Americas, the use of the Mesoamerican ballgame, and the worship of deities like the "Olmec dragon." Their legacy influenced later Mesoamerican cultures, including the Maya and the Aztecs.

The Zapotec Civilization: In the southern highlands of modern-day Oaxaca, the Zapotec civilization emerged around 500 BCE, making it one of the earliest complex societies in Mesoamerica. The city of Monte Albán served as their capital, boasting impressive architecture, ball courts, and hieroglyphic inscriptions. The Zapotecs are notable for their advanced understanding of mathematics and calendar systems, as well as their use of a hieroglyphic writing system. Their artistic achievements, including pottery and carved stone stelae, provide a window into their rich cultural traditions.

The Mixtec Civilization: The Mixtec civilization, neighbors to the Zapotecs in Oaxaca, thrived from around 900 CE to the Spanish conquest. They are known for their intricate codices, which are richly illustrated manuscripts that document their history, rituals, and genealogy. The Mixtec codices are renowned for their detailed pictorial narratives and hieroglyphic writing. This civilization developed complex social structures, including hereditary rulership, and produced magnificent gold jewelry and pottery. Their artistic expressions continue to captivate scholars and enthusiasts.

The Totonac Civilization: Situated in the eastern coastal region of modern Veracruz and northern Puebla, the Totonac civilization was known for its skilled craftsmanship, particularly in the realm of pottery and ceramic figurines. They were also recognized for their ritualistic practices, including the famous "Dance of the Flyers," a ceremonial performance involving dancers descending from tall poles while playing music. The Totonacs played a pivotal role in the trade of valuable resources like vanilla and cacao, which were highly sought after in Mesoamerica.

The Huastec Civilization: The Huastec civilization occupied the eastern coastal region of the Gulf of Mexico, encompassing parts of modern Veracruz and the Huasteca region. They were known for their distinctive ceramic artistry, which featured elaborate designs and vibrant colors. The Huastecs had a complex social structure, with hereditary rulers and priestly classes overseeing religious rituals and ceremonies. Their culture, influenced by the nearby Totonacs and Maya, demonstrates the interconnectedness of Mesoamerican societies.

The Tlatilco Culture: The Tlatilco culture, dating from around 1500 BCE to 600 BCE, existed in the Basin of Mexico, near what would later become the great city of Teotihuacan. This culture is renowned for its exquisite ceramic figurines, some of which depict intricate details of daily life, clothing, and rituals. Tlatilco ceramics are considered among the finest examples of early Mesoamerican art, showcasing the region's artistic prowess long before Teotihuacan's rise.

The Chupícuaro Culture: The Chupícuaro culture, which thrived in the Bajío region of modern Mexico from around 500 BCE to 200 CE, is celebrated for its distinctive ceramic traditions. Chupícuaro pottery is characterized by its elegant, slender figures and intricate designs. These ceramics served both utilitarian and ritualistic purposes, with some vessels containing intricate scenes and symbolic imagery. The Chupícuaro culture provides valuable insights into the artistic and cultural diversity of pre-Teotihuacan Mesoamerica.

The Cuicuilco Civilization: Cuicuilco was an ancient settlement located near present-day Mexico City. It emerged around 1400 BCE and was characterized by its circular pyramids and impressive architecture. The Cuicuilco culture is believed to have had extensive trade connections, including the exchange of obsidian and other goods. However, the eruption of the nearby Xitle volcano around 150 CE buried Cuicuilco under layers of lava and ash, leading to its abandonment. This event may have contributed to the rise of Teotihuacan as a regional power.

In summary, the pre-Teotihuacan cultures of Mesoamerica constitute a rich tapestry of human history, creativity, and innovation. These diverse civilizations laid the groundwork for the complex societies that would follow, leaving a lasting legacy in the form of art, architecture, writing systems, and cultural practices. Their achievements and contributions continue to be a source of fascination and inspiration, shedding light on the vibrant and interconnected world of ancient Mesoamerica before the rise

The founding of Teotihuacan represents a pivotal moment in the history of ancient Mesoamerica. This enigmatic city, whose name translates to "The Place of the Gods," would go on to become one of the most influential and iconic urban centers in the region. The story of Teotihuacan's origins is shrouded in mystery, with scholars and archaeologists continually piecing together fragments of evidence to unravel its enigma.

Early Settlements in the Teotihuacan Valley: The Teotihuacan Valley, located in the highlands of central Mexico, had been inhabited by various cultures for centuries before the rise of the city itself. Evidence of human settlements in the area dates back to as early as 2000 BCE, with agricultural communities engaging in maize cultivation and other subsistence activities. These early settlers laid the groundwork for what would eventually become Teotihuacan.

Cultural Influences: The region's cultural landscape was shaped by interactions with neighboring cultures, including the Maya to the south and the Zapotecs to the southeast. These interactions contributed to the exchange of ideas, technologies, and artistic styles, fostering cultural diversity in the Teotihuacan Valley.

Teotihuacan's Emergence: While the exact date of Teotihuacan's founding remains elusive, it is generally believed to have begun as a small settlement around 200 BCE. Over time, this settlement expanded and evolved into a complex urban center. The city's distinctive features, including its grid-like layout, monumental pyramids, and extensive apartment compounds, set it apart from other Mesoamerican cities of the era.

The Pyramid of the Sun and Pyramid of the Moon: Two of Teotihuacan's most iconic structures are the Pyramid of the Sun and the Pyramid of the Moon. The Pyramid of the Sun, one of the largest pyramids in the Americas, stands at the heart of the city and is a testament to Teotihuacan's architectural prowess. The Pyramid of the Moon, positioned at the northern end of the Avenue of the Dead, served as a prominent ceremonial and ritual site.

Multicultural Population: Teotihuacan's population was diverse and cosmopolitan, with evidence of people from various Mesoamerican regions residing within the city. This diversity is reflected in the city's art, architecture, and material culture, suggesting a complex and integrated society.

Ceremonial and Religious Significance: Teotihuacan's layout and architecture were designed with religious and ceremonial significance in mind. The city's urban plan was aligned with celestial phenomena, such as the movements of the sun, moon, and stars. The Avenue of the Dead, a central thoroughfare in the city, played a crucial role in religious processions and ceremonies.

Decline and Abandonment: Despite its grandeur and influence, Teotihuacan faced challenges during its later years. The exact reasons for its decline and eventual abandonment around the 7th century CE remain a subject of debate. Factors such as political unrest, social upheaval, environmental stress, and external pressures from neighboring groups may have contributed to its downfall.

Legacy and Influence: Although Teotihuacan's inhabitants left no written records, their legacy endures through their architectural achievements, art, and cultural influence. The city's grid layout, architectural styles, and religious symbolism left a profound mark on subsequent Mesoamerican civilizations, including the Maya and the Aztecs. Teotihuacan's artistic motifs, such as the feathered serpent deity Quetzalcoatl, continued to be revered and incorporated into the belief systems of later cultures.

Ongoing Exploration and Research: Archaeological investigations at Teotihuacan continue to shed light on its history and mysteries. Discoveries such as the hidden tunnel beneath the Pyramid of the Feathered Serpent, or the "Temple of the Snake," have offered new insights into the city's religious practices and may lead to a better understanding of its ultimate fate.

In summary, the founding of Teotihuacan represents a remarkable chapter in the annals of Mesoamerican history. This ancient city, whose origins are veiled in antiquity, emerged as a powerful and influential center of culture, religion, and architecture. Its legacy endures as a testament to the ingenuity and creativity of the people who built and inhabited it, leaving an indelible mark on the tapestry of Mesoamerican civilization.

The early society of Teotihuacan, one of the most significant ancient Mesoamerican civilizations, provides a window into the complex and vibrant culture that thrived in the highlands of central Mexico. Although much of Teotihuacan's early history remains shrouded in mystery, archaeological discoveries and research have shed light on the social, economic, and religious aspects of this enigmatic society.

Emergence of a Complex Society: Teotihuacan began as a small settlement around 200 BCE, and by 150 CE, it had evolved into a burgeoning urban center. This transformation marked the emergence of a complex society characterized by a structured social hierarchy, monumental architecture, and intricate religious practices.

Population Diversity: One of the remarkable features of early Teotihuacan society was its multicultural population. Archaeological evidence suggests that people from various Mesoamerican regions, including the Gulf Coast and Oaxaca, lived within the city. This diversity enriched the cultural tapestry of Teotihuacan and contributed to its cosmopolitan nature.

Social Hierarchy: Teotihuacan's society was stratified, with clear distinctions between different social classes. At the pinnacle of the social hierarchy were the elite, who likely held positions of political and religious authority. Beneath them were the commoners, who comprised the majority of the population and engaged in various occupations, including farming, crafting, and trade.

Residential Complexes: The city's layout featured expansive residential complexes, known as apartment compounds, which housed the majority of its population. These compounds consisted of multi-story apartment buildings arranged around central courtyards. Some of these compounds were intricately designed, with murals and frescoes adorning their walls.

Economic Activities: Teotihuacan's economy was based on a combination of agriculture, craft production, and trade. The fertile soils of the Teotihuacan Valley allowed for the cultivation of maize, beans, and other crops, sustaining the city's population. Skilled craftsmen produced a wide range of goods, including pottery, obsidian tools, textiles, and jewelry. The city's strategic location facilitated trade networks that extended across Mesoamerica.

Urban Planning: The layout of Teotihuacan was meticulously planned, with a grid-like street system and monumental architecture that reflected religious and cosmological beliefs. The city's central thoroughfare, known as the Avenue of the Dead, was flanked by pyramids, temples, and ceremonial structures. The Pyramid of the Sun and the Pyramid of the Moon were prominent landmarks, serving both religious and symbolic purposes.

Religious Practices: Religion played a central role in early Teotihuacan society. The city's religious complex included temples, pyramids, and open plazas where ceremonies and rituals were conducted. Deities such as the Feathered Serpent (Quetzalcoatl) and the Rain God (Tlaloc) were venerated. The presence of massive mural paintings, like those found at the Pyramid of the Feathered Serpent, suggests that these structures were sites of religious importance.

Art and Iconography: The art of early Teotihuacan is characterized by its distinctive iconography, including images of deities, animals, and geometric patterns. Mural paintings and sculptures adorned both public and private spaces. These artistic expressions conveyed religious and cosmological beliefs, as well as societal values.

Decline and Transformation: The early society of Teotihuacan eventually faced challenges and underwent transformations. The reasons for the city's decline, which began in the 7th century CE, are still a subject of debate among scholars. Factors such as political instability, environmental stress, and external pressures from neighboring groups may have contributed to its downfall.

In summary, the early society of Teotihuacan represents a remarkable chapter in the history of ancient Mesoamerica. This thriving urban center, with its multicultural population, structured social hierarchy, and intricate religious practices, left an indelible mark on the region's history. Although many mysteries surrounding Teotihuacan persist, ongoing archaeological research continues to provide valuable insights into the lives and culture of its early inhabitants.

Chapter 2: City of Pyramids: Teotihuacan's Architectural Marvels (100 CE - 300 CE)

The construction of the Pyramid of the Sun and the Pyramid of the Moon in Teotihuacan is a testament to the remarkable architectural achievements of the ancient Mesoamerican civilization that thrived in the highlands of central Mexico. These iconic pyramids, towering over the landscape, continue to inspire awe and fascination with their grandeur and significance in the history of Teotihuacan.

Pyramid of the Sun: The Pyramid of the Sun, or "Pirámide del Sol" in Spanish, is one of the most prominent structures in Teotihuacan and one of the largest pyramids in the Americas. Its construction is a testament to the engineering prowess of the ancient Teotihuacanos. This colossal edifice rises to a height of approximately 216 feet (66 meters) and covers an area of over 24,000 square meters at its base.

Design and Layout: The Pyramid of the Sun was meticulously designed with precise measurements and alignments. Its construction incorporated a massive earthen core, which was then covered with layers of adobe bricks and faced with large stone blocks. The pyramid's four sloping sides meet at a central staircase that leads to a temple platform at the summit. This temple platform was a sacred space, likely used for religious ceremonies and rituals.

Religious Significance: The Pyramid of the Sun held profound religious and cosmological significance for the Teotihuacanos. Its alignment with celestial events, such as the setting sun during certain times of the year, suggests its role in the city's cosmological beliefs. The pyramid was dedicated to deities associated with the sun and was part of a complex of religious structures that included the Avenue of the Dead and the Pyramid of the Moon.

Construction Techniques: Building the Pyramid of the Sun was a monumental undertaking that required immense labor and engineering expertise. The massive stone blocks used in its construction were transported from quarries located several kilometers away. Workers used ramps and a series of platforms to transport and position these massive stones. The construction process likely involved a significant labor force composed of skilled craftsmen, laborers, and possibly enslaved individuals.

Sacrificial Offerings: During archaeological excavations of the Pyramid of the Sun, researchers discovered numerous offerings buried beneath its layers. These offerings included pottery, obsidian blades, greenstone objects, and human remains. The presence of these offerings suggests that the pyramid had religious significance and was a site of rituals and ceremonies. Human sacrifices may have taken place atop the pyramid, further emphasizing its role in religious practices.

Pyramid of the Moon: The Pyramid of the Moon, or "Pirámide de la Luna," is another striking pyramid in Teotihuacan, located at the northern end of the Avenue of the Dead, opposite the Pyramid of the Sun. While not as massive as its counterpart, the Pyramid of the Moon is architecturally significant and serves as a crucial component of Teotihuacan's urban layout.

Design and Layout: The Pyramid of the Moon has a stepped pyramid design, consisting of several platforms with staircases leading to each level. The structure is smaller in scale compared to the Pyramid of the Sun, but it remains an imposing presence. The top of the pyramid features a small temple structure that likely had religious significance.

Ceremonial and Ritual Use: Like the Pyramid of the Sun, the Pyramid of the Moon played a vital role in Teotihuacan's religious and ceremonial activities. Its alignment with celestial events and its proximity to the Avenue of the Dead suggest its involvement in complex rituals and processions. The pyramid's stepped design allowed for distinct levels of elevation, providing different vantage points for viewing religious ceremonies and events in the city below.

Construction Methods: The construction of the Pyramid of the Moon employed similar techniques to those used for the Pyramid of the Sun. Workers transported stone blocks from quarries to the construction site, using ramps and platforms to move and position the stones. The layered construction style, consisting of adobe bricks and stone facades, was characteristic of Teotihuacan architecture.

Legacy and Significance: The Pyramid of the Moon, along with the Pyramid of the Sun, remains an enduring symbol of Teotihuacan's cultural and religious achievements. These monumental structures reflect the city's profound connection to celestial cycles, its religious beliefs, and the advanced engineering skills of its inhabitants. The complex layout and alignment of Teotihuacan's pyramids and temples continue to captivate scholars and visitors alike, offering glimpses into the spiritual and cosmological world of this ancient Mesoamerican civilization.

In summary, the construction of the Pyramid of the Sun and the Pyramid of the Moon in Teotihuacan stands as a remarkable testament to the architectural, religious, and cultural achievements of this ancient Mesoamerican civilization. These awe-inspiring structures continue to be a source of fascination and inspiration, inviting us to explore the mysteries of Teotihuacan's past and the significance of its monumental architecture.

The urban planning and layout of Teotihuacan, one of the most significant ancient Mesoamerican cities, are a testament to the meticulous design and organization of this ancient metropolis. Teotihuacan's well-structured layout, characterized by its grid-like streets and monumental architecture, played a crucial role in shaping the city's identity and functionality.

Avenue of the Dead: At the heart of Teotihuacan's urban design lies the Avenue of the Dead, or "Calzada de los Muertos" in Spanish. This grand thoroughfare stretches for approximately 2.4 kilometers (1.5 miles) through the center of the city, serving as its primary axis. The Avenue of the Dead is flanked by a series of monumental structures, including pyramids, temples, and palaces, which contribute to the city's imposing skyline. The name "Avenue of the Dead" was coined by the Aztecs, who believed that the structures along the avenue resembled tombs, although their original purpose was ceremonial and religious.

Grid Layout: Teotihuacan's urban plan features a precise grid layout, with streets and buildings aligned along a north-south and east-west axis. This grid pattern is especially evident in the design of the city's apartment compounds, which are characterized by multi-story apartment buildings arranged around central courtyards. The uniformity and regularity of the grid underscore the city's deliberate planning and architectural coordination.

Residential Areas: The city's residential areas, represented by these apartment compounds, are a significant component of Teotihuacan's urban fabric. These compounds housed a substantial portion of the city's population, and they varied in size and complexity. Some featured elaborately decorated murals, reflecting the artistic and cultural diversity of Teotihuacan's inhabitants. The presence of these residential complexes indicates that the city was home to a diverse and thriving population.

Ceremonial and Religious Spaces: Teotihuacan's urban layout prominently features ceremonial and religious spaces. The Pyramid of the Sun, the Pyramid of the Moon, and the Temple of the Feathered Serpent are key religious structures aligned along the Avenue of the Dead. These pyramids served as focal points for religious ceremonies and rituals, and their alignment with celestial events underscores their cosmological significance. The temple platforms atop these pyramids provided spaces for offerings and religious activities.

The Ciudadela: One of the most distinctive features of Teotihuacan's urban layout is the Ciudadela, or "Citadel" in Spanish. This massive enclosed complex is situated at the southern end of the Avenue of the Dead and is encircled by a thick wall. At its center stands the Temple of the Feathered Serpent, a pyramid adorned with intricate sculptures and carvings. The Ciudadela likely served as a political and religious center, and the Temple of the Feathered Serpent may have been dedicated to the worship of the deity Quetzalcoatl.

Alignment with Celestial Phenomena: One of the most intriguing aspects of Teotihuacan's urban planning is its alignment with celestial phenomena. The city's layout and architecture were carefully positioned to correspond with the movements of the sun, moon, and stars. For instance, the Pyramid of the Sun aligns with the setting sun during specific times of the year, highlighting the city's connection to solar worship and astronomical observations.

Trade and Commerce: Teotihuacan's well-organized streets and plazas also played a role in facilitating trade and commerce. The city's central location within the Mesoamerican region made it a hub for economic exchanges, and its wide avenues and open spaces provided ideal settings for marketplaces and trade activities. Valuable resources, such as obsidian, ceramics, textiles, and agricultural products, were likely traded within the city and with neighboring regions.

Sustainability and Infrastructure: The city's urban planning also considered elements of sustainability and infrastructure. Teotihuacan had a sophisticated drainage system that allowed for the efficient removal of rainwater, preventing flooding in the city. Additionally, the city's proximity to the fertile soils of the Teotihuacan Valley supported agricultural activities, contributing to its sustainability.

Legacy and Inspiration: Teotihuacan's urban planning and layout continue to captivate archaeologists, historians, and urban designers. The deliberate organization of streets, the alignment of structures with celestial events, and the integration of ceremonial and residential spaces showcase the city's advanced understanding of architecture and urban design. Teotihuacan's legacy can be seen in the later Mesoamerican civilizations, including the Maya and the Aztecs, who drew inspiration from its architectural and urban achievements.

In summary, the urban planning and layout of Teotihuacan stand as a remarkable example of ancient city planning and architectural coordination. The grid-like streets, monumental structures, and celestial alignments reveal a society that placed great importance on organization, cosmology, and religious practices. Teotihuacan's enduring legacy continues to offer valuable insights into the complex and interconnected world of ancient Mesoamerica.

Teotihuacan's pyramid complexes are among the most iconic and significant architectural achievements of the ancient

Mesoamerican world. These monumental structures, including the Pyramid of the Sun, the Pyramid of the Moon, and the Temple of the Feathered Serpent, continue to captivate scholars and visitors alike, offering insights into the religious, cosmological, and artistic aspects of Teotihuacan's civilization.

Pyramid of the Sun: The Pyramid of the Sun, or "Pirámide del Sol" in Spanish, is one of the most imposing pyramids in the Americas. Rising to a height of approximately 216 feet (66 meters), it dominates the Teotihuacan skyline. Its massive size and central location along the Avenue of the Dead make it a focal point of the city's layout. The pyramid is characterized by its stepped design, with a central staircase leading to a temple platform at its summit.

Architectural Marvel: The construction of the Pyramid of the Sun is a testament to the advanced engineering skills of the Teotihuacanos. Its core is composed of a massive earthen mound, which was then covered with layers of adobe bricks and faced with large stone blocks. These stone blocks were transported from quarries located several kilometers away, highlighting the logistical and organizational capabilities of the ancient builders.

Religious Significance: The Pyramid of the Sun held profound religious and cosmological significance for the Teotihuacanos. Its alignment with celestial events, such as the setting sun during certain times of the year, suggests its role in the city's cosmological beliefs. The pyramid was dedicated to deities associated with the sun and was likely a site for religious ceremonies, offerings, and rituals.

Pyramid of the Moon: The Pyramid of the Moon, or "Pirámide de la Luna," is another impressive structure situated at the northern end of the Avenue of the Dead, opposite the Pyramid of the Sun. While smaller in scale compared to its counterpart, the Pyramid of the Moon is architecturally significant and plays a crucial role in Teotihuacan's urban layout.

Stepped Pyramid Design: The Pyramid of the Moon features a stepped pyramid design, consisting of several platforms with staircases leading to each level. Although it is not as tall as the

Pyramid of the Sun, it remains an imposing structure. The top of the pyramid features a small temple structure that likely had religious significance. Its stepped design allowed for different vantage points for viewing religious ceremonies and events in the city below.

Ceremonial and Ritual Use: Like the Pyramid of the Sun, the Pyramid of the Moon played a vital role in Teotihuacan's religious and ceremonial activities. Its alignment with celestial events and its proximity to the Avenue of the Dead suggest its involvement in complex rituals and processions. The pyramid likely served as a stage for religious performances and offerings to the gods.

Temple of the Feathered Serpent: The Temple of the Feathered Serpent, also known as the "Templo de Quetzalcoatl," is located within the Ciudadela, a massive enclosed complex situated at the southern end of the Avenue of the Dead. This temple is adorned with intricate sculptures and carvings depicting the feathered serpent deity Quetzalcoatl. The temple's architectural style and artistic elements reflect the fusion of different Mesoamerican cultures and influences.

Sacrificial Offerings: Archaeological excavations around the pyramid complexes have unearthed numerous offerings, including pottery, obsidian blades, greenstone objects, and even human remains. These offerings provide evidence of the religious significance of these structures and suggest that they were central to various rituals and ceremonies. Human sacrifices may have taken place atop these pyramids, emphasizing their role in religious practices. The pyramid complexes of Teotihuacan continue to inspire awe and fascination. Their enduring legacy can be seen in the later Mesoamerican civilizations, including the Maya and the Aztecs, who drew inspiration from their architectural and religious significance. The precise alignment of these pyramids with celestial events highlights the city's advanced understanding of astronomy and its deep connection to religious beliefs. In summary, Teotihuacan's pyramid complexes stand as enduring symbols of the city's cultural, religious, and architectural achievements. These monumental structures, with their impressive scale and intricate designs, provide valuable insights into the rich and complex world of ancient Mesoamerica. Their significance goes beyond mere architecture, as they continue to captivate the imagination and curiosity of those who explore the mysteries of Teotihuacan's past.

Chapter 3: Art and Culture: Unveiling the Treasures of Teotihuacan (200 CE - 500 CE)

Teotihuacan's artistry and iconography represent a rich and complex visual language that reflects the culture, beliefs, and cosmology of this ancient Mesoamerican civilization. The city's artistic expressions, including mural paintings, sculptures, and intricate carvings, offer profound insights into the religious and cultural life of Teotihuacan's inhabitants.

Mural Paintings: Teotihuacan is renowned for its magnificent mural paintings that adorn the walls of various structures within the city. These murals provide a vivid canvas for understanding the artistic and symbolic language of the Teotihuacanos. They often depict scenes from daily life, mythological narratives, and deities.

Depictions of Deities: One of the recurring themes in Teotihuacan's mural art is the depiction of deities and supernatural beings. These divine figures are often portrayed with distinctive iconographic elements, such as headdresses, masks, and animal attributes. The Feathered Serpent deity, known as Quetzalcoatl, is a prominent figure in Teotihuacan art, and its representation is central to the city's cosmological beliefs.

Cosmic Imagery: Teotihuacan's murals are replete with cosmic imagery, reflecting the city's deep connection to the celestial realms. The sun, moon, stars, and celestial bodies frequently appear in mural compositions, emphasizing the importance of astronomy and cosmology in Teotihuacan culture. The Pyramid of the Sun's alignment with the setting sun during specific times of the year further underscores the city's cosmic focus.

Natural World: The Teotihuacanos had a profound reverence for the natural world, and this reverence is evident in their artistic representations. Murals often feature animals, plants, and agricultural scenes, highlighting the close relationship between the people of Teotihuacan and their environment. These depictions also underscore the importance of agriculture in sustaining the city's population.

Abstract Symbols and Geometric Patterns: Teotihuacan's artistry is not limited to representational imagery but also includes abstract symbols and geometric patterns. These symbols, which include spirals, crosses, and intricate designs, are believed to hold symbolic and ritualistic significance. They are thought to convey deeper meanings related to the city's cosmological and religious beliefs.

Color Palette: The vibrant and varied color palette used in Teotihuacan's murals adds depth and complexity to the artwork. Artists employed a wide range of pigments, including red, yellow, green, and blue, to create striking and visually engaging compositions. The use of color not only enhanced the aesthetic appeal of the murals but also conveyed specific meanings and symbolism.

Sculptures and Figurines: In addition to mural art, Teotihuacan is known for its sculptures and figurines, which provide further insights into the city's artistic expression. These sculptures often depict anthropomorphic figures, animals, and mythological beings. Some sculptures are intricately carved from stone, while others are made from clay or other materials.

Ceramic Figurines: Ceramic figurines from Teotihuacan are notable for their diversity and craftsmanship. These figurines often represent everyday people engaged in various activities, such as cooking, weaving, and farming. They provide a glimpse into the daily life and social dynamics of Teotihuacan's population.

Influence on Later Mesoamerican Art: The artistic traditions of Teotihuacan had a profound influence on later Mesoamerican civilizations, including the Maya and the Aztecs. Elements of Teotihuacan artistry, such as representations of the Feathered Serpent deity and cosmic symbolism, can be seen in the art of these subsequent cultures. This influence speaks to the enduring significance of Teotihuacan's artistic heritage.

Spiritual Significance and Ritual Context: Much of Teotihuacan's artistry was created within a spiritual and ritual context. The murals and sculptures were not merely decorative but played a crucial role in religious ceremonies and rituals. They served as visual aids in conveying cosmological beliefs, myths, and narratives that were central to Teotihuacan's religious practices.

Legacy of Teotihuacan Artistry: The artistry of Teotihuacan continues to be a source of fascination and inspiration for scholars, artists, and enthusiasts of Mesoamerican culture. These ancient artworks provide a window into the spiritual, cultural, and artistic world of a civilization that thrived over a thousand years ago. The intricate details, vibrant colors, and profound symbolism of Teotihuacan's artistry invite us to delve deeper into the mysteries of this ancient civilization and the enduring impact of its visual language.

In summary, Teotihuacan's artistry and iconography constitute a visual tapestry that reflects the intricate cosmology, religious beliefs, and daily life of its inhabitants. From murals depicting deities and celestial bodies to abstract symbols and representations of the natural world, these artworks convey the essence of Teotihuacan's rich and multifaceted culture. Their legacy endures as a testament to the enduring power of art to transcend time and connect us with the spiritual and cultural heritage of the past.

Ceramics and crafts were integral aspects of the material culture of ancient Mesoamerican civilizations, including the Olmec, Maya, Teotihuacan, Zapotec, Toltec, and Aztec societies. These ancient peoples were skilled artisans who created a wide range of ceramic vessels and intricate crafts that served various purposes in their daily lives, religious rituals, and trade activities.

Ceramic Vessels: Ceramic pottery was a fundamental craft in Mesoamerican societies, as it served both practical and ceremonial functions. Artisans crafted a diverse array of ceramic vessels, including jars, bowls, plates, and figurines. These vessels were used for storing food, water, and other essential substances, reflecting the significance of pottery in sustaining everyday life.

Decoration and Symbolism: Mesoamerican ceramics were often decorated with intricate designs, intricate patterns, and symbolic motifs. These decorations conveyed cultural symbolism and religious significance. Common motifs included representations of deities, animals, plants, and abstract geometric patterns. The choice of motifs and designs varied across different Mesoamerican cultures, reflecting their unique artistic traditions.

Polychrome Pottery: One of the remarkable features of Mesoamerican ceramics is the use of polychrome techniques, where multiple colors were applied to the pottery before firing. This allowed artisans to create vibrant and visually striking pieces. The Maya, in particular, were known for their exquisite polychrome ceramics, which featured complex scenes and hieroglyphic inscriptions.

Trade and Exchange: Ceramic vessels played a vital role in trade and exchange networks throughout Mesoamerica. Different regions produced distinct styles of ceramics, and these pottery items were often used as commodities for trade. The exchange of ceramics contributed to the cultural diffusion of artistic styles and ideas across Mesoamerica.

Craftsmanship and Artistry: Artisans in Mesoamerican societies demonstrated remarkable craftsmanship and artistry in their ceramic and craft production. They employed various techniques, such as coiling, modeling, and painting, to create vessels and objects of exceptional quality. The attention to detail and creativity displayed in these artifacts reflected the high level of skill and artistic innovation within these civilizations.

Utilitarian and Ritual Use: Ceramics and crafts served a dual purpose in Mesoamerican societies. While some items were purely utilitarian, others held profound ritual significance. Ceremonial vessels, for instance, were often used in religious rituals and offerings to deities. These vessels were adorned with specific symbols and designs associated with the respective rituals.

Figurines and Sculptures: In addition to pottery, Mesoamerican artisans crafted figurines and sculptures from various materials, including clay, stone, and jade. These figurines depicted deities, humans, animals, and mythical beings. They played roles in religious ceremonies, domestic rituals, and as items of personal adornment.

Symbolism and Cosmology: Many ceramic and crafted objects were imbued with symbolism and cosmological meaning. The intricate designs and motifs often related to Mesoamerican cosmology, such as the concept of the world tree, celestial bodies, and the duality of life and death. These symbols helped convey the spiritual beliefs and worldview of these ancient cultures.

Legacy and Continuity: The artistic traditions of ceramics and crafts in Mesoamerican civilizations left a lasting legacy. Even after the decline of these ancient cultures, their artistic motifs and techniques continued to influence later Mesoamerican societies, such as the Aztecs. Today, contemporary artisans in the region draw inspiration from these ancient traditions, preserving and revitalizing these artistic practices.

In summary, ceramics and crafts were integral to the cultural and artistic expressions of Mesoamerican civilizations. These artifacts not only served practical purposes but also conveyed the rich symbolism, cosmology, and artistic innovation of these ancient peoples. The legacy of Mesoamerican ceramics and crafts endures as a testament to the creativity and craftsmanship of these remarkable societies.

Religious and cultural practices were central to the lives of ancient Mesoamerican civilizations, including the Olmec, Maya, Teotihuacan, Zapotec, Toltec, and Aztec societies. These practices played a profound role in shaping the beliefs, values, and daily routines of the people, and they left a lasting legacy in the form of art, architecture, and social organization.

Polytheistic Beliefs: Mesoamerican civilizations were polytheistic, meaning they worshiped multiple deities or gods. Each deity held specific attributes and domains, and religious practices often revolved around appeasing these gods through rituals, offerings, and ceremonies. The pantheon of Mesoamerican deities included gods associated with agriculture, fertility, warfare, and the cosmos.

Cosmology and Ritual Calendar: Cosmology played a significant role in Mesoamerican religious practices. These societies developed complex cosmological beliefs and a ritual calendar based on celestial events, such as the movements of the sun, moon, and stars. Rituals and ceremonies were often timed to align with specific astronomical occurrences, emphasizing the connection between the terrestrial and celestial realms.

Pyramids and Temples: Religious and cultural centers in Mesoamerican cities featured prominent pyramids and temples dedicated to various deities. These structures served as sacred spaces for ceremonies, offerings, and religious pilgrimages. The architecture of these temples often reflected the beliefs and cosmological concepts of the society, with intricate carvings, sculptures, and symbolic designs.

Human Sacrifice: One of the most controversial aspects of Mesoamerican religious practices was human sacrifice. Some civilizations, notably the Aztecs, practiced human sacrifice as part of their religious rituals. The belief was that offering human blood to the gods would ensure the balance of the cosmos and the continuation of life. Captives from warfare were often chosen as sacrificial victims.

Bloodletting Rituals: Bloodletting rituals were another common religious practice in Mesoamerica. Nobility and rulers would engage in self-mutilation by drawing their own blood, which was collected on paper or textiles and offered to the gods. Bloodletting was seen as a means of communication with the deities and a way to gain their favor.

Shamans and Priests: Religious leaders, such as shamans and priests, held significant roles in Mesoamerican societies. They acted as intermediaries between the human world and the spiritual realm, conducting rituals, interpreting omens, and communicating with the gods. These individuals played a crucial role in maintaining the spiritual and cultural fabric of their civilizations.

Ceremonial Ballgames: Ceremonial ballgames were a unique cultural practice in Mesoamerica and often had religious significance. These games, played with rubber balls, were held in ball courts and were associated with creation myths and religious rituals. The games sometimes had a ritualistic element, with winners often receiving honors or sacrificial offerings.

Offerings and Altars: Altars and offering tables were common features in Mesoamerican religious spaces. These were used to present offerings such as food, incense, flowers, and symbolic objects to the gods. The act of offering was essential to maintaining harmony between humans and the divine.

Dance and Music: Dance and music played roles in Mesoamerican religious ceremonies. Ritual dances, accompanied by drums, flutes, and other instruments, were performed to invoke the presence of deities or to celebrate important events. These artistic expressions were integral to the cultural and spiritual identity of Mesoamerican societies.

Legacy and Continuity: The religious and cultural practices of Mesoamerican civilizations left a lasting legacy. Many elements of these practices, including deities, cosmological beliefs, and rituals, persisted in the cultural traditions of later Mesoamerican societies, such as the Aztecs and their successors. Today, aspects of Mesoamerican religion and culture continue to be practiced and celebrated by indigenous communities in the region, demonstrating the enduring influence of these ancient traditions.

In summary, religious and cultural practices were fundamental to the identity and worldview of Mesoamerican civilizations. These practices encompassed a diverse range of rituals, ceremonies, and beliefs, all of which played pivotal roles in shaping the societies and leaving a lasting impact on the cultural heritage of Mesoamerica.

The discovery of murals in various ancient Mesoamerican sites has been a momentous and insightful endeavor, shedding light on the rich cultural, artistic, and historical aspects of these civilizations. These murals, often hidden beneath layers of time and civilization, have offered significant contributions to our understanding of Mesoamerican life, beliefs, and practices.

Unearthing the Past: The uncovering of these murals is, in many ways, akin to uncovering the past itself. These artworks are not only aesthetically striking but serve as time capsules, preserving the thoughts, beliefs, and cultural expressions of the people who created them. The process of their discovery involves careful excavation, preservation, and analysis by archaeologists, historians, and art experts.

Colorful and Intricate Compositions: One of the most striking aspects of these murals is their vivid and intricate compositions. The use of color, form, and detail in Mesoamerican mural art is nothing short of breathtaking. These murals often depict scenes from everyday life, religious ceremonies, and mythological narratives, providing a window into the world of these ancient civilizations.

Religious and Mythological Themes: Religious and mythological themes are prevalent in many Mesoamerican murals. These artworks often depict deities, supernatural beings, and cosmological elements. The murals reveal the spiritual beliefs and practices of these societies, emphasizing the central role of religion in their lives. The Feathered Serpent deity, Quetzalcoatl, is a recurring figure in many murals, signifying its importance in Mesoamerican cosmology.

Daily Life and Society: Beyond the realm of religion and mythology, Mesoamerican murals also offer glimpses into the daily life and society of these civilizations. Scenes of agriculture, trade, and social interactions provide valuable insights into the economic and social dynamics of these societies. They depict the roles of men, women, and children in various aspects of life.

Techniques and Materials: The techniques and materials used in Mesoamerican mural painting are remarkable. Artists employed a combination of mineral pigments, organic binders, and plaster to create these masterpieces. The pigments included a wide range of colors, allowing for the creation of vibrant and visually striking compositions. Mesoamerican muralists used brushes made from natural fibers, such as maguey leaves, to apply the pigments to the walls.

Alignment with Cosmic Events: One of the fascinating aspects of Mesoamerican mural art is its alignment with cosmic events. Many murals are positioned and designed to correspond with celestial phenomena, such as the solstices and equinoxes. This indicates the deep connection between the people of Mesoamerica and their understanding of the heavens. The Pyramid of the Sun's alignment with the setting sun during specific times of the year is a testament to this cosmic awareness.

Ritual Context: Mesoamerican murals were often created within a ritual context. They adorned temples, palaces, and other ceremonial structures, serving as backdrops for religious ceremonies and rituals. These murals were not mere decorations; they played an active role in the religious and spiritual life of these societies. They helped convey cosmological beliefs, myths, and narratives that were central to Mesoamerican religious practices.

Legacy and Interpretation: The discovery of Mesoamerican murals has had a profound impact on our understanding of these ancient cultures. These artworks have provided scholars with valuable clues about the beliefs, rituals, and daily life of the Olmec, Maya, Teotihuacan, Zapotec, Toltec, and Aztec civilizations. They have also fueled ongoing research and interpretation, offering new perspectives and insights into the past.

Preservation and Conservation: Preservation and conservation efforts are crucial in ensuring the longevity of Mesoamerican murals. Once uncovered, these artworks require meticulous care to protect them from environmental factors, such as humidity, erosion, and pollution. Preservationists employ advanced techniques to stabilize and protect the murals while allowing researchers to continue their study.

Educational and Cultural Significance: Mesoamerican murals hold immense educational and cultural significance. They provide a tangible connection to the past and help bridge the gap between ancient civilizations and modern understanding. These artworks are not only valuable for scholars but also for the communities and descendants of these ancient cultures, who can reconnect with their heritage through the murals.

In summary, the discovery of Mesoamerican murals has been a transformative journey into the heart of ancient civilizations. These artworks serve as vibrant and intricate windows into the lives, beliefs, and practices of the Olmec, Maya, Teotihuacan, Zapotec, Toltec, and Aztec peoples. Their discovery and continued study contribute to the preservation and appreciation of Mesoamerican cultural heritage, enriching our understanding of human history and artistic expression.

Themes and symbolism in Teotihuacan murals provide profound insights into the beliefs, cosmology, and cultural expressions of this ancient Mesoamerican civilization. These vibrant and intricate artworks are rich with symbolism, conveying a complex visual language that reflects the spiritual and cultural fabric of Teotihuacan society.

Celestial Themes: One of the prominent themes in Teotihuacan murals is the celestial realm. These murals often depict celestial bodies, such as the sun, moon, stars, and planets. The celestial motifs highlight the significance of astronomy and cosmology in Teotihuacan culture. The city's alignment with the sun and the Pyramid of the Sun's role in marking solar events underscore the deep cosmic connection of Teotihuacanos.

Feathered Serpent Deity (Quetzalcoatl): The Feathered Serpent deity, known as Quetzalcoatl, is a recurrent and central figure in Teotihuacan murals. Depictions of Quetzalcoatl are characterized by its feathered headdress, serpentine body, and bird-like features. The presence of Quetzalcoatl underscores its importance in Mesoamerican cosmology and suggests that Teotihuacan played a significant role in disseminating the worship of this deity to other cultures.

Water Imagery: Murals in Teotihuacan often incorporate water imagery, symbolizing the importance of water in sustaining life and fertility. Scenes of flowing water, aquatic creatures, and water deities convey the idea of a watery underworld and the role of water in agricultural abundance. The balance between water and earth was integral to Teotihuacan's agricultural practices.

Agricultural Scenes: Agricultural themes are prevalent in Teotihuacan murals, reflecting the agrarian nature of the society. Scenes of planting, harvesting, and tending to crops underscore the importance of agriculture in sustaining the city's population. These murals highlight the interconnectedness of humans with the natural world and the agricultural cycles.

Animal Symbolism: Teotihuacan murals frequently incorporate animal symbolism, with various animals appearing as both realistic depictions and stylized representations. Jaguars, birds, serpents, and other animals hold symbolic significance, often associated with deities or mythological narratives. These animals serve as intermediaries between the human and divine realms.

Geometric and Abstract Patterns: In addition to representational imagery, Teotihuacan murals feature intricate geometric and abstract patterns. These patterns, which include spirals, crosses, and intricate designs, are believed to hold symbolic and ritualistic significance. They convey deeper meanings related to the city's cosmological and religious beliefs.

Human Figures: Human figures and characters are also central to Teotihuacan mural art. These figures often engage in various activities, such as rituals, dance, and social interactions. They provide glimpses into the daily life and society of Teotihuacan, showcasing the roles of men, women, and children in different aspects of the civilization.

Mythological Narratives: Teotihuacan murals depict mythological narratives and stories. These narratives may include creation myths, heroic tales, and cosmological journeys. They serve as a means of transmitting cultural and religious knowledge from one generation to another, reinforcing the spiritual and historical identity of the civilization.

Ritual Context and Offerings: Many of the murals in Teotihuacan were created within a ritual context. They adorned temples and ceremonial spaces, serving as visual aids in religious ceremonies and offerings to the gods. The murals helped convey cosmological beliefs, sacred narratives, and the connection between the terrestrial and celestial realms.

Continued Research and Interpretation: The study of Teotihuacan murals continues to be an active area of research and interpretation. Scholars and archaeologists work diligently to unravel the symbolic meanings and cultural contexts of these artworks. Each new discovery and analysis deepens our understanding of Teotihuacan's complex belief system and cultural heritage.

In summary, themes and symbolism in Teotihuacan murals reveal a multi-layered tapestry of beliefs and expressions. From celestial motifs to agricultural scenes and mythological narratives, these murals convey the intricate cosmology and cultural identity of Teotihuacan society. Their significance goes beyond aesthetics, serving as a testament to the spiritual and artistic legacy of this ancient civilization.

Artistic techniques and preservation efforts play crucial roles in safeguarding the rich cultural heritage represented by the ancient Mesoamerican murals and artworks. These remarkable artistic achievements are not only valuable for their aesthetic qualities but also for the insights they offer into the beliefs, lifestyles, and history of the Olmec, Maya, Teotihuacan, Zapotec, Toltec, and Aztec civilizations.

Pigments and Binders: The creation of Mesoamerican murals involved the use of various pigments and binders to produce the vibrant and enduring colors that still captivate us today. Mineral pigments, derived from minerals like hematite and malachite, were skillfully mixed with organic binders, such as plant resins and agave sap, to form the paint used for mural creation. These pigments were carefully chosen for their color stability and longevity.

Brushes and Tools: Artists in Mesoamerican civilizations employed a range of brushes and tools to create their murals. Brushes were typically made from natural materials, such as maguey leaves or animal hair, and were selected based on their suitability for different painting techniques. These brushes allowed for intricate details and fine lines, contributing to the sophistication of Mesoamerican mural art.

Plaster Preparation: Before painting, mural surfaces were prepared with plaster, which served as the canvas for the artwork. The plaster was expertly applied in multiple layers to create a smooth and even surface. Artists meticulously smoothed and leveled the plaster to ensure an ideal foundation for their work. The thickness and quality of the plaster contributed to the durability of the murals.

Mural Creation Techniques: Mesoamerican muralists employed various techniques to create their artworks. They used both fresco and secco techniques. Fresco painting involved applying paint to wet plaster, allowing the pigments to bond with the surface as the plaster dried. Secco painting, on the other hand, involved applying paint to dry plaster. These techniques allowed for different levels of detail and color vibrancy.

Layering and Overpainting: Muralists often used layering and overpainting to achieve depth and complexity in their compositions. By applying multiple layers of paint and allowing certain areas to dry before adding additional details, artists created subtle shading, highlights, and intricate patterns. This layering technique contributed to the visual richness of Mesoamerican murals.

Symbolism and Cultural Significance: Every stroke of paint on a Mesoamerican mural held symbolic and cultural significance. Artists were not merely decorating walls but conveying complex narratives, spiritual beliefs, and cultural messages. The choice of colors, motifs, and placement of elements conveyed specific meanings related to cosmology, mythology, and daily life.

Preservation Challenges: Preserving Mesoamerican murals presents significant challenges due to their age, delicate nature, and exposure to environmental factors. Over time, these artworks have been subjected to deterioration caused by humidity, temperature fluctuations, pollution, and physical damage. The conservation of these murals requires a delicate balance of protecting them while allowing for ongoing research and public access.

Conservation and Restoration: Preservation efforts involve the careful conservation and restoration of Mesoamerican murals. Skilled conservators employ techniques such as cleaning, stabilization, and repair to ensure the long-term survival of these artworks. Advanced imaging technologies, including digital photography and multispectral imaging, assist in documenting and analyzing the murals.

Environmental Controls: To mitigate environmental damage, conservationists implement environmental controls in mural sites. These measures include humidity and temperature regulation, as well as measures to limit exposure to natural light and pollutants. Conservation teams work to create controlled environments that mimic the conditions necessary for the murals' preservation.

Education and Public Engagement: Public education and engagement are integral to the preservation of Mesoamerican murals. By raising awareness about the value of these artworks and their cultural significance, communities, scholars, and institutions can work together to ensure their protection. Public engagement also fosters a sense of responsibility for preserving cultural heritage.

Ethical Considerations: Preservation efforts must be conducted ethically and with respect for the cultural heritage of indigenous communities. Collaboration with local communities and descendants of the civilizations represented by the murals is essential. Ethical guidelines for excavation, restoration, and research aim to balance the preservation of heritage with cultural sensitivity.

Continued Research and Documentation: Mesoamerican mural preservation goes hand in hand with ongoing research and documentation. Researchers continue to study these artworks to gain deeper insights into the history, culture, and artistic techniques of the ancient civilizations. Documentation efforts, including detailed records and digital databases, aid in the long-term conservation of mural sites.

In summary, the artistic techniques used in the creation of Mesoamerican murals demonstrate the sophistication and skill of ancient artists. These murals provide invaluable glimpses into the beliefs and cultural expressions of Mesoamerican civilizations. Preserving these artworks requires a multidisciplinary approach that combines conservation, research, education, and ethical considerations to ensure that future generations can continue to marvel at their beauty and significance.

Chapter 5: Social Hierarchy and Daily Life in Teotihuacan (400 CE - 700 CE)

Teotihuacan, one of the most significant and influential ancient Mesoamerican cities, exhibited a complex social structure with distinct social classes that shaped the daily lives and interactions of its inhabitants. Understanding these social classes provides insight into the organization, governance, and cultural dynamics of Teotihuacan society.

Elite Class: At the top of Teotihuacan's social hierarchy was the elite class, comprising rulers, high-ranking priests, and nobility. These individuals enjoyed privileges, including access to luxurious goods, fine clothing, and grand residences. They held significant political and religious power, often participating in state ceremonies and rituals. The elite played pivotal roles in governance and religious activities, reflecting their authority within the city-state.

Priesthood: The priesthood held a prominent place in Teotihuacan society. Priests were responsible for conducting elaborate religious ceremonies, maintaining temples, and interpreting celestial events. Their role was essential in upholding the city's religious beliefs, including the veneration of deities like the Feathered Serpent (Quetzalcoatl). Priests also played a crucial role in mediating between the spiritual and earthly realms, ensuring the favor of the gods.

Artisans and Craftsmen: Artisans and craftsmen constituted another important segment of Teotihuacan society. They were skilled in various trades, including pottery, textiles, obsidian tool-making, and mural painting. These skilled individuals produced a wide range of goods, from utilitarian pottery to intricate jewelry, reflecting the city's vibrant artistic and economic life. Artisans contributed to the material wealth and cultural richness of Teotihuacan.

Commoners: The majority of Teotihuacan's population belonged to the commoner class. These individuals engaged in diverse occupations, such as agriculture, construction, trade, and daily labor. Commoners formed the backbone of the city's economy, sustaining it through their agricultural efforts, market activities, and contributions to monumental construction projects like the Pyramid of the Sun and Pyramid of the Moon. Their labor was crucial in shaping the physical landscape of Teotihuacan.

Slaves or Servants: While slavery existed in Teotihuacan, it was not as extensive or brutal as in some other ancient civilizations. Slaves or servants typically served the elite and were considered the lowest social class. They performed various domestic and labor-intensive tasks, such as household chores, agricultural work, and construction labor. Despite their lower status, some slaves could earn their freedom through various means.

Residential Distinctions: Residential areas within Teotihuacan reflected social stratification. Elite members inhabited impressive compounds with courtyards, murals, and architectural sophistication. Commoners lived in multi-family residential compounds, which often featured shared courtyards and simple living quarters. These distinctions in housing underscored the social disparities within the city.

Economic Interactions: Teotihuacan's social classes interacted through economic exchanges, trade, and tribute systems. The elite class benefited from tribute collected from outlying regions, which contributed to their wealth and power. Artisans and craftsmen played a pivotal role in producing goods for both local consumption and long-distance trade networks, which facilitated economic connections with distant Mesoamerican cultures.

Religious Roles: Religion played a unifying role in Teotihuacan society, with various social classes participating in religious rituals and ceremonies. The priesthood, in particular, had a central role in conducting elaborate ceremonies dedicated to the city's deities. Commoners also participated in religious activities, making offerings and seeking the favor of the gods for agricultural success and protection.

Cultural Identity: Teotihuacan's social classes contributed to the city's unique cultural identity. The diversity of roles and occupations within the city enriched its artistic expressions, technological achievements, and religious practices. This dynamic interaction of social classes fostered a sense of collective identity and a shared connection to the city's monumental architecture and symbolic landscape.

Influence on Later Civilizations: Teotihuacan's social structure and cultural achievements left a lasting impact on subsequent Mesoamerican civilizations, including the Maya and Aztecs. The city's architectural designs, religious beliefs, and social hierarchies influenced the development of these later societies, attesting to the enduring legacy of Teotihuacan's social classes.

In summary, Teotihuacan's social structure was marked by a hierarchical arrangement that included elites, priests, artisans, commoners, and servants. Each class played a distinct role in shaping the city's culture, economy, and religious practices. This social diversity contributed to the city's prosperity, cultural richness, and lasting influence on Mesoamerican civilizations.

Family life and household activities in ancient Mesoamerican civilizations, including the Olmec, Maya, Teotihuacan, Zapotec, Toltec, and Aztec, were characterized by distinct cultural practices, roles, and daily routines that reflected the values and traditions of each society. Understanding these aspects provides a glimpse into the domestic lives of these ancient peoples.

Family Structure: Family structures in Mesoamerican civilizations varied but often included extended families. These families typically consisted of parents, children, grandparents, and sometimes other relatives. The importance of extended family networks extended beyond the nuclear family, with aunts, uncles, and cousins playing significant roles in the lives of individuals.

Roles and Gender: Gender roles in Mesoamerican societies were clearly defined. Men were primarily responsible for activities such as agriculture, hunting, warfare, and trade. Women played key roles in food preparation, weaving, and childcare. However, women also had economic responsibilities, such as participating in market activities and trading.

Agriculture and Food Production: Agriculture was central to Mesoamerican life, and many household activities revolved around farming. Families cultivated maize (corn), beans, squash, and other crops. Women often planted and tended to these crops, which were staples of the Mesoamerican diet. Men engaged in hunting and fishing to supplement the family's diet.

Cooking and Food Preparation: Cooking was a significant household activity. Women were responsible for preparing meals, which typically involved grinding maize into masa (dough) to make tortillas, tamales, and other dishes. Traditional Mesoamerican cuisine featured a variety of ingredients, including chili peppers, tomatoes, chocolate, and avocados.

Domestic Arts and Crafts: Mesoamerican women were skilled in various domestic arts and crafts. They were known for their expertise in pottery-making, weaving, and textile production. Pottery served both utilitarian and decorative purposes, while textiles were used for clothing and household items.

Childcare and Education: Childcare was a shared responsibility within extended families. Grandparents often played an active role in raising and educating children. Education in Mesoamerican societies was primarily oral, with elders passing down knowledge, stories, and traditions to younger generations.

Religious Practices at Home: Religion played a significant role in household life. Families often had household altars or shrines dedicated to deities and ancestors. Offerings and rituals were conducted to seek blessings, protection, and guidance from the spiritual realm. The household was considered a sacred space, and religious ceremonies were an integral part of daily life.

Community and Social Interaction: Households were not isolated units but integral parts of their communities. Families participated in communal activities, such as religious ceremonies, festivals, and trade. Social interaction within the community strengthened social bonds and cultural ties.

Housing and Architecture: The design of Mesoamerican households varied among the different civilizations. Common features included multi-family compounds, central courtyards, and living spaces arranged around open areas. The architecture often incorporated artistic elements, such as murals and carvings, which reflected the culture and beliefs of the inhabitants.

Marriage and Family Life: Marriage was an important institution in Mesoamerican societies. Marriages were often arranged by families, and ceremonies varied in complexity. Families sought to create alliances and strengthen social ties through marital unions. The birth of children was celebrated and marked important milestones in family life.

Burial Practices: Burial practices were intertwined with family life and religious beliefs. Families buried their deceased loved ones with care, often including grave goods and offerings to accompany the deceased into the afterlife. Ancestor veneration was a common practice, and families maintained connections with their ancestors through rituals and offerings.

In summary, family life and household activities in ancient Mesoamerican civilizations were deeply rooted in cultural traditions and social structures. Gender roles were well-defined, with men and women contributing to the family's well-being in distinct ways. Agriculture, food preparation, domestic arts, and religious practices were central to daily life. Families were interconnected with their communities, and the household served as a space for the transmission of cultural values and traditions from one generation to the next.

Food, trade, and the economy were interconnected aspects of life in ancient Mesoamerican civilizations, each playing a vital role in shaping the culture, society, and daily routines of the Olmec, Maya, Teotihuacan, Zapotec, Toltec, and Aztec civilizations. Understanding the dynamics of food production, trade networks, and economic activities provides insight into the complexities of these ancient societies.

Agriculture and Staple Crops: Agriculture formed the foundation of Mesoamerican economies. Maize (corn) was the primary staple crop and the most essential food source for Mesoamerican peoples. It was often cultivated alongside beans and squash, a farming technique known as the "Three Sisters." Other crops included chili peppers, tomatoes, amaranth, and avocados. Agricultural knowledge was passed down through generations, with each civilization developing its agricultural techniques and crop varieties.

Domestication of Plants and Animals: Mesoamerican civilizations made significant contributions to the domestication of plants and animals. Beyond maize, they cultivated various crops like cacao (cocoa), vanilla, and cotton. The domestication of animals, such as turkeys and dogs, also played a role in their societies. Cacao, in particular, held immense cultural and economic value and was used to make chocolate beverages.

Trade Networks: Trade networks were extensive and facilitated the exchange of goods among Mesoamerican civilizations. Trade routes connected different regions, enabling the transfer of commodities like obsidian, jade, feathers, pottery, textiles, and other craft goods. Long-distance trade played a pivotal role in cultural diffusion, as it allowed for the exchange of ideas, art styles, and technologies between different civilizations.

Marketplaces and Economic Hubs: Marketplaces were essential economic hubs in Mesoamerican cities. They were vibrant centers of trade and commerce where a wide range of goods was bought and sold. Local and regional markets allowed for the exchange of agricultural produce, crafts, and specialty items. Some marketplaces also served as religious and social gathering places.

Barter and Currency: While barter was a common method of trade, some Mesoamerican civilizations developed currency systems. The Aztecs, for instance, used cacao beans as a form of currency. These cacao beans were often traded in standardized units known as "cacao nibs." Copper bells, cotton textiles, and other items were also used as currency in various regions.

Economic Specialization: Mesoamerican societies had economic specialization, with individuals and families often focusing on specific occupations. Artisans and craftsmen produced goods such as pottery, textiles, obsidian tools, and jewelry. Agricultural laborers cultivated crops, while traders facilitated long-distance commerce. This specialization contributed to the diversity and complexity of the economy.

Tribute Systems: Many Mesoamerican civilizations employed tribute systems as a means of resource collection and control over conquered regions. Conquered cities or regions would pay tribute in the form of goods, such as food, textiles, and valuable items, to the ruling city or state. Tribute played a significant role in maintaining the wealth and power of the ruling elite.

Economic Impact on Social Structure: Economic activities were closely tied to social structure. The ruling elite often benefited from tribute and controlled valuable resources, while commoners engaged in agricultural and craft production. Trade provided opportunities for individuals to accumulate wealth and rise in social status. The economic divisions within society were reflected in the allocation of resources and access to luxury goods.

Diet and Cuisine: The availability of diverse crops and trade networks influenced Mesoamerican cuisine. Common dishes included tortillas, tamales, stews, and chili-based sauces. Maize-based foods were central to the diet, along with chocolate-based beverages. The cuisine often incorporated local ingredients and spices, resulting in a rich and flavorful culinary tradition.

In summary, food, trade, and the economy were fundamental components of life in ancient Mesoamerican civilizations. Agriculture provided the sustenance needed for survival, while trade networks facilitated the exchange of goods and cultural influences. Economic activities were intricately linked to social structure and cultural practices, shaping the identities and legacies of these remarkable civilizations.

Chapter 6: Trade and Influence: Teotihuacan's Reach Across Mesoamerica (600 CE - 750 CE)

Teotihuacan, one of the most influential ancient Mesoamerican cities, maintained extensive and far-reaching trade networks that played a pivotal role in shaping its economy, culture, and influence across the region. These trade networks allowed Teotihuacan to access valuable resources, exchange goods with distant regions, and establish itself as a major economic and cultural center. Here's an overview of Teotihuacan's trade networks:

Regional Trade: Teotihuacan was strategically located in the heart of the Mesoamerican region, which enabled it to engage in extensive regional trade. The city's agricultural surplus, produced through advanced farming techniques, allowed it to trade maize, beans, squash, and other agricultural products with neighboring cities and regions. This trade in staple crops was crucial for sustaining the city's population and for establishing diplomatic and economic ties with nearby settlements.

Obsidian Trade: One of Teotihuacan's most significant trade commodities was obsidian, a volcanic glass highly valued for its sharpness and use in tool-making. Teotihuacan controlled several obsidian sources in the nearby region of Pachuca. The city's skilled artisans transformed raw obsidian into various tools, including blades, knives, and projectile points. These tools were traded throughout Mesoamerica and became highly sought after by neighboring civilizations.

Crafts and Artifacts: Teotihuacan was renowned for its skilled artisans who produced a wide range of crafts and artifacts. These included pottery, textiles, jewelry, ceramics, and decorative items. Teotihuacan's craftsmen created high-quality goods that were traded not only within the city but also across long-distance trade networks. These crafted items showcased the city's artistic prowess and cultural influence.

Teotihuacan's Influence on Trade: Teotihuacan's dominance in trade was not solely based on the exchange of goods but also on its cultural and political influence. The city's monumental architecture, murals, and religious practices left a lasting impression on neighboring regions. Many cities sought to emulate Teotihuacan's architectural styles, religious beliefs, and artistic traditions. As a result, Teotihuacan's cultural influence extended beyond its trade network.

Cacao Trade: Cacao beans, used to make chocolate beverages, were another valuable trade item in Mesoamerica. Teotihuacan played a role in cacao trade, as evidenced by the presence of cacao residues found at the city's archaeological sites. This commodity was traded and consumed as a luxury item among the elite.

Long-Distance Trade: Teotihuacan's trade networks extended far beyond its immediate vicinity. The city engaged in long-distance trade with regions such as the Gulf Coast, the Oaxaca Valley, the Maya lowlands, and even as far south as Guatemala. The exchange of goods and ideas through these networks contributed to cultural diffusion and the spread of Teotihuacan's influence.

Tribute and Alliance: In addition to trade, Teotihuacan also collected tribute from conquered regions and formed alliances with neighboring cities. Tribute was a means of resource extraction and a sign of political control. Cities that paid tribute to Teotihuacan often received protection and access to Teotihuacan's trade networks in return.

Impact on Successor Cultures: Teotihuacan's trade networks and cultural influence had a lasting impact on successor civilizations, including the Maya and the Toltecs. The architectural styles, artistic traditions, and religious beliefs of Teotihuacan were adopted and adapted by these civilizations, demonstrating the enduring legacy of Teotihuacan's trade and cultural exchange.

In summary, Teotihuacan's trade networks were instrumental in establishing its economic dominance and cultural influence in ancient Mesoamerica. These networks allowed for the exchange of goods, ideas, and cultural practices, contributing to the city's significance as a major center of trade and civilization in the region.

Cultural exchange and influence were integral aspects of life in ancient Mesoamerican civilizations, including the Olmec, Maya, Teotihuacan, Zapotec, Toltec, and Aztec societies. These civilizations interacted through trade, diplomacy, and shared cultural practices, leading to the exchange of ideas, technologies, and artistic styles. Here's an exploration of how cultural exchange and influence shaped these ancient Mesoamerican cultures:

Trade Networks and Commerce: Trade played a central role in cultural exchange. Mesoamerican civilizations engaged in extensive trade networks that facilitated the movement of goods, materials, and ideas across vast regions. Valuable commodities such as obsidian, jade, textiles, pottery, and cacao beans were exchanged among these cultures. Teotihuacan, in particular, served as a major trade hub and disseminated its cultural elements through commerce.

Artistic Exchange: Artistic traditions were a significant medium of cultural exchange. Iconic art styles, symbolism, and iconography were shared and adopted by various civilizations. For instance, the influence of Teotihuacan's murals and architectural designs extended to other regions, including the Maya lowlands. This exchange of artistic ideas enriched the visual language of Mesoamerican cultures.

Architectural Influences: Architectural innovations and designs were frequently shared and adapted. Teotihuacan's monumental pyramids, platforms, and urban planning influenced neighboring cities, as seen in the adoption of similar architectural elements and city layouts. Maya cities, in particular, incorporated Teotihuacan-style platforms and pyramids into their own urban centers.

Religious Syncretism: Cultural exchange often led to the syncretism of religious beliefs and practices. Deities, rituals, and religious symbolism were shared and blended. The Feathered Serpent deity, known as Quetzalcoatl in Central Mexico, was revered across Mesoamerica, demonstrating the cross-cultural influence of religious figures. This syncretism enriched the spiritual landscape of the region.

Writing and Glyphs: Writing systems and glyphic traditions were also exchanged and adapted. The Maya script, for example, drew upon earlier Mesoamerican writing systems, including those of the Zapotec and Olmec. These writing systems evolved over time and contributed to the recording of history, religious texts, and astronomical knowledge.

Astronomy and Calendar Systems: Astronomical knowledge and calendar systems were shared and adapted by various civilizations. The Maya, renowned for their precise calendar and astronomical observations, influenced neighboring cultures in the development of their own calendar systems. Teotihuacan's celestial alignments and architectural orientations also reflected its astronomical knowledge, which influenced later civilizations.

Cultural Diffusion Through Trade: Trade routes served as conduits for the diffusion of cultural elements. Teotihuacan's influence, for instance, extended to the Maya lowlands through trade connections. As goods were exchanged, cultural practices, technologies, and religious beliefs were shared, leading to a more interconnected Mesoamerican world.

Political and Diplomatic Relations: Political interactions and alliances often facilitated cultural exchange. Diplomatic marriages, tribute systems, and alliances between city-states and empires led to the transfer of cultural elements. For instance, the Aztec Triple Alliance's control over neighboring regions allowed for the dissemination of Aztec culture and religion.

Legacy and Enduring Influence: The cultural exchange and influence among Mesoamerican civilizations left a profound legacy. The art, architecture, religious beliefs, and scientific knowledge of these cultures continue to influence contemporary Mesoamerican societies and inspire scholars and enthusiasts worldwide. The enduring legacy of cultural exchange serves as a testament to the richness and complexity of ancient Mesoamerican civilizations.

In summary, cultural exchange and influence were dynamic forces that shaped the identities and achievements of ancient Mesoamerican civilizations. The interconnectedness of these cultures through trade, art, religion, and other facets of life contributed to the vibrancy and diversity of Mesoamerican civilization, leaving a lasting imprint on the history of the region.

Teotihuacan, the ancient Mesoamerican city known for its monumental pyramids, grand avenues, and rich cultural heritage, boasts a legacy that continues to captivate scholars, archaeologists, and enthusiasts. This remarkable city, located in what is now central Mexico, flourished during its heyday from approximately 100 BCE to 750 CE. Its enduring legacy encompasses several facets that shed light on the profound impact it had on subsequent Mesoamerican civilizations and the world at large.

Architectural Marvels: Teotihuacan's architectural legacy stands as a testament to its grandeur and innovation. The city's monumental structures, particularly the Pyramid of the Sun and the Pyramid of the Moon, remain iconic symbols of ancient Mesoamerican engineering and urban planning. These colossal pyramids, meticulously aligned with celestial bodies, have inspired awe and admiration for centuries. The enduring presence of Teotihuacan's architectural marvels serves as a reminder of the city's once-thriving urban center and its contribution to Mesoamerican urban planning.

Urban Planning and Layout: Teotihuacan's meticulously planned urban layout has influenced subsequent Mesoamerican cities. Its gridded streets, central avenues, and well-organized residential and ceremonial districts set a precedent for urban design in the region. The concept of an urban core featuring a central pyramid flanked by temples and plazas found in Teotihuacan influenced the layouts of later Mesoamerican cities like Chichen Itza and Tenochtitlan. This legacy of urban planning and architectural design continues to shape our understanding of ancient urbanism.

Cultural and Religious Influence: Teotihuacan's religious and cultural practices had a profound and lasting impact on Mesoamerican societies. The city's pantheon of deities, including the Feathered Serpent (Quetzalcoatl), were revered across the region. Teotihuacan's religious iconography, symbolism, and rituals were adopted and adapted by neighboring civilizations, including the Maya and the Aztecs. The religious syncretism that emerged from these exchanges enriched the spiritual landscape of

Mesoamerica, creating a lasting legacy of shared beliefs and practices.

Artistic Traditions: Teotihuacan was renowned for its artistic achievements, particularly its vibrant murals and frescoes. These intricate artworks adorned the walls of elite residences and temples, depicting scenes of daily life, mythology, and cosmology. The city's artistic traditions influenced the visual language of subsequent Mesoamerican cultures. Notably, Teotihuacan-style murals have been discovered in Maya cities, attesting to the wide-reaching influence of Teotihuacan's artistic heritage.

Astronomical Knowledge: Teotihuacan's precise astronomical alignments and celestial observations left an indelible mark on Mesoamerican calendars and astronomical systems. The city's understanding of celestial phenomena, reflected in its architectural orientations, informed the development of the Mesoamerican calendar. Teotihuacan's legacy in astronomy is evident in the continued use of its calendar and its influence on later civilizations' astronomical pursuits.

Trade and Cultural Exchange: Teotihuacan's central location made it a vital hub for trade and cultural exchange. The city's extensive trade networks connected it to distant regions, facilitating the exchange of goods, ideas, and technologies. This cultural diffusion enriched the fabric of Mesoamerican societies, leading to the adoption and adaptation of Teotihuacan's cultural elements by neighboring civilizations. The legacy of cultural exchange is evident in the shared practices, iconography, and artistic styles that transcended regional boundaries.

Influence on Successor Civilizations: The influence of Teotihuacan extended to successor civilizations, including the Toltecs and the Aztecs. These later societies drew upon Teotihuacan's architectural, religious, and artistic traditions. Tula, the capital of the Toltec civilization, featured architecture reminiscent of Teotihuacan, and the Feathered Serpent deity was central to Toltec religion. The Aztecs, upon establishing their capital, Tenochtitlan, incorporated elements of Teotihuacan's urban planning and religion into their own city. This enduring influence underscores the enduring impact of Teotihuacan on the cultural and political landscape of Mesoamerica.

Legacy in Modern Understanding: The study of Teotihuacan continues to shape our understanding of ancient Mesoamerican civilizations. Archaeological excavations, ongoing research, and conservation efforts at the site provide valuable insights into the daily lives, religious practices, and societal organization of the city's inhabitants. The preservation of Teotihuacan's legacy is crucial for unraveling the mysteries of Mesoamerican history and advancing our knowledge of the region's rich cultural heritage.

In summary, Teotihuacan's legacy transcends time, leaving an indelible mark on the tapestry of Mesoamerican history. Its architectural achievements, cultural influence, and enduring impact on subsequent civilizations serve as a testament to the city's significance in the ancient world. The study and preservation of Teotihuacan's legacy continue to illuminate the complexities of Mesoamerican civilization and inspire a sense of wonder about the achievements of our ancient ancestors.

Chapter 7: The Mysterious Collapse of Teotihuacan (700 CE - 750 CE)

The decline of Teotihuacan, one of the most iconic ancient Mesoamerican cities, has been the subject of much speculation and scholarly debate. Various theories have been proposed to explain the factors that contributed to the city's eventual abandonment and fall from prominence. While the exact causes of Teotihuacan's decline remain a subject of ongoing research, several key theories shed light on the complex processes that may have played a role:

1. Environmental Factors:

Drought and Agricultural Decline: Some researchers suggest that prolonged periods of drought and environmental stress may have impacted Teotihuacan's ability to sustain its large population. A decline in agricultural productivity due to water shortages could have strained resources and led to food shortages.

2. Socio-Political Factors:

Internal Conflict: Internal conflicts, power struggles, or class tensions within Teotihuacan's society may have weakened its political stability. This could have resulted in social unrest, declining authority, and a loss of centralized control.

Excessive Centralization: The city's centralized government and economy, while effective in its heyday, may have become inefficient or inflexible over time. A rigid bureaucratic structure could have hindered adaptability and responsiveness to changing circumstances.

3. External Factors:

Military Conflict: The possibility of external invasions or conflicts with neighboring city-states is another theory. Teotihuacan's influence extended across Mesoamerica, and its control over distant regions might have sparked resistance or aggression from rival powers.

Trade Disruption: Disruptions in trade networks or the collapse of long-distance trade routes could have affected Teotihuacan's economic stability. A decline in the exchange of valuable goods might have undermined the city's prosperity.

4. Cultural and Religious Factors:

Religious Change: Shifts in religious beliefs or practices could have played a role in Teotihuacan's decline. Changes in the pantheon of deities or religious reforms might have influenced the city's sociopolitical dynamics.

Cultural Shifts: Cultural shifts or the emergence of new ideologies within the city might have caused internal divisions and weakened its unity.

5. Epidemics and Health Issues:

Disease and Epidemics: The spread of diseases, possibly introduced by external contacts or internal factors, could have had devastating effects on Teotihuacan's population. Epidemics might have led to a decline in labor force and social disruption.

6. Volcanic Activity:

Volcanic Eruptions: The eruption of nearby volcanoes, such as the Popocatepetl or the Xitle volcano, might have caused damage to Teotihuacan's infrastructure, disrupted agricultural practices, and created an inhospitable environment.

7. Migration and Urban Shift:

Population Movement: Some theories propose that the city's residents gradually migrated away from Teotihuacan to other regions, leading to the city's depopulation. This could have been driven by a combination of factors, including environmental challenges and social upheaval.

8. Combination of Factors:

Multifactorial Decline: It's important to recognize that Teotihuacan's decline was likely influenced by a combination of several factors rather than a single cause. Environmental stress, internal conflict, external pressures, and cultural changes may have all played a role.

The exact sequence of events and the relative significance of these factors in Teotihuacan's decline continue to be subjects of research and debate. Ongoing archaeological investigations, scientific analyses, and interdisciplinary studies aim to provide a more comprehensive understanding of the complex processes that led to the city's ultimate decline and abandonment. Teotihuacan's enigmatic past continues to intrigue scholars and enthusiasts alike, offering a window into the intricate dynamics of ancient Mesoamerican civilizations.

The end of the Teotihuacan civilization, one of the most prominent and mysterious ancient Mesoamerican cultures, remains a subject of intrigue and scholarly debate. Teotihuacan, characterized by its monumental pyramids and sophisticated urban planning, experienced a decline and eventual collapse around the 7th and 8th centuries CE. While the exact reasons for its downfall are still a matter of investigation, several key factors are often considered in understanding the end of Teotihuacan civilization:

1. Decline in Population:
One of the most evident signs of Teotihuacan's decline is the significant reduction in its population. The once-thriving city, with an estimated population of over 100,000 inhabitants at its peak, experienced a sharp decline in the number of residents. Abandoned residential areas and structures point to a dwindling population.

2. Abandonment of Urban Core:
The ceremonial and administrative center of Teotihuacan, which included the Pyramid of the Sun, Pyramid of the Moon, and the central Avenue of the Dead, was gradually abandoned. These iconic structures were no longer maintained, suggesting a loss of central authority and religious significance.

3. Looting and Destruction:
Evidence of looting and deliberate destruction of buildings and temples has been found at Teotihuacan. This suggests that the city faced internal strife, possibly including social unrest or conflict that led to damage to its infrastructure.

4. Environmental Stress:
Environmental factors, such as prolonged droughts, may have played a role in Teotihuacan's decline. A series of dry periods could have led to agricultural difficulties, resource shortages, and

food insecurity. Environmental stress might have contributed to social unrest and population movements.

5. Changing Trade Networks:

The disruption of trade networks that connected Teotihuacan to other Mesoamerican regions might have had economic repercussions. A decline in the exchange of goods and resources could have weakened the city's economic foundation.

6. Sociopolitical Factors:

Internal conflicts, power struggles, or a loss of centralized authority might have contributed to Teotihuacan's unraveling. Inefficiencies in governance and changes in leadership may have weakened the city's ability to respond to challenges effectively.

7. Potential Migrations:

Some theories propose that Teotihuacan's residents gradually migrated away from the city, possibly due to the aforementioned factors. This population movement could have led to the abandonment of the urban core.

8. External Pressures:

Teotihuacan's expansion and influence across Mesoamerica might have provoked resistance from neighboring city-states or external powers. Conflict or external pressures could have hastened the city's decline.

9. Cultural Shifts:

Changes in religious beliefs, cultural practices, or social norms may have contributed to internal divisions and shifts in Teotihuacan's identity and cohesion.

It is important to note that the decline of Teotihuacan was likely a complex interplay of multiple factors rather than a single cause. Moreover, the exact chronology and sequence of events leading to its decline remain subjects of ongoing research and debate.

Despite its eventual fall, Teotihuacan's legacy endures in the form of its iconic architecture, art, and cultural influence on successor civilizations like the Aztecs. The mysterious and enigmatic nature of Teotihuacan continues to captivate researchers and enthusiasts, offering glimpses into the intricate dynamics of ancient Mesoamerican societies and their complex histories.

Amid the ruins of Teotihuacan, the ancient Mesoamerican city that once thrived with grandeur and sophistication, lies a profound and enduring legacy that continues to captivate the imagination of people around the world. Teotihuacan, which flourished between roughly 100 BCE and 750 CE, was known for its monumental pyramids, grand avenues, and rich cultural heritage. Although the city's inhabitants departed long ago, leaving behind a silent urban expanse, its legacy endures in several key aspects:

Architectural Marvels and Urban Planning: Teotihuacan's architectural legacy is perhaps its most iconic contribution to Mesoamerican civilization. The monumental pyramids, including the Pyramid of the Sun and the Pyramid of the Moon, stand as enduring symbols of ancient engineering and urban planning. These colossal structures, aligned with celestial bodies and precisely designed, continue to inspire awe and admiration.

The city's urban layout, characterized by gridded streets, central avenues, and well-organized residential and ceremonial districts, set a standard for urban design that influenced subsequent Mesoamerican cities. The concept of an urban core featuring a central pyramid flanked by temples and plazas, as seen in Teotihuacan, became a blueprint for city planning in the region.

Cultural and Religious Influence: Teotihuacan's cultural and religious practices had a profound and lasting impact on Mesoamerican societies. The city's pantheon of deities, including the Feathered Serpent deity (known as Quetzalcoatl), were revered across the region. The religious iconography, symbolism, and rituals of Teotihuacan were adopted and adapted by neighboring civilizations, including the Maya and the Aztecs. This religious syncretism enriched the spiritual landscape of Mesoamerica, creating a lasting legacy of shared beliefs and practices.

Teotihuacan's religious influence extended to its art and iconography, which featured elaborate murals and frescoes depicting scenes of daily life, mythology, and cosmology. These intricate artworks, discovered in elite residences and temples, influenced the visual language of subsequent Mesoamerican cultures. Teotihuacan-style murals have even been found in Maya cities, underscoring the wide-reaching influence of the city's artistic heritage.

Astronomical Knowledge and Calendar Systems: The precision of Teotihuacan's astronomical alignments and celestial observations left an indelible mark on Mesoamerican calendars and astronomical systems. The city's understanding of celestial phenomena, reflected in its architectural orientations, informed the development of the Mesoamerican calendar. Teotihuacan's legacy in astronomy is evident in the continued use of its calendar and its influence on later civilizations' astronomical pursuits.

Trade and Cultural Exchange: Teotihuacan's central location made it a vital hub for trade and cultural exchange. The city's extensive trade networks connected it to distant regions, facilitating the exchange of goods, ideas, and technologies. This cultural diffusion enriched the fabric of Mesoamerican societies, leading to the adoption and adaptation of Teotihuacan's cultural elements by neighboring civilizations. The legacy of cultural exchange is evident in the shared practices, iconography, and artistic styles that transcended regional boundaries.

Influence on Successor Civilizations: The influence of Teotihuacan extended to successor civilizations, including the Toltecs and the Aztecs. These later societies drew upon Teotihuacan's architectural, religious, and artistic traditions. The Toltec capital, Tula, featured architecture reminiscent of Teotihuacan, and the Feathered Serpent deity was central to Toltec religion. The Aztecs, upon establishing their capital, Tenochtitlan, incorporated elements of Teotihuacan's urban planning and religion into their own city. This enduring influence underscores the lasting impact of Teotihuacan on the cultural and political landscape of Mesoamerica.

Legacy in Modern Understanding: The study of Teotihuacan continues to shape our understanding of ancient Mesoamerican civilizations. Archaeological excavations, ongoing research, and conservation efforts at the site provide valuable insights into the daily lives, religious practices, and societal organization of the city's inhabitants. The preservation of Teotihuacan's legacy is crucial for unraveling the mysteries of Mesoamerican history and advancing our knowledge of the region's rich cultural heritage.

In summary, Teotihuacan's legacy endures amid its silent ruins, leaving an indelible mark on the tapestry of Mesoamerican history. Its architectural achievements, cultural influence, and enduring impact on subsequent civilizations serve as a testament to the city's significance in the ancient world. The study and preservation of Teotihuacan's legacy continue to illuminate the complexities of Mesoamerican civilization and inspire a sense of wonder about the achievements of our ancient ancestors.

BOOK 4
ZAPOTEC RESILIENCE
A JOURNEY THROUGH ANCIENT OAXACA (500 BCE - 800 CE)

BY A.J. KINGSTON

Chapter 1: Origins and Early Settlements: The Birth of the Zapotec Culture (500 BCE - 200 CE)

The region of Oaxaca, located in modern-day southern Mexico, has a rich and diverse history that predates the rise of the Zapotec civilization. Before the emergence of the Zapotec culture, several pre-Zapotec cultures thrived in this region, leaving behind a legacy that contributes to our understanding of Oaxaca's ancient past.

Early Settlements and Societies: Oaxaca's history can be traced back to as early as 1500 BCE when the first human settlements began to appear in the region. These early settlers engaged in agricultural activities, cultivating crops like maize, beans, and squash. Their villages were typically small and scattered across the landscape.

Over time, these scattered settlements began to coalesce into larger communities, marking the transition from simple agricultural societies to more complex ones. As communities grew, they developed a more structured social organization and began to engage in trade and exchange with neighboring groups.

San José Mogote Culture: One of the prominent pre-Zapotec cultures in Oaxaca was the San José Mogote culture, which flourished from approximately 1500 BCE to 500 BCE. San José Mogote is considered one of the earliest urban centers in the Oaxaca Valley.

This culture is known for its distinctive pottery, which featured intricate designs and symbols. The presence of ceremonial structures and evidence of long-distance trade suggest that San José Mogote had a well-developed societal structure with connections to other Mesoamerican cultures.

San José Mogote is also significant because it represents a transition period in Oaxacan history, marking the shift from scattered villages to larger, more centralized settlements.

Monte Albán: The First Zapotec Capital: While Monte Albán is often associated with the Zapotec civilization, it is important to note that its early phases were influenced by the pre-Zapotec cultures that preceded it. Monte Albán was founded around 500 BCE, and it became the first capital of the Zapotec civilization.

The establishment of Monte Albán marked a significant consolidation of power and resources in the region. This city became a center of political, religious, and economic activity. Monte Albán's impressive stone architecture, including its pyramids and temples, reflected the advanced engineering skills of its inhabitants.

The incorporation of elements from earlier cultures into Monte Albán's art and iconography illustrates the continuity of cultural traditions from the pre-Zapotec period.

Mixtec Influence: While the Zapotecs are often credited with the rise of Monte Albán, the Mixtecs, another Mesoamerican civilization, also had a significant presence in Oaxaca. The Mixtec culture, known for its skilled craftsmanship, intricate codices, and distinctive art, coexisted with the Zapotecs in the region.

The Mixtecs established their own centers, such as Lambityeco and Mitla, and their influence extended beyond Oaxaca. The Mixtecs engaged in complex trade networks and diplomatic relations with other Mesoamerican civilizations.

It's important to recognize that Oaxaca's history was not solely shaped by the Zapotecs but was influenced by interactions and cultural exchanges with neighboring groups like the Mixtecs.

Legacy of Pre-Zapotec Cultures: The pre-Zapotec cultures of Oaxaca played a crucial role in shaping the region's history and laying the foundation for the subsequent rise of the Zapotec civilization. Their contributions are evident in the development of early settlements, the emergence of urban centers like San José Mogote, and the incorporation of cultural elements into Monte Albán.

The legacy of these pre-Zapotec cultures can also be seen in the rich artistic traditions, pottery styles, and iconography that persisted throughout Oaxaca's history. The intricate designs and symbols found in their art continue to inspire contemporary artists and scholars, shedding light on the diverse cultural tapestry of Oaxaca's ancient past.

Additionally, the interactions between pre-Zapotec cultures, the Zapotecs, and the Mixtecs highlight the dynamic and interconnected nature of Mesoamerican societies. These exchanges contributed to the region's cultural richness and complexity.

In summary, the pre-Zapotec cultures of Oaxaca represent an integral part of the region's history, contributing to its cultural and societal development. While they may not be as well-known as their Zapotec successors, their legacy endures in the archaeological record and serves as a testament to the enduring human presence in this vibrant and historically significant region of southern Mexico.

The emergence of Zapotec identity is a complex and fascinating journey that spans millennia and is deeply intertwined with the history, culture, and civilization of the Zapotec people in Oaxaca, Mexico. While it is challenging to pinpoint a single moment or factor that gave rise to Zapotec identity, this narrative seeks to explore the multifaceted aspects that contributed to its development and evolution over time.

Ancient Roots and Ancestral Heritage: To understand the emergence of Zapotec identity, one must begin with the ancient roots of the Zapotec civilization. The Zapotecs are one of the indigenous Mesoamerican groups with a rich and ancient history that dates back over 2,500 years. This historical depth lays the foundation for their identity.

The Zapotecs' ancestral heritage is rooted in the Oaxaca Valley, where they first settled and developed their distinctive culture. Their deep connection to the land, traditions, and language created a sense of continuity with their ancestors, fostering a strong cultural identity.

Language as a Cultural Marker: Language plays a pivotal role in shaping identity, and for the Zapotec people, their unique Zapotec language (Didxsaj) serves as a crucial cultural marker. The Zapotec language is a testament to their distinct linguistic heritage and has been spoken in the region for millennia.

The preservation and continued use of the Zapotec language have played a significant role in maintaining a sense of cultural identity among Zapotec communities. It serves as a vehicle for the transmission of traditional knowledge, stories, and oral histories that are integral to their identity.

Religious and Spiritual Practices: The religious and spiritual practices of the Zapotec people have also contributed to the formation of their identity. Traditional Zapotec spirituality is deeply connected to the land, ancestors, and natural world. Ceremonies, rituals, and the veneration of deities are central to their belief system.

The Zapotec worldview, which incorporates concepts of reciprocity and harmony with nature, reflects their unique identity. These spiritual practices not only define their cultural identity but also influence their relationship with the environment and their communities.

Cultural Expressions and Artistic Traditions: Zapotec identity is expressed and reinforced through various cultural forms and artistic traditions. The Zapotec people have a rich tradition of pottery, weaving, painting, and sculpture, which reflect their artistic creativity and distinct aesthetic sensibilities.

Zapotec art often features intricate designs, symbolism, and representations of the natural world. These artistic expressions serve as visual manifestations of their cultural identity and heritage. Additionally, Zapotec textiles are renowned for their intricate patterns and vibrant colors, showcasing the pride and identity of the weavers.

Community and Social Organization: Zapotec identity is deeply rooted in community and social organization. Traditional Zapotec communities are often organized around shared customs, governance systems, and collective decision-making processes. These communities, known as "pueblos," are the heart of Zapotec identity.

The strong sense of belonging to a specific pueblo is a fundamental aspect of Zapotec identity. Each pueblo has its own traditions, celebrations, and practices that contribute to a unique local identity within the broader Zapotec culture.

Resistance and Resilience: Throughout their history, the Zapotec people have faced external pressures and challenges, including Spanish colonization, land dispossession, and cultural assimilation efforts. Despite these adversities, Zapotec identity has demonstrated resilience and resistance.

Zapotec communities have actively preserved their cultural practices, languages, and traditions, resisting attempts to erode their identity. This resilience is a testament to the strength and determination of the Zapotec people to maintain their distinct way of life.

Contemporary Zapotec Identity: Today, Zapotec identity continues to evolve and adapt in response to contemporary challenges and opportunities. While many Zapotec communities maintain their traditional practices and values, they also engage with the modern world.

Zapotec identity is not static; it is a dynamic and living expression of the culture, heritage, and values of the Zapotec people. Efforts to revitalize the Zapotec language, promote cultural education, and assert indigenous rights contribute to the ongoing development and preservation of Zapotec identity.

The emergence of Zapotec identity is a complex and multifaceted journey that encompasses language, spirituality, art, community, and resilience. It reflects the enduring connection of the Zapotec people to their ancestral land, culture, and heritage.

Zapotec identity is not a fixed concept but a dynamic and evolving expression of a proud and resilient indigenous civilization that continues to shape the cultural landscape of Oaxaca, Mexico, and contribute to the rich tapestry of human diversity in the world.

The early Zapotec communities in the Oaxaca Valley of southern Mexico were the cradle of a rich and enduring civilization that would leave an indelible mark on Mesoamerican history. The Zapotec people, who are known for their complex societies and cultural achievements, gradually emerged as a distinct group over thousands of years. This narrative explores the formation and characteristics of these early Zapotec communities, shedding light on the foundations of their civilization.

Ancient Beginnings: The roots of Zapotec communities can be traced back to the early agricultural settlements that began to appear in the Oaxaca Valley around 1500 BCE. These early communities engaged in subsistence farming, cultivating crops like maize, beans, and squash. Their existence marked the transition from nomadic hunter-gatherer societies to settled agricultural communities.

Over time, these scattered settlements began to coalesce into larger villages and towns, which laid the groundwork for the development of more complex Zapotec communities. This period of transition saw the emergence of social hierarchies, as some individuals specialized in craft production, trade, or religious roles.

Monte Albán: The First Urban Center: One of the most significant early Zapotec communities was Monte Albán, which was founded around 500 BCE. Monte Albán would later become the capital of the Zapotec civilization. The establishment of Monte Albán marked a pivotal moment in the region's history, signifying the shift from scattered agricultural villages to a centralized urban center.

The rise of Monte Albán was influenced by earlier cultures in the Oaxaca Valley, such as the San José Mogote culture. This transition period was marked by increased complexity in social organization, architectural innovation, and cultural exchange.

Architectural Achievements: One of the defining features of early Zapotec communities, including Monte Albán, was their remarkable architectural achievements. The construction of monumental buildings and temples, often adorned with intricate carvings and stelae, showcased the advanced engineering skills of the Zapotec people.

The Zapotecs' architectural innovations were not only practical but also held profound cultural and religious significance. Pyramids, temples, and plazas served as focal points for religious ceremonies, civic gatherings, and political activities. The orientation of these structures often had celestial alignments, demonstrating the Zapotecs' sophisticated understanding of astronomy.

Social Organization and Governance: The social organization of early Zapotec communities was characterized by emerging hierarchies and specialized roles. While agricultural activities were fundamental to their subsistence, certain individuals took on roles as craftsmen, traders, priests, and political leaders.

The governance of these communities was likely carried out by a ruling elite or council of elders who oversaw religious rituals, resource allocation, and decision-making. The existence of a ruling class is evident in the elaborate tombs and burials discovered in the Oaxaca Valley, reflecting the social stratification of these early Zapotec communities.

Religion and Cosmology: Religion played a central role in the lives of early Zapotec communities. Their belief system was closely tied to the natural world, celestial events, and the cycle of agricultural seasons. The Zapotecs worshipped a pantheon of deities, including gods associated with agriculture, rain, and fertility.

Ceremonial centers, such as Monte Albán, featured temples and altars where religious rituals were performed. The Zapotecs believed in the interconnectedness of the spiritual and material realms, and their religious practices were integral to maintaining harmony with the cosmos.

Trade and Exchange: Early Zapotec communities were active participants in trade networks that extended across Mesoamerica. The Oaxaca Valley's strategic location facilitated interactions with neighboring regions, allowing for the exchange of goods, ideas, and cultural influences.

Trade items such as obsidian, ceramics, and textiles have been found in archaeological excavations, providing insights into the interconnected nature of Mesoamerican societies during this period. The Zapotecs' engagement in trade contributed to the exchange of technological innovations, artistic styles, and cultural practices.

Continuity and Legacy: The early Zapotec communities laid the foundation for the flourishing Zapotec civilization that would later emerge at Monte Albán. Their achievements in agriculture, architecture, governance, and religion set the stage for the cultural and societal developments that would follow.

While the specific identities and structures of these early communities may have evolved and transformed over time, their legacy endures in the enduring traditions, artistic expressions, and cultural practices of the Zapotec people. The emergence of early Zapotec communities marked the beginning of a remarkable journey that would shape the history of the Oaxaca Valley and contribute to the mosaic of Mesoamerican civilizations.

Chapter 2: Monte Albán: The Majestic Zapotec Capital (200 CE - 500 CE)

The founding of Monte Albán, one of the most significant archaeological sites in Mexico, marks a pivotal moment in the history of the Zapotec civilization. Located in the Oaxaca Valley of southern Mexico, Monte Albán's emergence as a major urban center around 500 BCE represents the culmination of centuries of cultural development and innovation. This narrative explores the founding of Monte Albán, shedding light on its historical significance and the factors that contributed to its rise.

Early Agricultural Settlements: The story of Monte Albán's founding begins with the early agricultural settlements that appeared in the Oaxaca Valley as far back as 1500 BCE. These settlements were inhabited by the Zapotec people, who engaged in subsistence farming and gradually transitioned from nomadic hunter-gatherer lifestyles to settled agricultural communities.

Over time, these scattered agricultural villages began to coalesce into larger communities, setting the stage for the eventual rise of Monte Albán. The fertile lands of the Oaxaca Valley and its temperate climate provided favorable conditions for agriculture, contributing to the region's population growth and cultural development.

Emergence of Complex Society: The transition from small agricultural settlements to a complex society was a gradual process that spanned centuries. During this period, the Zapotec people developed more sophisticated social hierarchies, specialized roles, and increasingly complex religious and political structures.

As communities grew in size and complexity, so did their need for centralized leadership and organization. This period of social evolution laid the groundwork for the emergence of urban centers like Monte Albán.

Monte Albán's Strategic Location: The location of Monte Albán played a crucial role in its founding and subsequent significance.

Perched on a flattened mountaintop overlooking the Oaxaca Valley, Monte Albán's strategic position provided several advantages.

Firstly, it offered a vantage point from which to oversee and control the surrounding landscape, making it an ideal location for a capital city. Additionally, the elevated terrain offered natural defensive advantages, safeguarding the city from potential threats.

Furthermore, the geographic centrality of Monte Albán within the Oaxaca Valley facilitated trade and communication with neighboring communities and regions, contributing to its prominence as a political and economic hub.

Architectural and Urban Innovation: The construction of Monte Albán's monumental architecture reflects the advanced engineering skills and innovative spirit of its founders. The city's layout featured a complex of temples, pyramids, ball courts, plazas, and ceremonial spaces, all meticulously planned and constructed.

The iconic structures of Monte Albán showcased a sophisticated understanding of architecture and urban planning. Pyramid-like platforms, known as "mound-like buildings," and intricate stelae adorned with hieroglyphics and carvings contributed to the city's grandeur.

The orientation of these architectural features often had celestial alignments, emphasizing the Zapotecs' deep connection to astronomy and cosmology.

Cultural and Religious Significance: Monte Albán held profound cultural and religious significance for the Zapotec people. The city served as a center for religious ceremonies, political gatherings, and cultural expression. Its temples and altars were sites of worship and ritual, where offerings were made to appease deities associated with agriculture, rain, and fertility.

The Zapotecs' religious beliefs were deeply intertwined with their agricultural practices and the cyclical rhythms of nature. Monte Albán's role as a religious and ceremonial center underscored the spiritual connection between the city's inhabitants and the cosmos.

The Founding Myth: Although the precise details of Monte Albán's founding remain shrouded in history, Zapotec oral traditions and later codices provide a founding myth that speaks of a legendary priest named Danibáá, who is credited with the city's establishment. According to legend, Danibáá's vision led to the selection of Monte Albán's mountaintop location.

While the founding myth may contain elements of truth, it is also a testament to the Zapotec people's cultural pride and the significance they attached to Monte Albán's founding.

Continued Development and Legacy: Monte Albán continued to thrive and evolve for over a millennium, eventually becoming one of Mesoamerica's most important urban centers. Its influence extended far beyond its mountaintop borders, shaping the cultural and political landscape of the Oaxaca Valley and influencing neighboring regions.

Today, Monte Albán stands as a UNESCO World Heritage Site and a testament to the ingenuity, cultural richness, and enduring legacy of the Zapotec civilization. Its founding represents not only the birth of a city but also the embodiment of a complex and vibrant civilization that left an indelible mark on the history of Mesoamerica.

The ancient city of Monte Albán, perched on a flattened mountaintop in the Oaxaca Valley of southern Mexico, is renowned for its remarkable architectural wonders. As one of the most significant archaeological sites in Mexico, Monte Albán's architecture reflects the advanced engineering skills, artistic creativity, and cultural significance of the Zapotec civilization that thrived there for centuries. This narrative explores the architectural wonders of Monte Albán and their contributions to Mesoamerican history and culture.

1. Pyramid-like Platforms: One of the most iconic features of Monte Albán's architecture is its pyramid-like platforms, often referred to as "mound-like buildings." These raised platforms served both practical and symbolic purposes. They were constructed using stone and clay, and their terraces were used for various functions.

These platforms were not tombs, as they lacked burial chambers, but rather served as stages for ceremonies, rituals, and public gatherings. The largest of these platforms, known as the South Platform, is especially notable for its grandeur and size, providing a commanding view of the surrounding valley.

2. Ball Courts: Monte Albán boasts several ball courts, which were significant architectural features in Mesoamerican societies. These ball courts were constructed for the popular Mesoamerican ballgame, a ritualistic and athletic activity played throughout the region.

The ball courts at Monte Albán featured sloping walls and a narrow playing alley, challenging players to use their hips to propel a rubber ball through stone hoops. These courts served both recreational and ceremonial purposes, with the game often associated with religious symbolism and cosmic beliefs.

3. Temples and Altars: The city's religious and ceremonial centers featured temples and altars dedicated to various deities. These structures were characterized by their distinctive architectural style, often adorned with intricate carvings and stelae that depicted gods, mythological creatures, and hieroglyphics.

Temple 4, for example, is a prominent structure at Monte Albán, and its summit is graced by a carved stone altar known as the Danzantes ("Dancers") relief, featuring mysterious, contorted figures believed to depict prisoners, sacrificial victims, or individuals engaged in ritual dances.

4. Hieroglyphic Stelae: Monte Albán is renowned for its hieroglyphic stelae, which provide valuable insights into the Zapotec script and their historical narratives. These stelae are large stone slabs carved with intricate hieroglyphs and images.

Stela 3, also known as the "Stela of the Dancers," is a prime example. It features a complex arrangement of hieroglyphics surrounding a central image of a human figure in a ceremonial pose. These stelae likely served as markers of important events, such as royal decrees, calendar dates, and historical records.

5. Observatory: Monte Albán's architecture also includes an observatory known as Building J, reflecting the Zapotecs' advanced knowledge of astronomy and celestial observations. This structure features a small rectangular room with a narrow slit or opening in its roof, allowing for precise observations of celestial events.

The observatory was likely used for tracking the movement of celestial bodies, including the sun and moon, which played crucial roles in Mesoamerican cosmology, religious rituals, and calendar systems.

6. Plaza of the Columns: The Plaza of the Columns is an architectural marvel at Monte Albán, characterized by a row of stone columns arranged in a T-shape. These columns were positioned around a central platform and likely served as a ceremonial space.

The Plaza of the Columns showcases the Zapotecs' architectural prowess in constructing complex and aesthetically pleasing spaces for communal gatherings and religious activities.

7. Water Management: Monte Albán's architecture also included advanced water management systems, such as cisterns and channels that directed rainwater for agricultural and domestic use. These systems highlight the city's ingenuity in managing water resources in an arid environment.

The combination of architectural achievements and water management systems allowed Monte Albán to sustain a thriving urban population.

8. Residential Complexes: In addition to its monumental architecture, Monte Albán had residential areas where its inhabitants lived. These residential complexes featured smaller, multi-roomed buildings arranged around courtyards.

These dwellings provide insights into the daily lives of the Zapotec people, including their domestic activities, family structures, and social organization.

Monte Albán's architectural wonders stand as a testament to the Zapotec civilization's cultural sophistication, technological achievements, and spiritual beliefs. The city's layout and structures not only served practical purposes but also held profound cultural and religious significance, shaping the identity and legacy of the Zapotec people in the Mesoamerican landscape.

The Zapotec civilization, centered in the Oaxaca Valley of southern Mexico, was characterized by a complex system of governance and leadership that evolved over centuries. Unlike centralized empires like the Aztecs or Maya, the Zapotecs developed a decentralized political structure with numerous independent city-states. This narrative delves into the intricate world of Zapotec rulers and governance, exploring the roles of leaders, their political systems, and the challenges they faced.

City-States and Decentralization: The Zapotecs were organized into multiple city-states, each governed independently and ruled by a local elite. These city-states were often characterized by distinct cultures, traditions, and hierarchies. While some, like Monte Albán, were more prominent and powerful, others were smaller and less influential.

This decentralized structure allowed for a degree of autonomy among city-states but also led to political fragmentation and competition for resources and territory. Zapotec city-states frequently engaged in alliances and conflicts, leading to a dynamic political landscape.

Civic Leaders and Priests: At the heart of Zapotec governance were civic leaders and priests who held significant power within their respective city-states. Civic leaders, often referred to as rulers or lords, played a pivotal role in decision-making, resource allocation, and maintaining social order. Their authority extended to military matters, religious ceremonies, and trade agreements.

Priests were equally influential, as religion played a central role in Zapotec society. They officiated religious rituals, interpreted celestial events, and ensured the spiritual well-being of their communities. The relationship between civic leaders and priests was often intertwined, with rulers frequently holding religious roles as well.

The Council of Elders: In many Zapotec city-states, governance was further guided by a council of elders known as "Tlazocamatl." These respected individuals, often chosen for their wisdom and experience, advised rulers and helped shape political decisions. The council provided a system of checks and balances, ensuring that power was not concentrated in the hands of a single individual.

The council's role extended beyond political matters; they also had influence in settling disputes, maintaining social harmony, and upholding the customary laws and traditions of their city-state.

Inheritance and Succession: Succession in Zapotec leadership was typically based on hereditary principles, with rulership passing from one generation to the next within noble families. This dynastic system reinforced the social hierarchy, as ruling families held both political and economic power.

The process of succession often involved rituals and ceremonies to legitimize the new ruler's authority. In some cases, a ruler's legitimacy was further reinforced by their association with divine or celestial forces.

Challenges to Stability: The decentralized nature of Zapotec governance, while allowing for local autonomy, also presented challenges to political stability. Rivalries and conflicts between city-states were common, as each vied for control of fertile lands, trade routes, and other valuable resources.

Additionally, external pressures from neighboring civilizations, such as the Mixtec or Teotihuacan, posed threats to Zapotec autonomy. These interactions could lead to alliances, trade agreements, or conflicts, further shaping the political landscape.

Cultural and Religious Role of Rulers: Zapotec rulers held a dual role as political leaders and religious figures. They were often regarded as intermediaries between the earthly realm and the divine, responsible for conducting important religious ceremonies and ensuring the favor of gods associated with agriculture, fertility, and celestial events.

Rulers' actions were closely tied to the well-being of their city-state and its people. Their ability to maintain agricultural fertility and harmony with the cosmos was believed to influence the prosperity and survival of their communities.

Decline and Transformation: The Zapotec civilization went through periods of growth, decline, and transformation. While some city-states, like Monte Albán, experienced periods of political and cultural flourishing, others faced challenges that led to their decline.

External pressures, environmental factors, and internal conflicts contributed to the changing political landscape of the Oaxaca Valley. Some city-states were abandoned, while others were absorbed by emerging regional powers, such as the Mixtec or later, the Aztecs.

Legacy and Cultural Continuity: Despite the eventual decline of the Zapotec city-states as independent political entities, their legacy endured. Zapotec cultural traditions, art, architecture, and religious practices persisted in the region. The Zapotec language, a rich and ancient Mesoamerican tongue, continued to be spoken by their descendants.

Today, Zapotec communities maintain a strong sense of cultural identity and pride, keeping alive the memory of their ancestors and the governance systems that shaped their history.

In summary, the governance of the Zapotec civilization was characterized by a decentralized system of city-states, each with its own rulers, priests, and councils of elders. Rulers held dual roles as political leaders and religious figures, responsible for maintaining harmony with the cosmos and ensuring the well-being of their communities. While the Zapotec civilization faced challenges and transformations over time, its legacy endures in the cultural continuity and traditions of contemporary Zapotec communities.

Chapter 3: Zapotec Art and Innovation (300 CE - 600 CE)

The Zapotec civilization, flourishing in the Oaxaca Valley of southern Mexico, left behind a rich legacy of artistic traditions that provide profound insights into their culture, beliefs, and way of life. These artistic traditions spanned a wide range of forms, from sculpture and ceramics to textiles and architecture, and they played a central role in Zapotec society. This narrative explores the multifaceted world of Zapotec artistic traditions and their significance within the broader context of Mesoamerican art.

Sculpture and Monumental Art: Zapotec sculpture is renowned for its intricate detailing and remarkable craftsmanship. The city of Monte Albán, as the political and cultural heart of the Zapotec civilization, boasts an array of monumental sculptures and stelae that grace its temples and plazas.

One of the most iconic examples is the "Danzantes" (Dancers) relief found on Stela 3 at Monte Albán. These carvings depict distorted, contorted figures in various poses, thought to represent captives or individuals involved in ritual dances. The meaning of these figures remains a subject of debate among scholars, but they undoubtedly convey a sense of motion and narrative.

Ceramics and Pottery: Zapotec pottery is celebrated for its exquisite craftsmanship and diverse forms. Artisans created utilitarian vessels as well as intricate ceremonial pieces that often featured intricate painted designs.

The Monte Albán II phase (200-600 CE) witnessed the development of distinctive Zapotec pottery styles. Blackware ceramics, characterized by their polished black surfaces and intricate incised designs, were prevalent. These vessels served both functional and ritual purposes and were often adorned with symbolic motifs representing deities, animals, and geometric patterns.

Textiles and Weaving: Zapotec weaving traditions were highly developed and played a vital role in the culture's social and economic fabric. Women were primarily responsible for weaving textiles, which were not only used for clothing but also as tribute and trade items.

The Zapotecs used a backstrap loom to create intricate textile patterns, often incorporating symbolic designs that conveyed social status, identity, and mythology. The use of natural dyes and intricate weaving techniques allowed for a wide range of colors and patterns in textiles.

Architecture and Urban Planning: Zapotec architecture is best exemplified by the city of Monte Albán. The layout of the city itself is an architectural marvel, perched atop a mountain plateau and featuring pyramids, plazas, ball courts, and other ceremonial spaces.

The buildings and structures within Monte Albán exhibited intricate architectural detailing, with carved reliefs, friezes, and columns adorned with symbolic motifs. These architectural elements were not only functional but also held deep religious and cosmological significance, aligning with the Zapotec's celestial beliefs.

Hieroglyphic Writing: Zapotec hieroglyphic writing, known as the "Zapotec script," is an integral part of the civilization's artistic and intellectual heritage. Although less understood than some Mesoamerican writing systems, the Zapotec script has been deciphered to a certain extent, allowing researchers to unlock portions of Zapotec history and culture.

Hieroglyphic inscriptions can be found on stelae, altars, and other monumental structures, often recounting historical events, names of rulers, and dates of significant ceremonies. These inscriptions blend art and writing, adding a layer of complexity to the Zapotec artistic tradition.

Symbolism and Religious Imagery: Much of Zapotec art is imbued with symbolic meaning, reflecting the civilization's deep connection to religion and cosmology. Deities associated with agriculture, fertility, and celestial phenomena were frequently depicted in art and sculpture.

The Zapotecs believed that their rulers were intermediaries between the divine and earthly realms, and this belief is reflected in the art, where rulers were often depicted in religious and ritualistic contexts. The placement and orientation of art within ceremonial spaces were meticulously planned to align with celestial events, underscoring the importance of astronomy in Zapotec culture.

Legacy and Contemporary Art: The artistic traditions of the Zapotec civilization continue to influence contemporary Zapotec artists. Many contemporary Zapotec weavers, potters, and painters draw inspiration from their cultural heritage, incorporating traditional techniques and motifs into their work.

Zapotec art also holds a special place in the cultural identity of modern-day Zapotec communities, reinforcing their connection to their ancestors and their unique heritage. It serves as a means of preserving and celebrating their rich cultural legacy.

In summary, Zapotec artistic traditions encompassed a wide array of forms and mediums, from sculpture and ceramics to textiles and architecture. These artistic expressions not only showcased the creativity and craftsmanship of the Zapotec people but also served as a means of conveying their cultural and religious beliefs. The legacy of Zapotec art endures in contemporary Zapotec communities and continues to be a source of cultural pride and inspiration.

In the heart of the Oaxaca Valley, the Zapotec civilization cultivated a rich artistic tradition that included various innovations, pushing the boundaries of Mesoamerican art during its heyday. These artistic innovations reflected the Zapotecs' ingenuity, creativity, and cultural significance. This narrative delves into the groundbreaking innovations in Zapotec art that left an indelible mark on Mesoamerican artistic heritage.

1. Polychrome Pottery: One of the notable innovations in Zapotec art was the development of polychrome pottery. The Zapotec artisans were among the first in Mesoamerica to experiment with a wide range of colors and intricate painted designs on their ceramics.

Polychrome pottery involved the use of multiple colors, often derived from natural pigments, to decorate utilitarian and ceremonial vessels. These vibrant ceramics featured intricate patterns, mythological motifs, and scenes from daily life. The use of color and detailed painting techniques set Zapotec pottery apart from the more monochromatic styles of neighboring cultures.

2. Complex Iconography: Zapotec art was characterized by its complex and highly symbolic iconography. This innovation included the depiction of mythological creatures, deities, and celestial symbols in a sophisticated and often abstract manner.

Symbols and motifs found in Zapotec art conveyed narratives, beliefs, and social status. Artisans incorporated these symbols into various mediums, including pottery, textiles, and monumental sculpture. These intricate narratives were an essential part of Zapotec art's cultural and religious significance.

3. Hieroglyphic Writing and Codices: The Zapotecs developed their hieroglyphic writing system, known as the Zapotec script. While not as extensively deciphered as some other Mesoamerican scripts, the Zapotec script was used to record historical events, dates, and names of rulers on stelae and in codices.

Zapotec codices, such as the Codex Nuttall and Codex Selden, contained intricate illustrations and hieroglyphic texts that provided insights into Zapotec history, religion, and cosmology. These codices are considered masterpieces of pre-Columbian manuscript art and are invaluable sources for understanding Zapotec culture.

4. Architectural Innovation: The architectural innovations of the Zapotecs can be seen in their construction techniques, which included the use of stone and clay for pyramids, plazas, and ball courts. One remarkable architectural feature was the use of raised platforms and pyramids, which served both practical and ceremonial purposes.

Zapotec architectural innovations extended to the incorporation of artistic elements into their buildings. Carved reliefs, stelae, and sculpted friezes adorned temple facades, conveying the civilization's cosmological beliefs and religious narratives.

5. Textile Artistry: Zapotec textile art was another arena of innovation. Skilled weavers employed intricate techniques and bold designs to create textiles that held both utilitarian and symbolic value.

Zapotec textiles featured geometric patterns, animals, and celestial symbols. The use of natural dyes allowed for a wide spectrum of colors, further enhancing the visual appeal of their woven creations. Zapotec textiles were highly sought-after trade items and were often used for clothing and ceremonial regalia.

6. Ceremonial Centers and Alignment: Zapotec art often integrated cosmological and astronomical principles into architectural and artistic designs. Ceremonial centers, like Monte Albán, were meticulously oriented to align with celestial events such as solstices and equinoxes.

This alignment underscored the Zapotecs' connection between the physical and spiritual worlds, reinforcing their belief that rulers were intermediaries between the earthly realm and the divine.

7. Influence on Neighboring Cultures: The innovations in Zapotec art had a profound impact on neighboring cultures, including the Mixtec and Aztec civilizations. The Mixtecs, in particular, adopted and adapted Zapotec artistic styles and techniques, incorporating them into their own rich artistic traditions.

This cultural exchange influenced the broader Mesoamerican artistic landscape and demonstrates the enduring legacy of Zapotec art.

In summary, Zapotec art was characterized by its remarkable innovations, from polychrome pottery and complex iconography to hieroglyphic writing and architectural alignment with celestial events. These artistic innovations not only showcased the creativity and skill of Zapotec artisans but also played a crucial role in conveying the cultural, religious, and historical narratives of the Zapotec civilization. The influence of Zapotec art extended beyond its borders, shaping the artistic traditions of neighboring cultures and leaving an enduring mark on Mesoamerican art and heritage.

Artistic expression has always played a central role in human rituals and ceremonies, serving as a powerful means of conveying cultural, religious, and social messages. Throughout history and across cultures, rituals have been enriched by a wide array of artistic forms, from music and dance to visual arts and architecture. This narrative explores the profound relationship between artistic expression and rituals, highlighting how art has been woven into the fabric of human ceremonies and traditions.

Visual Arts and Sacred Spaces: One of the most striking ways in which art intertwines with rituals is through the creation of sacred spaces. Across civilizations, people have built temples, shrines, and altars adorned with intricate carvings, paintings, and sculptures that serve as focal points for religious ceremonies.

For example, in ancient Egypt, temples like the Karnak Temple complex were adorned with colossal statues, hieroglyphic inscriptions, and vivid murals depicting gods, pharaohs, and sacred events. These artistic elements not only celebrated the divine but also provided a backdrop for rituals, adding depth and spiritual significance to the ceremonies held within.

Ceremonial Costumes and Textiles: The use of textiles and costumes is another significant aspect of artistic expression in rituals. Elaborate garments, often handwoven and adorned with intricate patterns, have been worn during ceremonies around the world.

In Japan, the kimono is a prime example of such artistic attire. Kimonos are not only beautiful garments but also powerful symbols of cultural identity and heritage. They are worn during various ceremonies, including weddings, tea ceremonies, and religious rituals, where they contribute to the visual splendor and solemnity of the occasion.

Music and Instruments: Music is a universal language that transcends cultural boundaries and holds a special place in rituals and ceremonies. Across cultures, musical instruments like drums, flutes, bells, and stringed instruments have been used to create rhythmic and melodic accompaniments to ceremonies.

In Native American cultures, the powwow is a vibrant example of how music and dance are integrated into rituals. The beat of the drum and the melodies of the flute and vocals fill the air, connecting participants with the spirits and ancestors, making the ceremony a profound sensory experience.

Dance and Movement: Dance is a dynamic form of artistic expression that plays a central role in many rituals. Traditional dances often carry deep cultural and spiritual significance, with each movement conveying a specific message or story.

The Maasai people of East Africa, for instance, perform the adumu, or "jumping dance," as part of their coming-of-age rituals. The dance involves high jumps and intricate footwork, and it symbolizes the transition from boyhood to warriorhood. Through this dance, the Maasai preserve their cultural identity and pass down traditions to the next generation.

Ritual Objects and Artifacts: Rituals frequently involve the use of sacred objects and artifacts that are imbued with artistic significance. These objects may include chalices, incense burners, masks, and sculptures, all carefully crafted to serve specific ritual functions.

The intricate masks used in African tribal ceremonies are a prime example. These masks are not only visually striking but also represent ancestral spirits, deities, and mythological beings. They are believed to embody the spiritual essence of the rituals they are a part of, connecting participants with the divine.

Body Art and Tattoos: Body art, including tattoos, scarification, and body painting, has been a common form of artistic expression in rituals and rites of passage. These practices often mark important life events, transitions, or affiliations with cultural or religious groups.

The indigenous peoples of the Pacific Islands, such as the Maori of New Zealand, have a long history of using intricate facial tattoos called moko. These tattoos are not only visually striking but also serve as markers of status, identity, and genealogy within the community.

Narrative Art and Storytelling: Art has been a medium for storytelling within rituals, preserving cultural myths, legends, and histories. In indigenous Australian cultures, for example, "Dreamtime" paintings and rock art depict ancestral stories and landscapes.

These narrative artworks are a means of passing down cultural knowledge and connecting generations with their heritage. They are often used in ceremonies to reinforce the oral traditions and spiritual beliefs of the community.

Contemporary and Evolving Traditions: In the modern world, artistic expression in rituals continues to evolve. New forms of artistic expression, including multimedia presentations, digital art, and performance art, are incorporated into contemporary ceremonies and rituals.

For instance, the Burning Man festival in the United States combines elements of performance art, sculpture, and music in a week-long event that culminates in the burning of a large wooden effigy. This event reflects the fusion of artistic expression and communal ritual in a contemporary context.

In summary, artistic expression in rituals serves as a bridge between the tangible and the intangible, the physical and the spiritual. Whether through visual arts, music, dance, or narrative, art enriches and elevates human ceremonies, connecting participants with their cultural heritage, spirituality, and the profound moments that define their lives. Across time and cultures, the relationship between art and rituals remains a testament to the enduring power of creativity and symbolism in the human experience.

Chapter 4: The Zapotec Writing System: A Glimpse into Ancient Oaxacan Knowledge (400 CE - 700 CE)

The Zapotec script, also known as the Zapotec writing system, is a remarkable and enigmatic aspect of Zapotec culture and history. Unlike some of the more well-known Mesoamerican writing systems like Maya hieroglyphics or Aztec pictograms, the Zapotec script is less deciphered and understood. Nevertheless, it represents an essential part of the Zapotec civilization's intellectual and cultural heritage, offering tantalizing glimpses into their history, language, and worldview.

The Zapotec script is believed to have been in use as early as the Zapotec civilization's classical period, which dates back to around 500 BCE to 750 CE. However, it was most prevalent during the Late Classic period, from approximately 750 CE to 1000 CE. This period saw the proliferation of inscriptions, primarily on stelae, altars, and other stone monuments in Zapotec ceremonial centers, notably the city of Monte Albán.

One of the defining characteristics of the Zapotec script is its use of glyphs or symbols to represent words or syllables. These glyphs can vary in complexity, from simple symbols to more intricate combinations. Researchers have identified over 160 unique Zapotec glyphs, each with its own potential meaning or phonetic value.

One of the challenges in deciphering the Zapotec script lies in its complexity and the limited number of surviving texts. Unlike the Maya script, which has a considerable corpus of inscriptions and codices, Zapotec texts are relatively rare. As a result, scholars have faced difficulties in piecing together a comprehensive understanding of the script.

One of the key breakthroughs in deciphering the Zapotec script came with the discovery of the "Tomb 7" inscriptions at Monte Albán in the 1930s. These inscriptions, found within the tomb, contained a series of glyphs that provided a crucial starting point for decipherment efforts. They included dates and names, allowing scholars to begin to crack the code of the script.

It's important to note that the Zapotec script exhibits a degree of variability across different Zapotec communities and time periods. This suggests that there may have been regional variations or adaptations of the script to suit specific dialects or linguistic nuances.

The function of the Zapotec script is believed to have been multifaceted. It likely served as a means of recording historical events, such as the reigns of rulers, the construction of buildings, and the occurrence of important ceremonies. These inscriptions also provided a way to record calendrical and astronomical information, aligning with the Zapotec's keen interest in celestial events.

One of the most significant challenges in deciphering the Zapotec script has been the lack of a full bilingual text, which would provide a Rosetta Stone-like key to unlocking the script's meaning. Without a direct translation or comparative text in a known language, researchers have had to rely on context, the presence of known symbols, and educated guesswork to interpret the inscriptions.

The Zapotec script's enigmatic nature has led to various hypotheses regarding its structure and function. Some researchers believe that it was a logosyllabic script, combining logograms (symbols representing whole words) and syllabic elements. Others posit that it may have been a primarily syllabic script, where each glyph represented a syllable in the Zapotec language.

The Zapotec script's legacy can be seen in modern-day Zapotec communities, where it continues to be a source of cultural pride and scholarly exploration. While the script's full decipherment remains a work in progress, efforts to understand its intricacies have shed light on Zapotec history and culture.

In summary, the Zapotec script is a complex and fascinating aspect of Zapotec civilization, reflecting their intellectual achievements and cultural identity. Despite the challenges in deciphering it fully, ongoing research and interdisciplinary collaboration offer hope for a deeper understanding of this script and its contributions to our knowledge of Mesoamerican history. The Zapotec script remains a testament to the enduring legacy of indigenous cultures and their rich heritage.

The decipherment of Zapotec hieroglyphs has been a complex and ongoing process, driven by the desire to unlock the mysteries of the Zapotec script and gain insights into the history, language, and culture of the Zapotec civilization. While significant progress has been made, deciphering Zapotec hieroglyphs remains a challenging endeavor due to the limited number of surviving texts and the absence of a full bilingual inscription for direct comparison. Nevertheless, dedicated scholars and researchers have made significant strides in deciphering this enigmatic writing system.

The Rosetta Stone of Zapotec Decipherment: A crucial development in the decipherment of Zapotec hieroglyphs came with the discovery of the "Tomb 7" inscriptions at Monte Albán in the 1930s. These inscriptions provided a key starting point for researchers, as they contained elements that could be compared to known symbols and dates. The inscriptions included names, dates, and other contextual information, offering vital clues for decipherment.

Context and Syllabic Patterns: Scholars analyzing Zapotec hieroglyphs have observed patterns in the way glyphs are used within texts. These patterns suggest that the script is syllabic in nature, with each glyph representing a syllable in the Zapotec language. This discovery has allowed researchers to make progress in assigning phonetic values to certain glyphs.

By comparing the patterns of symbols in various inscriptions and contexts, researchers have been able to identify recurring elements that likely represent common syllables or words. This comparative approach, combined with the analysis of the context in which hieroglyphs appear, has been instrumental in decipherment efforts.

Epigraphic Dictionaries and Resources: To aid in the decipherment of Zapotec hieroglyphs, epigraphic dictionaries and resources have been developed. These resources compile known hieroglyphs, their proposed meanings, and their phonetic values based on current research and analysis. Epigraphic dictionaries serve as valuable references for researchers and provide a foundation for further decipherment work.

Regional Variations and Dialects: It's important to acknowledge that Zapotec hieroglyphs may exhibit regional variations or adaptations to suit specific dialects or linguistic nuances. This variability has added complexity to decipherment efforts, as researchers must account for potential regional differences in the script.

Ongoing Research and Collaboration: Deciphering Zapotec hieroglyphs remains an ongoing and collaborative effort among scholars, linguists, archaeologists, and epigraphers. Interdisciplinary approaches, including the combination of linguistic analysis, archaeological context, and comparative studies, have been crucial in advancing our understanding of the script.

The Role of Comparative Texts: One of the challenges in deciphering Zapotec hieroglyphs is the absence of a direct bilingual text that would provide a clear translation key. Researchers have often turned to comparative studies with related Mesoamerican scripts, such as the Mixtec or Maya hieroglyphs, to identify potential similarities and shared symbols. These comparative studies have offered valuable insights into Zapotec script structure and function.

Cultural and Historical Insights: While decipherment efforts have focused on the linguistic aspects of Zapotec hieroglyphs, the script also provides cultural and historical insights. Hieroglyphic inscriptions often record significant events, such as the reigns of rulers, important ceremonies, and celestial observations. These inscriptions offer a window into the Zapotec civilization's worldview, beliefs, and achievements.

In summary, deciphering Zapotec hieroglyphs is an ongoing journey marked by significant progress and ongoing challenges. The script's complexity, regional variations, and the absence of a full bilingual text continue to pose hurdles for researchers. However, the dedication of scholars and the collaborative nature of decipherment efforts offer hope for further insights into the

Zapotec script, shedding light on this remarkable civilization and its contributions to Mesoamerican history and culture. The ongoing work to decipher Zapotec hieroglyphs stands as a testament to the enduring curiosity and determination of those seeking to unlock the secrets of the past.

The role of writing in Zapotec society was a multifaceted and significant aspect of their civilization, offering a means of preserving and transmitting knowledge, recording historical events, and expressing cultural and religious beliefs. While the Zapotec writing system, known as Zapotec hieroglyphs, is less well-understood compared to some other Mesoamerican scripts like Maya or Aztec, it played a crucial role in shaping Zapotec culture and society.

Preservation of Knowledge and History: Writing in Zapotec society served as a vital tool for preserving knowledge and documenting the history of the civilization. Through inscriptions on stelae, altars, and other monumental structures, the Zapotecs recorded important events, such as the reigns of rulers, significant ceremonies, and the construction of buildings. These inscriptions acted as historical records, allowing future generations to learn about their ancestors and the achievements of their society.

The writing system also played a role in preserving the Zapotec language itself. It allowed for the documentation of linguistic elements, phonetics, and grammatical structures, contributing to the preservation of the Zapotec language across generations.

Religious and Ritual Significance: Writing was closely tied to religious and ritual practices in Zapotec society. Many inscriptions featured references to religious deities, celestial events, and the spiritual significance of certain locations. These inscriptions were often found on altars and temple facades, highlighting the connection between writing and religious beliefs.

In some cases, Zapotec hieroglyphs were used to record calendrical information related to religious ceremonies and celestial observations. The accurate tracking of celestial events was essential for determining the timing of religious rituals, agricultural activities, and other aspects of Zapotec life.

Cultural Expression and Identity: Writing also played a role in expressing Zapotec cultural identity. Inscriptions often contained symbols and motifs that were specific to Zapotec culture, including depictions of Zapotec rulers, gods, and mythological beings. These symbols served to reinforce cultural identity and convey a sense of pride in Zapotec heritage.

Zapotec hieroglyphs were not limited to monumental inscriptions; they were also used in the creation of ceramic vessels, textiles, and other artifacts. These artistic expressions showcased the integration of writing with other forms of art and craft, reflecting the Zapotec's appreciation for aesthetics and symbolism.

Interactions with Other Mesoamerican Cultures: The Zapotec civilization had interactions with neighboring Mesoamerican cultures, such as the Mixtecs and the Maya. These interactions influenced the development and adaptation of the Zapotec writing system. Scholars have noted similarities and shared symbols between Zapotec hieroglyphs and those of other Mesoamerican cultures, suggesting cultural exchanges and the transmission of knowledge.

These interactions highlight the interconnectedness of Mesoamerican civilizations and the role of writing as a medium for communication and cultural exchange.

Challenges in Decipherment and Understanding: Deciphering Zapotec hieroglyphs has been a challenging and ongoing process. Unlike some Mesoamerican scripts with a substantial corpus of texts and codices, Zapotec hieroglyphs are relatively rare. The absence of a full bilingual text, similar to the Maya Rosetta Stone, has made decipherment efforts more complex.

Researchers have relied on context, comparative studies with related scripts, and the identification of recurring symbols and patterns to decipher Zapotec hieroglyphs. Despite progress, there is still much work to be done to fully understand the script's intricacies and nuances.

Legacy and Continuation: The legacy of Zapotec writing continues to be celebrated and explored in modern-day Zapotec communities. Efforts to preserve and revitalize the Zapotec language and script are ongoing, reflecting the importance of cultural heritage and identity.

Zapotec hieroglyphs serve as a reminder of the rich history and achievements of the Zapotec civilization. As scholars continue to decipher and interpret these inscriptions, new insights into Zapotec culture, history, and worldview emerge, contributing to a deeper understanding of this remarkable Mesoamerican civilization.

In summary, writing played a vital and multifaceted role in Zapotec society, encompassing historical preservation, religious expression, cultural identity, and interactions with neighboring cultures. Despite the challenges of decipherment, Zapotec hieroglyphs remain a testament to the intellectual and artistic achievements of the Zapotec civilization, offering a window into their rich and complex history.

Chapter 5: Society and Rituals: Life in Ancient Oaxaca (600 CE - 800 CE)

The social structure of the Zapotec civilization was organized and hierarchical, reflecting the complex society that thrived in the region of Oaxaca, Mexico. The Zapotecs, like many ancient Mesoamerican cultures, had a well-defined social hierarchy that influenced various aspects of their lives, including politics, religion, and daily activities.

Rulers and Elite Class: At the top of Zapotec society were the rulers and the elite class. The rulers, often referred to as kings or lords, held significant political and religious power. They were responsible for governing the Zapotec city-states, overseeing religious ceremonies, and maintaining social order. The elite class, which included nobles, high-ranking priests, and military leaders, enjoyed privileges such as land ownership and access to valuable resources.

The rulers and elites often resided in palatial structures within the city centers, emphasizing their elevated status within Zapotec society. Their authority was bolstered by religious roles, as they were often seen as intermediaries between the gods and the people.

Priests and Religious Specialists: Religion played a central role in Zapotec society, and priests held considerable influence. Religious specialists were responsible for conducting rituals, overseeing temple activities, and interpreting celestial events. They played a pivotal role in maintaining the spiritual well-being of the community and ensuring favorable outcomes for agricultural endeavors.

The religious calendar and celestial observations were essential components of Zapotec religious practices, and priests were experts in these areas. Their knowledge allowed them to determine auspicious times for planting and harvesting crops, as well as for conducting religious ceremonies.

Commoners and Artisans: Below the elite and priestly classes were the commoners and artisans. Commoners made up the majority of the population and were engaged in various occupations, including farming, craft production, and trade. They were responsible for providing food, goods, and services to support both the ruling class and the broader community.

Artisans played a crucial role in Zapotec society, producing a wide range of items, including pottery, textiles, jewelry, and sculptures. Their craftsmanship contributed to the cultural and artistic richness of Zapotec civilization. Artisans often organized themselves into specialized craft guilds, passing down their skills and knowledge through generations.

Slavery and Captives: Slavery was present in Zapotec society, as in many other ancient cultures. Slaves were typically individuals captured in warfare or obtained through other means. They performed labor-intensive tasks such as agriculture, construction, and domestic work. Slavery was a significant source of labor for the ruling elite and contributed to the economic and agricultural productivity of the Zapotec city-states.

Social Mobility: While Zapotec society had a hierarchical structure, there was some degree of social mobility. Exceptional individuals could rise in status through achievements in warfare, religious service, or craftsmanship. Marriages between individuals of different social strata also occurred, potentially allowing for the exchange of resources and the advancement of social standing.

Community Organization: Zapotec society was organized into city-states, each with its ruler and elite class. These city-states often engaged in complex alliances, conflicts, and trade networks with neighboring communities, such as the Mixtecs and the Maya. The city-states served as centers of political, economic, and religious activity, and their leaders played pivotal roles in regional affairs.

Legacy: The social structure of the Zapotec civilization left a lasting legacy that can still be observed in the modern-day communities of Oaxaca, Mexico. The cultural richness and historical significance of the Zapotecs continue to be celebrated, and efforts are made to preserve their heritage and traditions.

In summary, the social structure of the Zapotec civilization was characterized by a hierarchical organization, with rulers and elites at the top, followed by priests, commoners, and slaves. Religion played a central role in Zapotec society, and artisans contributed to its cultural and artistic vibrancy. While the social structure had elements of rigidity, there were opportunities for social mobility, and the legacy of the Zapotec civilization endures as a testament to their achievements in ancient Mesoamerica.

Religious practices and beliefs were central to the Zapotec civilization, shaping their worldview, societal organization, and cultural expressions. The Zapotecs held a complex and multifaceted belief system that revolved around the veneration of deities, celestial observations, and rituals conducted by priests. These religious practices played a vital role in maintaining the spiritual well-being of the community and were deeply interwoven with daily life.

Polytheism and Deities: The Zapotec religion was polytheistic, meaning they worshipped a pantheon of deities. These gods and goddesses represented various aspects of life, nature, and the cosmos. Some of the prominent deities in Zapotec religion included Cocijo, the rain god; Pitao Cozobi, the maize god; and Xipe Totec, the god of agriculture and fertility.

Each deity had specific roles and attributes, and their worship was essential for ensuring favorable conditions for agriculture, rain, and protection from natural and supernatural forces. The Zapotecs believed that the gods played a direct role in the well-being and prosperity of their society.

Celestial Observations and Calendars: Zapotec religious practices were closely tied to celestial observations and the tracking of celestial events. The Zapotecs had a complex calendrical system that included both solar and lunar calendars. These calendars guided religious ceremonies, agricultural activities, and other important events.

Priests were responsible for interpreting celestial phenomena, such as eclipses and solstices, to determine auspicious times for rituals and agricultural activities. The accurate tracking of celestial events was seen as a way to maintain harmony with the natural world and the gods.

Rituals and Ceremonies: Rituals and ceremonies were fundamental to Zapotec religious life. These ceremonies encompassed a wide range of activities, including offerings, feasts, dances, and processions. Ceremonial centers and temples were constructed for these rituals, and priests played a central role in their execution.

Some of the key ceremonies in Zapotec religion included those dedicated to agricultural deities to ensure successful harvests, as well as ceremonies related to the changing of seasons and celestial events. The timing and execution of these rituals were meticulously planned to align with the religious calendar.

Ancestor Veneration: Ancestor veneration was another important aspect of Zapotec religious beliefs. The Zapotecs believed in the continuity of life beyond death and maintained a connection with their ancestors. Ancestral spirits were honored through offerings and rituals, and they were believed to provide guidance and protection to the living.

Ancestral imagery was often incorporated into religious art and sculpture, further emphasizing the importance of this belief in Zapotec culture.

Shamans and Divination: In addition to priests, shamans and diviners played a role in Zapotec religious practices. Shamans were believed to have the ability to communicate with the spirit world and provide insights into various aspects of life, including healing, divination, and prophecy. Divination practices, such as reading omens from natural phenomena, were used to make important decisions and foresee future events.

Interaction with Other Mesoamerican Cultures: The Zapotecs had interactions with neighboring Mesoamerican cultures, such as the Mixtecs and the Maya. These interactions influenced their religious practices and iconography, resulting in shared symbols and beliefs. Cultural exchanges enriched the religious tapestry of the Zapotec civilization.

Legacy and Continuation: While the Zapotec civilization declined, elements of their religious practices and beliefs continue to be observed in modern Zapotec communities. Efforts are made to preserve and revitalize Zapotec spirituality and traditions, emphasizing the enduring cultural significance of their religious heritage.

In summary, religious practices and beliefs were integral to the Zapotec civilization, encompassing polytheism, celestial observations, rituals, ancestor veneration, and the guidance of priests and shamans. Zapotec religion played a central role in their societal organization and cultural expressions, leaving a lasting legacy that continues to be celebrated and honored in modern times.

Daily life in Zapotec society was characterized by a complex and organized way of living that revolved around agriculture, social hierarchy, religious practices, and community engagement. The Zapotecs, residing in the region of Oaxaca, Mexico, created a thriving civilization with well-defined roles and activities for its members.

Agriculture as the Backbone: Agriculture played a pivotal role in Zapotec daily life. The fertile valleys of Oaxaca allowed for the cultivation of maize (corn), beans, squash, and various other crops. Maize, in particular, held immense importance and was considered a staple food. The agricultural calendar was closely tied to celestial observations, and priests provided guidance on when to plant and harvest crops.

Social Hierarchy and Roles: Zapotec society had a hierarchical structure, with rulers and elites at the top, followed by priests, commoners, and slaves. Social roles were well-defined, and individuals were expected to fulfill their obligations based on their status.

Rulers and elites were responsible for governing the city-states, overseeing religious ceremonies, and managing resources. Priests played a crucial role in conducting rituals, interpreting celestial events, and maintaining the spiritual well-being of the community. Commoners engaged in various occupations, including farming, craft production, and trade, to provide for their families and contribute to the community's welfare.

Slavery was present in Zapotec society, with enslaved individuals performing labor-intensive tasks such as agriculture and construction.

Family Life and Household Activities: Family life was central to Zapotec society, and households were typically extended, with multiple generations living together. The family unit served as the primary social and economic unit.

Daily activities in Zapotec households included cooking, cleaning, and childcare. Meals were prepared using maize and other locally grown ingredients, with cooking methods such as grinding maize to make tortillas, stews, and tamales. Zapotec cuisine incorporated a variety of flavors, including chili peppers, chocolate, and various spices.

Textiles also played a significant role in Zapotec daily life. Women were skilled weavers and created intricate textiles using traditional techniques, producing garments, blankets, and other items.

Craftsmanship and Artistry: Craftsmanship and artistic expression were integral to Zapotec daily life. Artisans produced a wide range of items, including pottery, textiles, jewelry, and sculptures. These artistic creations were both functional and aesthetically pleasing, reflecting the Zapotec's appreciation for aesthetics and symbolism.

Craftsmen organized themselves into specialized craft guilds, passing down their skills and knowledge through generations. This system contributed to the high quality and diversity of Zapotec artistry.

Religious Rituals and Ceremonies: Religious practices were woven into the fabric of daily life. Zapotec religious rituals and ceremonies occurred regularly, with priests conducting ceremonies, offerings, and processions. The religious calendar guided the timing of these events, which were closely tied to celestial observations and agricultural cycles.

These rituals were conducted in ceremonial centers and temples, which were central to Zapotec city-states. Religious activities were not limited to priests; community participation was encouraged, reinforcing the sense of shared spiritual responsibility.

Community Engagement and Governance: Zapotec communities were organized into city-states, each with its ruler and elite class. These city-states served as centers of political, economic, and religious activity. Community engagement was essential, as individuals were expected to contribute to the welfare of their city-state.

Governance was in the hands of rulers and elites who managed city affairs, made decisions about resource allocation, and maintained social order. The community's well-being depended on effective governance and cooperation among its members.

Trade and Exchange: Trade networks were another vital aspect of Zapotec daily life. The Zapotecs engaged in trade with neighboring Mesoamerican cultures, such as the Mixtecs and the Maya. Trade routes facilitated the exchange of goods, including agricultural products, craft items, and exotic goods like precious stones and feathers.

Trade not only served as an economic activity but also fostered cultural exchanges and interactions with neighboring societies.

Legacy and Continuation: The legacy of Zapotec daily life and culture continues to be celebrated in modern Zapotec communities. Traditional practices, including agriculture, craftsmanship, and religious ceremonies, are preserved and passed down through generations. Efforts are made to honor the cultural heritage of the Zapotecs and maintain the connection to their rich history.

In summary, daily life in Zapotec society was characterized by a strong emphasis on agriculture, a well-defined social hierarchy, family-centered households, craftsmanship, religious practices, community engagement, and trade networks. These elements collectively contributed to the vibrancy and resilience of the Zapotec civilization, leaving a lasting legacy that continues to be cherished in contemporary times.

Chapter 6: Trade Routes and Zapotec Influence (700 CE - 800 CE)

Zapotec trade networks were an essential aspect of their civilization, facilitating the exchange of goods, ideas, and culture with neighboring Mesoamerican societies. The Zapotecs, who inhabited the Oaxaca region in what is now modern-day Mexico, engaged in extensive trade networks that played a crucial role in their economic prosperity and cultural development.

Geographic Location and Trade Routes: The Zapotecs' geographic location in the Oaxaca Valley was strategically positioned to connect various regions of Mesoamerica. The Oaxaca Valley's fertile land allowed for the cultivation of maize, beans, squash, and other crops, making it an agricultural hub. This abundance of resources attracted traders from both nearby and distant regions.

Trade routes radiated from the Oaxaca Valley in multiple directions, connecting the Zapotecs to neighboring cultures. These routes extended to regions such as the Gulf Coast, the Pacific Coast, the Central Highlands, and even as far south as Central America. The Zapotecs became intermediaries, facilitating trade between different Mesoamerican groups.

Trade Goods and Commodities: The Zapotecs traded a wide range of goods and commodities. Agricultural products, such as maize, beans, and cacao (chocolate), were among the primary items exchanged. These staples were essential for sustenance and served as valuable trade commodities.

Craftsmanship was another cornerstone of Zapotec trade. Artisans in Zapotec society produced intricate textiles, pottery, jewelry, and sculptures. These artisanal goods were highly sought after and contributed to the cultural richness of Zapotec civilization.

Precious stones, feathers, and exotic items like jaguar pelts were also traded, reflecting the diversity of resources available in the Oaxaca Valley and surrounding regions. These luxury items played a significant role in both trade and cultural exchanges.

Cultural Exchanges and Influences: Zapotec trade networks facilitated cultural exchanges and influences between the

Zapotecs and their trading partners. The interactions with neighboring Mesoamerican societies, such as the Mixtecs and the Maya, resulted in the sharing of ideas, artistry, and even religious beliefs.

Iconography and artistic styles were often influenced by these exchanges. Symbols and motifs from different cultures found their way into Zapotec art and pottery, creating a unique blend of artistic expression. Religious practices and rituals also bore the imprint of cultural interactions.

Trade Centers and Marketplaces: Trade centers and marketplaces were integral to Zapotec trade networks. These were bustling hubs where merchants and traders from various regions converged to exchange goods. One of the most well-known trade centers in the Oaxaca Valley was Monte Albán, the Zapotec capital. Monte Albán had a central role in the region's trade networks, serving as a vital trading and economic hub.

Marketplaces were vibrant spaces where not only goods but also ideas and news were exchanged. The lively atmosphere of these marketplaces contributed to the sense of community and connectedness among the Zapotecs and their trading partners.

Economic Significance: Zapotec trade networks had significant economic implications for their society. Trade brought in valuable resources, such as exotic materials, that were used for craftsmanship and artistic expression. It also provided access to goods that were not locally available, enriching the quality of life for Zapotec individuals.

Additionally, trade networks fostered economic interdependence among Mesoamerican societies. The exchange of goods created economic ties that promoted stability and cooperation in the region. Trade was not solely about economic gain; it was a means of forging relationships and alliances.

Continuation and Legacy: The legacy of Zapotec trade networks is still evident in modern-day Oaxaca. The region continues to be known for its vibrant markets, where traditional goods, crafts, and culinary delights are traded and enjoyed. Zapotec communities take pride in their heritage, preserving the cultural richness and economic significance of their ancestors' trade networks.

In summary, Zapotec trade networks were instrumental in shaping the economic, cultural, and social dynamics of the Zapotec civilization. These networks connected the Oaxaca Valley to various regions of Mesoamerica, facilitating the exchange of goods and ideas. The legacy of Zapotec trade continues to thrive in contemporary Oaxaca, embodying the enduring cultural significance of these ancient trade connections.

Cultural exchange beyond Oaxaca was a dynamic and transformative process that enriched the Zapotec civilization by connecting them with neighboring Mesoamerican cultures. The exchange of ideas, artistry, and traditions contributed to the cultural diversity and complexity of the Zapotec society, leaving a lasting impact on their civilization.

Neighboring Mesoamerican Cultures: The Zapotecs inhabited the Oaxaca region, which positioned them as intermediaries between various neighboring Mesoamerican cultures. These neighboring cultures included the Mixtecs, the Maya, the Teotihuacan civilization, and others. Each of these cultures had its unique customs, languages, and artistic expressions.

Artistic Influences: Cultural exchange led to the blending of artistic styles and influences. The Zapotecs, like other Mesoamerican societies, created intricate artwork, including pottery, textiles, and sculptures. Through interactions with neighboring cultures, the Zapotecs incorporated new artistic motifs, symbols, and techniques into their own creations.

For example, Zapotec pottery might feature Maya-inspired glyphs, or Mixtec-influenced patterns could be woven into Zapotec textiles. This artistic fusion resulted in a unique and diverse artistic heritage within the Zapotec civilization.

Religious and Spiritual Connections: Religion played a pivotal role in Mesoamerican societies, and cultural exchange often had a profound impact on religious beliefs and practices. The Zapotecs, while maintaining their own religious traditions, were exposed to the deities, rituals, and cosmologies of neighboring cultures.

This exchange sometimes led to the assimilation of certain beliefs or the syncretism of religious practices. It wasn't uncommon for

Zapotec deities to be depicted in a style influenced by Maya or Mixtec iconography, reflecting the interconnectedness of Mesoamerican spirituality.

Language and Communication: Language was a significant aspect of cultural exchange. The Zapotec language had its own distinct linguistic characteristics, but interactions with neighboring cultures resulted in the borrowing of words and phrases. Communication became more fluid, enabling people from different linguistic backgrounds to engage with one another.

Trade and Economic Cooperation: Cultural exchange went hand in hand with trade and economic cooperation. The exchange of goods and resources facilitated the movement of people, ideas, and traditions. Valuable items like precious stones, metals, and textiles traversed trade routes, forging economic ties between different Mesoamerican regions.

Shared Practices and Rituals: Cultural exchange led to the sharing of practices and rituals. Certain ceremonies and traditions became common across different cultures. For example, the ballgame, a ritualistic sport with religious significance, was played in various Mesoamerican societies, including the Zapotecs. The rules and symbolism of the game might vary from one culture to another, but the shared practice itself was a unifying element.

Diversity and Complexity: The cultural exchange beyond Oaxaca contributed to the diversity and complexity of the Zapotec civilization. It enriched their worldview, broadened their artistic repertoire, and deepened their understanding of the interconnectedness of Mesoamerican societies.

This diversity was not just a matter of adopting external elements but also of adapting and reinterpreting them within the Zapotec context. It showcased the ability of the Zapotecs to engage with and embrace the richness of their Mesoamerican neighbors while maintaining their cultural identity.

Legacy of Cultural Exchange: The legacy of cultural exchange beyond Oaxaca continues to be celebrated in modern Zapotec communities. It reminds contemporary generations of the enduring connections between Mesoamerican cultures and the importance of preserving and honoring their diverse heritage.

In summary, cultural exchange beyond Oaxaca was a dynamic and transformative process that enriched the Zapotec civilization by connecting them with neighboring Mesoamerican cultures. It fostered artistic innovation, spiritual connections, linguistic influences, and economic cooperation, contributing to the cultural diversity and complexity of the Zapotec society. This legacy of exchange continues to be a source of cultural pride and celebration in modern Zapotec communities.

The legacy of the Zapotec civilization extended beyond the borders of Oaxaca, influencing nearby regions and leaving a profound mark on the cultural, artistic, and architectural landscapes of Mesoamerica. This enduring legacy is a testament to the Zapotecs' rich history and their significant contributions to the broader Mesoamerican world.

Artistic and Architectural Influence: One of the most striking aspects of the Zapotec legacy is their influence on the artistic and architectural traditions of neighboring regions. The iconic Zapotec architectural style, characterized by intricate stone carvings and elaborate buildings, served as an inspiration for other Mesoamerican cultures.

The Mixtecs, who occupied the region of modern-day Oaxaca alongside the Zapotecs, were particularly influenced by Zapotec artistry. Mixtec codices and manuscripts, known for their detailed pictorial representations, were influenced by Zapotec iconography and artistic techniques. This fusion of artistic styles created a unique and vibrant artistic tradition that continues to be celebrated in the Mixtec region.

Architectural Marvels: Zapotec architectural innovations also left a lasting legacy in nearby regions. The grand city of Monte Albán, the Zapotec capital, featured impressive structures, plazas, and pyramids. These architectural marvels set a precedent for the construction of ceremonial centers and urban planning in Mesoamerica.

The architectural influence of Monte Albán extended to other city-states and cultures. The layout of plazas, the use of pyramids as religious and administrative centers, and the integration of celestial alignments into architectural design were elements that neighboring cultures adopted and adapted to their own cities.

Cultural Syncretism: The Zapotecs' interactions with neighboring cultures led to cultural syncretism, a blending of beliefs and practices. Religious and spiritual traditions were among the most affected by this syncretism. While the Zapotecs had their own pantheon of deities and rituals, they also incorporated elements from other Mesoamerican cultures.

The fusion of religious beliefs and practices resulted in a rich tapestry of spirituality. Deities and rituals from different cultures coexisted, and individuals often engaged in syncretic ceremonies that honored both traditional Zapotec beliefs and those of neighboring cultures.

Artistic Traditions and Craftsmanship: Zapotec craftsmanship and artistic traditions had a profound influence on the nearby regions. The production of intricate textiles, pottery, jewelry, and sculptures was a hallmark of Zapotec culture. The Mixtecs, in particular, embraced and integrated these artistic traditions into their own craftsmanship.

Mixtec artisans, like their Zapotec counterparts, produced finely detailed jewelry and intricate codices. The use of precious metals, gemstones, and intricate filigree work in Mixtec jewelry was a testament to the legacy of artistic excellence inherited from the Zapotecs.

Language and Communication: Linguistic exchange was another facet of the Zapotec legacy. The Zapotec language, like other Mesoamerican languages, influenced neighboring languages through shared vocabulary and linguistic interactions. This linguistic exchange fostered communication and cultural connections among diverse Mesoamerican communities.

Cultural Celebrations and Festivals: The legacy of the Zapotecs is celebrated in various cultural festivals and traditions in nearby regions. These celebrations often incorporate elements of Zapotec culture, including traditional dances, music, and cuisine. Festivals provide an opportunity for communities to pay homage to the enduring influence of the Zapotecs and their contributions to Mesoamerican culture.

Continuity and Preservation: Modern Zapotec communities in Oaxaca continue to preserve and honor their cultural heritage, passing down traditions and knowledge to future generations. Efforts to revitalize the Zapotec language, maintain artistic craftsmanship, and uphold religious practices ensure the continuity of the Zapotec legacy.

Additionally, archaeological excavations and research in the Oaxaca region have shed light on the Zapotec civilization's history and contributions, further enhancing our understanding of their legacy in nearby regions.

An Enduring Legacy: The Zapotec legacy in nearby regions is a testament to the resilience and creativity of this ancient civilization. Their influence on art, architecture, spirituality, and culture continues to resonate across Mesoamerica, reminding us of the interconnectedness of Mesoamerican societies and the enduring impact of the Zapotecs. In summary, the Zapotec legacy in nearby regions is a multifaceted testament to their contributions to Mesoamerican culture. From art and architecture to spirituality and language, the Zapotecs left an indelible mark on neighboring cultures, enriching the cultural tapestry of Mesoamerica and ensuring the enduring legacy of their civilization.

Chapter 7: The Legacy of Zapotec Civilization (800 CE and Beyond)

The enduring influences of the Zapotec civilization continue to shape the cultural, artistic, and social landscapes of Oaxaca and neighboring regions in Mesoamerica. The legacy of this ancient civilization, which thrived in the Oaxaca Valley for centuries, is a testament to the enduring power of their traditions, innovations, and cultural heritage.

Cultural Resilience: One of the most remarkable aspects of Zapotec influences is the cultural resilience of modern-day Zapotec communities. Despite centuries of societal changes, conquests, and external pressures, the Zapotec culture has persisted and thrived. The preservation of their language, traditions, and customs is a testament to the deep-rooted connection to their ancestors and the resilience of their cultural identity.

Zapotec communities continue to celebrate traditional festivals, such as the Guelaguetza, which showcase their rich heritage through dance, music, and artisanal craftsmanship. These celebrations are not only a source of pride but also a way of passing down their cultural legacy to younger generations.

Language and Identity: The Zapotec language, which belongs to the Oto-Manguean language family, remains a vital part of Zapotec identity. While Spanish is widely spoken in the region, efforts to preserve and revitalize the Zapotec language have gained momentum in recent years. Bilingual education programs, language immersion initiatives, and the creation of written materials in Zapotec contribute to the preservation of this linguistic heritage.

Language plays a central role in Zapotec identity, connecting individuals to their cultural roots and facilitating intergenerational communication. It serves as a vehicle for the transmission of oral traditions, folklore, and historical narratives.

Artistic Traditions and Craftsmanship: The artistic traditions of the Zapotec civilization continue to flourish in contemporary

Oaxaca. Zapotec artisans create intricate textiles, pottery, woodwork, and jewelry that reflect the deep-rooted artistic heritage of their ancestors. The use of traditional techniques and designs is a testament to the enduring influence of Zapotec craftsmanship.

Zapotec weavers, known for their skill in creating intricate and vibrant textiles, produce garments and fabrics that are not only functional but also works of art. These textiles often feature intricate patterns and motifs inspired by nature, mythology, and ancestral knowledge.

Architectural and Urban Legacy: The architectural and urban planning innovations of the Zapotecs left a lasting imprint on the physical landscape of Oaxaca. Monte Albán, the Zapotec capital, serves as a tangible reminder of their architectural prowess. The layout of the city, with its pyramidal structures, plazas, and ceremonial centers, continues to inspire urban planning and design in contemporary Oaxacan cities.

The use of celestial alignments in Zapotec architecture, such as the orientation of buildings to astronomical events, has also influenced modern-day architectural practices. The significance of celestial observations in Zapotec culture has left an enduring mark on the region's architectural heritage.

Religious Syncretism: The Zapotec spiritual and religious traditions, which integrated elements from neighboring cultures, continue to shape contemporary belief systems. While many Zapotecs practice a syncretic form of Catholicism that incorporates indigenous elements, there are also communities that maintain traditional Zapotec religious practices.

Ceremonies and rituals, often linked to agricultural cycles and celestial events, remain central to Zapotec spirituality. These practices provide a sense of continuity with their ancestral heritage and a connection to the natural world.

Social Cohesion: The enduring Zapotec influences extend to the social fabric of contemporary communities. Social cohesion, community bonds, and a strong sense of collective identity are hallmarks of Zapotec society. These values are evident in communal work projects, mutual support networks, and community decision-making processes.

The Guelaguetza, a Zapotec term that translates to "reciprocal exchange of gifts and services," encapsulates the spirit of community and mutual aid. It involves sharing resources, labor, and support among community members, reinforcing social ties and solidarity.

Cultural Tourism and Revitalization: The enduring Zapotec influences have also contributed to the cultural tourism industry in Oaxaca. Visitors from around the world are drawn to the region to experience the vibrant traditions, artistry, and historical sites associated with the Zapotecs. This tourism not only generates economic opportunities but also promotes the preservation and revitalization of cultural practices.

Cultural festivals, artisan markets, and heritage sites attract travelers interested in exploring the rich tapestry of Zapotec culture. These experiences offer a window into the enduring legacy of the Zapotecs and their contributions to Mesoamerican civilization.

Environmental Stewardship: The Zapotec civilization's deep connection to the natural world continues to influence contemporary attitudes toward environmental stewardship. Traditional knowledge of local ecosystems, agricultural practices, and sustainable resource management is passed down through generations. This ecological wisdom contributes to the preservation of the region's biodiversity and the sustainable use of natural resources.

Zapotec communities often implement conservation initiatives and reforestation projects to protect their ancestral lands and maintain ecological balance. These efforts align with the ancient Zapotec philosophy of living in harmony with nature.

In summary, the enduring Zapotec influences in Oaxaca and neighboring regions serve as a testament to the resilience of their culture, language, artistic traditions, and societal values. The Zapotec legacy not only enriches the lives of contemporary Zapotec communities but also offers a glimpse into the enduring contributions of an ancient civilization to the cultural tapestry of

Mesoamerica. It is a reminder that the echoes of the past continue to shape the present and inspire the future.

Archaeological discoveries and ongoing research in Mesoamerica have played a pivotal role in unraveling the mysteries of ancient civilizations, shedding light on their intricate societies, and expanding our understanding of their cultural and historical significance. The rich archaeological landscape of Mesoamerica has yielded a treasure trove of artifacts, structures, and insights that continue to captivate scholars and enthusiasts alike.

The Olmec Enigma Unearthed: Archaeological excavations in the tropical lowlands of what is now Mexico have unearthed some of the most iconic Olmec artifacts and monumental sculptures. The colossal stone heads of La Venta, which stand as enigmatic sentinels of the Olmec civilization, were discovered in the mid-20th century. These immense stone carvings, some weighing up to 24 tons, represent colossal human heads adorned with distinctive helmet-like headdresses.

The discovery of these colossal heads, along with other Olmec artifacts such as jade figurines and intricate pottery, has sparked intense fascination and debate among archaeologists and historians. These findings have prompted questions about the origins and significance of the Olmec civilization, often considered the "mother culture" of Mesoamerica.

The Maya: Unveiling Their Secrets: Maya archaeology has revealed a complex and sophisticated civilization that thrived for centuries in the Yucatan Peninsula, Guatemala, Belize, and parts of Honduras and El Salvador. Research efforts have uncovered extensive city-states, monumental pyramids, temples, and intricate hieroglyphic writing systems.

One of the most notable discoveries in Maya archaeology is the decipherment of the Maya script, which has provided invaluable insights into their history, mythology, and political systems. Hieroglyphic inscriptions on stelae, monuments, and codices have unveiled the stories of Maya rulers, religious ceremonies, and astronomical knowledge.

Teotihuacan: City of the Gods Revealed: The ancient city of Teotihuacan, located in the Valley of Mexico, has been a focal point of archaeological research for decades. The monumental pyramids of the Sun and Moon, the sprawling layout of the city, and the exquisite murals found in residential complexes have all contributed to our understanding of this ancient metropolis.

Excavations at Teotihuacan have revealed the complexity of its society, its urban planning, and its religious and ritual practices. The murals, in particular, offer a glimpse into the artistic and cultural expressions of its inhabitants.

Zapotec Treasures in Monte Albán: The archaeological site of Monte Albán, once the capital of the Zapotec civilization in Oaxaca, has yielded a wealth of artifacts and insights into Zapotec culture. Excavations in this ancient city have unearthed intricate tombs, carved stone stelae, and a ballcourt that reflects the significance of ritualistic ball games in Mesoamerican societies.

The archaeological research at Monte Albán has revealed the social hierarchy, governance structures, and artistic achievements of the Zapotecs. It provides a window into their complex society and the enduring influence of their civilization on subsequent cultures in the region.

Toltec Legacy and Tula: The archaeological exploration of Tula, the capital of the Toltec civilization, has unveiled impressive architectural features such as the Pyramid of Quetzalcoatl and the Temple of the Warriors. These structures, adorned with intricate sculptures and carvings, reflect the Toltec's artistic prowess.

Research at Tula has also shed light on the Toltec military and political influence in Mesoamerica. The legend of Quetzalcoatl, the feathered serpent deity, is intertwined with the history of Tula and has captivated the imaginations of scholars and enthusiasts alike.

Aztec Civilization Rediscovered: The Aztec civilization, which rose to prominence in the 14th century and established the grand city of Tenochtitlan, has been a subject of extensive archaeological investigation. The Templo Mayor, the main temple of Tenochtitlan, was rediscovered in the heart of modern-day Mexico

City. Excavations at this site have revealed layers of construction and offerings that provide insights into Aztec religious practices.

The Aztecs' engineering feats, including the construction of chinampas (floating gardens) and intricate causeways, have been uncovered through archaeological research. The Codex Mendoza, a pictorial manuscript created in the early colonial period, offers a visual record of Aztec life and history.

Interdisciplinary Approaches: Modern archaeological research in Mesoamerica embraces interdisciplinary approaches that incorporate advanced technologies and scientific methods. Remote sensing technologies, such as LiDAR (Light Detection and Ranging), have allowed archaeologists to map vast landscapes and identify hidden archaeological features beneath dense vegetation. Radiocarbon dating, isotopic analysis, and DNA studies have provided precise dating and insights into the diets, migrations, and interactions of ancient Mesoamerican populations. These scientific advancements continue to refine our understanding of the chronology and dynamics of Mesoamerican civilizations.

Preservation and Ethical Considerations: The preservation of archaeological sites and artifacts is of paramount importance in Mesoamerica. Conservation efforts and collaboration with indigenous communities aim to protect cultural heritage while respecting the rights and beliefs of local populations. Ethical considerations in archaeological research involve engaging with descendant communities and acknowledging their perspectives and knowledge.

In summary, archaeological discoveries and ongoing research in Mesoamerica have illuminated the histories of diverse ancient civilizations, from the enigmatic Olmec culture to the majestic Maya city-states, the cosmopolitan Teotihuacan, the innovative Zapotecs, the influential Toltecs, and the mighty Aztecs. These excavations and investigations have not only deepened our understanding of Mesoamerican cultures but have also highlighted the importance of preserving and respecting the legacies of these ancient civilizations for future generations. Archaeology continues to be a dynamic and evolving field, promising new revelations and insights into the mysteries of Mesoamerica.

Modern-day Zapotec cultural heritage is a vibrant tapestry that weaves together the ancient traditions, language, arts, and customs of the Zapotec people, who have inhabited the Oaxaca region of Mexico for thousands of years. This rich cultural legacy, deeply rooted in the history of the Zapotec civilization, continues to thrive and evolve in contemporary Zapotec communities.

Language and Linguistic Revitalization: At the heart of Zapotec cultural heritage is the Zapotec language, a branch of the Oto-Manguean language family. Despite the challenges posed by globalization and the dominance of Spanish, Zapotec communities are actively engaged in linguistic revitalization efforts. Bilingual education programs, language immersion initiatives, and the creation of written materials in Zapotec are crucial for preserving and transmitting this indigenous language to younger generations. The Zapotec language serves as a vehicle for the transmission of oral traditions, folklore, and historical narratives, reinforcing cultural identity and connecting individuals to their ancestral heritage.

Ceremonies and Festivals: Traditional Zapotec ceremonies and festivals are vibrant expressions of cultural heritage. The Guelaguetza, a Zapotec term that translates to "reciprocal exchange of gifts and services," is one of the most celebrated events. It involves sharing resources, labor, and support among community members, reinforcing social ties and solidarity.

During the Guelaguetza, communities come together to showcase their traditional dances, music, and artisanal craftsmanship. These celebrations not only serve as a source of cultural pride but also provide a platform for preserving and sharing Zapotec heritage with a broader audience.

Artisanal Traditions: The artistic traditions of the Zapotec civilization are alive and well in contemporary Oaxaca. Zapotec artisans are known for their exquisite textiles, pottery, woodwork, and jewelry, which reflect the deep-rooted artistic heritage of their ancestors. These artisans employ traditional techniques and designs inspired by nature, mythology, and ancestral knowledge.

Zapotec weavers, in particular, are renowned for their skill in creating intricate and vibrant textiles. These textiles often feature complex patterns and motifs that tell stories, convey cultural symbols, and capture the essence of Zapotec identity.

Cultural Tourism and Economic Opportunities: Zapotec cultural heritage has also become a significant driver of cultural tourism in Oaxaca. Visitors from around the world are drawn to the region to experience the vibrant traditions, artistry, and historical sites associated with the Zapotecs. Cultural festivals, artisan markets, and heritage sites attract travelers interested in exploring the rich tapestry of Zapotec culture.

This influx of tourists generates economic opportunities for Zapotec communities, providing income for artisans, local businesses, and cultural initiatives. It also promotes the preservation and revitalization of cultural practices as they become integral to the region's tourism offerings.

Environmental Stewardship and Ethical Practices: The Zapotec cultural heritage emphasizes a profound connection to the natural world, and this ecological wisdom continues to shape contemporary attitudes toward environmental stewardship. Traditional knowledge of local ecosystems, agricultural practices, and sustainable resource management is passed down through generations.

Zapotec communities often implement conservation initiatives and reforestation projects to protect their ancestral lands and maintain ecological balance. These efforts align with the ancient Zapotec philosophy of living in harmony with nature, reflecting a holistic approach to cultural heritage that encompasses the environment.

Social Cohesion and Community Bonds: Another hallmark of Zapotec cultural heritage is the strong sense of social cohesion, community bonds, and a collective identity that persists in contemporary Zapotec society. These values are evident in communal work projects, mutual support networks, and community decision-making processes.

The Guelaguetza, which symbolizes reciprocity and mutual aid, serves as a reminder of the importance of community ties in Zapotec culture. It fosters solidarity and a sense of responsibility toward fellow community members.

Religious Syncretism and Spirituality: Zapotec spiritual and religious traditions, often syncretic in nature, continue to shape contemporary belief systems. While many Zapotecs practice a form of Catholicism that incorporates indigenous elements, there are also communities that maintain traditional Zapotec religious practices.

Ceremonies and rituals, often linked to agricultural cycles and celestial events, remain central to Zapotec spirituality. These practices provide a sense of continuity with their ancestral heritage and a connection to the natural world.

Social Change and Adaptation: Zapotec cultural heritage is not static; it evolves alongside changing social, economic, and political landscapes. Zapotec communities are adept at adapting their traditions and practices to meet contemporary challenges while preserving their core cultural values.

The interplay between tradition and adaptation is a testament to the resilience of Zapotec cultural heritage, allowing it to remain relevant in a rapidly changing world.

Cross-Cultural Exchange: Zapotec cultural heritage is not confined to the Oaxaca region alone. As Zapotec communities engage with the broader world, they contribute to cross-cultural exchange and enrich the global cultural mosaic. The artistry, craftsmanship, and cultural expressions of the Zapotecs find appreciation beyond their local communities.

International recognition of Zapotec heritage fosters pride and awareness of their culture, creating opportunities for collaboration and cultural dialogue on a global scale.

In summary, modern-day Zapotec cultural heritage is a living testament to the resilience, adaptability, and vibrancy of this ancient civilization. It thrives in contemporary Zapotec communities, encompassing language, ceremonies, artisanal traditions, and a profound connection to the natural world. Zapotec cultural heritage serves as a source of cultural pride, economic opportunity, and environmental stewardship, contributing to the region's rich cultural tapestry and fostering cross-cultural exchange with the wider world. It is a legacy that continues to evolve while remaining deeply rooted in the enduring traditions of the Zapotec people.

BOOK 5
TOLTEC WARRIORS
RISE AND FALL OF AN EMPIRE (900 CE - 1200 CE)

BY A.J. KINGSTON

Chapter 1: The Emergence of the Toltecs: Origins and Early Power (900 CE - 950 CE)

The Pre-Toltec period in Mesoamerica represents a fascinating and dynamic epoch in the region's history, characterized by the emergence and development of several influential cultures that paved the way for the later Mesoamerican civilizations. This era, which predates the rise of the Toltec Empire, spans a significant timeframe and encompasses a variety of cultural achievements, innovations, and interactions.

Early Cultures and the Olmec Influence: The Pre-Toltec period is often associated with the influence of the Olmec civilization, which thrived between 1500 BCE and 400 BCE in what is now the Gulf Coast of Mexico. The Olmec, renowned for their colossal stone heads and intricate art, played a foundational role in shaping Mesoamerican cultures that followed. Their impact extended beyond their heartland, influencing neighboring societies in terms of art, religion, and societal organization.

Zapotec and Monte Albán: In the Oaxaca region, the Zapotec civilization began to flourish during the Pre-Toltec period. One of the most prominent Zapotec centers during this time was Monte Albán, which served as the capital of their burgeoning empire. Monte Albán's strategic location atop a mountain plateau allowed it to control key trade routes and interact with neighboring cultures.

The Zapotecs developed sophisticated architectural techniques, including the construction of monumental stone buildings and tombs. Monte Albán's complex layout, adorned with intricate carvings and stelae, attests to their advanced urban planning and artistic achievements.

The Teotihuacan Enigma: Another enigmatic Pre-Toltec culture is Teotihuacan, which thrived in the Valley of Mexico and reached its zenith between 100 BCE and 750 CE. The massive pyramids, broad avenues, and intricate murals found at Teotihuacan testify to the city's grandeur. Yet, despite its significance, the identity of the people who built Teotihuacan remains a mystery.

Teotihuacan was a hub of trade, art, and culture in Mesoamerica. The city's extensive trade networks brought exotic goods and materials from distant regions, facilitating the exchange of ideas and technologies. Teotihuacan's multi-ethnic population likely contributed to its cultural diversity and innovation.

Maya Beginnings: In the lowland jungles of present-day Guatemala and Mexico's Yucatan Peninsula, the Pre-Toltec period witnessed the emergence of the Maya civilization. Although the Classic Maya period would come later, during the Pre-Toltec era, early Maya communities began to develop agricultural systems, establish settlements, and lay the foundation for the sophisticated society that would follow.

These early Maya settlements featured rudimentary architectural structures, and the first inklings of Maya hieroglyphic writing began to appear on monuments and stelae, signifying the beginning of a rich literary and intellectual tradition.

Interactions and Trade: Throughout the Pre-Toltec period, interactions between these diverse cultures were not uncommon. Trade routes crisscrossed Mesoamerica, facilitating the exchange of goods such as obsidian, cacao, and valuable metals. These exchanges not only contributed to the economic prosperity of various societies but also promoted cultural diffusion and the spread of knowledge and artistic styles.

The Olmec, in particular, played a significant role as cultural intermediaries, transmitting their artistic motifs and religious symbolism to other Mesoamerican cultures. The iconic Olmec colossal heads, believed to represent rulers or deities, have been discovered in various regions, illustrating the wide-reaching influence of the Olmec civilization.

Religion and Rituals: Religion and ritual practices were central to Pre-Toltec Mesoamerican cultures. These societies venerated a pantheon of gods and spirits and conducted elaborate ceremonies to appease and honor them. Offerings, sacrifices, and sacred places, such as pyramids and temples, were integral components of these rituals.

The precise details of these religious practices varied among cultures. Teotihuacan, for example, featured the Pyramid of the Sun and the Pyramid of the Moon as important ceremonial centers, while the Zapotec civilization incorporated sacred ball games into their religious rituals.

Decline and Transformation: As the Pre-Toltec period unfolded, several of these cultures underwent transformations and shifts in power. Teotihuacan experienced a mysterious decline around 750 CE, marked by significant disruption and population decline. The reasons for this decline remain a subject of scholarly debate, with factors such as political unrest, environmental stress, and invasion theories proposed.

The Zapotec civilization continued to thrive but evolved over time, with Monte Albán gradually losing its prominence as the capital. The Maya, too, underwent significant societal changes, setting the stage for the development of the Classic Maya civilization in subsequent centuries.

Legacy and Continuity: The Pre-Toltec period in Mesoamerica left a lasting legacy that influenced the subsequent great civilizations of the region, including the Toltec, Aztec, and Classic Maya. The cultural exchange, innovations in architecture and agriculture, and religious practices developed during this era formed the building blocks of Mesoamerican civilization.

The Pre-Toltec period serves as a testament to the resilience and adaptability of ancient Mesoamerican societies. Despite the challenges and transformations they faced, these cultures laid the groundwork for the magnificent civilizations that would follow, leaving an indelible mark on the history and cultural heritage of Mesoamerica.

The rise of Toltec identity marked a pivotal period in Mesoamerican history, characterized by the emergence of a dynamic and influential civilization that played a significant role in shaping the cultural landscape of the region. This era, which spanned from the 10th to the 12th centuries CE, witnessed the ascent of the Toltecs as a dominant force in central Mexico, leading to the establishment of their capital city, Tula, and the flourishing of their unique cultural identity.

Origins and Early Power: The origins of the Toltec civilization are shrouded in myth and legend, with the Toltecs often traced back to a mythical homeland called Tollan. Their legendary journey from this ancestral home to the highlands of central Mexico is a central narrative in their identity. It is believed that the Toltecs arrived in the region around the 10th century CE, where they encountered and absorbed elements of the cultures that preceded them.

Tula, located in the modern-day state of Hidalgo, served as the capital of the Toltec Empire during this period. Its strategic position allowed the Toltecs to control key trade routes and engage in extensive interactions with neighboring civilizations.

Tula: The Glorious Toltec Capital: Tula was a marvel of urban planning and architecture. The city was characterized by its monumental pyramids, palaces, and a ceremonial ball court, all constructed with precise alignments to celestial events. The Pyramid of Quetzalcoatl, adorned with intricately carved serpentine columns and sculptures, remains an iconic symbol of Toltec artistry.

The city's layout and architectural achievements reflected the Toltecs' advanced understanding of urban planning, influenced by their predecessors, such as Teotihuacan. Tula's greatness extended beyond its physical structures; it was also a center of learning, culture, and religious practices.

Toltec Artistry and Warfare: The Toltecs were renowned for their artistic achievements, which were characterized by intricate carvings, pottery, and metalwork. The masterful craftsmanship displayed in their sculptures and ceramics demonstrated their dedication to artistic expression. Toltec artisans often depicted war-related themes, reflecting the militaristic aspect of their society.

Quetzalcoatl, the feathered serpent deity, held significant religious and symbolic importance for the Toltecs. Depictions of Quetzalcoatl adorned many of their artworks, emphasizing his role as a deity associated with creation, knowledge, and culture.

Quetzalcoatl and Toltec Religion: Quetzalcoatl's importance in Toltec culture cannot be overstated. He was not only a deity but also a legendary figure believed to be the founder of civilization, credited with bringing knowledge, agriculture, and the arts to humanity. The Toltecs worshipped Quetzalcoatl and sought to emulate his qualities of wisdom and cultural refinement.

Religious practices in Tula included ceremonies, rituals, and offerings to honor the gods. Toltec religion was polytheistic, with a pantheon that featured deities associated with various aspects of life, including fertility, war, and the cycles of the natural world.

The Toltec Military Machine: The Toltecs were known for their martial prowess, and warfare played a central role in their identity. They expanded their influence through military campaigns, conquering neighboring territories and establishing a network of tributary states. The Toltec army was well-organized and equipped, and their military successes solidified their dominance in the region.

Toltec warriors were characterized by their distinctive attire, which often featured feathered headdresses and elaborate costumes. These warriors were highly disciplined and trained in various forms of combat, reflecting the militaristic ethos of Toltec society.

Influence and Disintegration: The Toltec Empire's influence extended beyond its borders, shaping the cultures of surrounding regions. The Toltecs established a far-reaching trading network, facilitating the exchange of goods, ideas, and cultural practices. Their artistic styles and religious beliefs left an enduring impact on Mesoamerican civilization.

However, like many great civilizations, the Toltec Empire eventually faced challenges and internal strife. Factors such as political instability, environmental stress, and conflicts with neighboring groups contributed to its decline. By the 12th century CE, Tula had been abandoned, marking the end of the Toltec capital.

The Last Stand and Legacy: The fall of Tula was accompanied by a period of upheaval, during which the Toltec identity began to fragment. Some Toltec descendants migrated to other regions, such as the Yucatan Peninsula, where they contributed to the cultural development of the Maya civilization. Others sought refuge in cities like Cholula and continued to practice Toltec traditions.

Despite the decline of the Toltec Empire, their cultural legacy endured. Their architectural and artistic achievements continued to influence subsequent Mesoamerican civilizations, including the Aztecs. The legend of Quetzalcoatl and the idealized image of the Toltecs as a cultural and intellectual beacon persisted in the collective memory of Mesoamerica.

In summary, the rise of Toltec identity represents a fascinating chapter in Mesoamerican history. The Toltecs' achievements in art, architecture, religion, and warfare left an indelible mark on the cultural landscape of the region. While their empire eventually crumbled, their legacy lived on in the traditions, beliefs, and artistic expressions of subsequent civilizations. The Toltec civilization stands as a testament to the dynamic and ever-evolving nature of Mesoamerican culture.

Chapter 2: Tula: The Glorious Toltec Capital (950 CE - 1000 CE)

The early achievements of the Toltec civilization, which emerged in Mesoamerica during the 10th century CE, reflect a dynamic and influential society that made significant contributions to the region's cultural, artistic, and architectural heritage. During this formative period, the Toltecs laid the foundation for their future greatness, with their accomplishments leaving an indelible mark on the history of Mesoamerica.

Founding and Early Developments: The Toltec civilization is believed to have originated in the highlands of central Mexico, in the region around Tula. The exact origins of the Toltecs are shrouded in myth and legend, with tales of their migration from a mythical homeland, Tollan, forming a central part of their cultural identity. The early Toltecs settled in the fertile basin of the Tula River, where they began to establish their society.

Tula, the capital city of the Toltec Empire, played a pivotal role in their early achievements. The city's strategic location allowed the Toltecs to control key trade routes and engage in interactions with neighboring cultures. It was in Tula that many of the Toltecs' cultural, artistic, and architectural innovations took root.

Artistic Excellence: Early Toltec achievements in the realm of art were marked by a commitment to precision, detail, and craftsmanship. Toltec artisans excelled in various forms of artistic expression, including sculpture, ceramics, and metalwork. They created intricate carvings and sculptures that showcased their artistic prowess.

The iconic Pyramid of Quetzalcoatl in Tula serves as a testament to Toltec artistry. Adorned with serpentine columns, feathered serpent sculptures, and intricately carved reliefs, this pyramid stands as a prime example of Toltec architectural and artistic excellence. The reverence for Quetzalcoatl, the feathered serpent deity, was a central theme in Toltec art, reflecting their religious and cultural values.

Urban Planning and Architecture: Tula's urban planning and architectural achievements during this early period were striking. The city featured monumental pyramids, palaces, and ceremonial ball courts, all designed with precise alignments to celestial events. This attention to astronomical and calendar-based planning revealed the Toltecs' advanced knowledge of the cosmos.

The city's layout and architectural innovations displayed a level of sophistication influenced by their predecessors, such as Teotihuacan. The Pyramid of Quetzalcoatl, with its distinctive serpentine columns and intricate reliefs, exemplified the Toltecs' architectural ingenuity.

Religion and Rituals: Religion played a central role in the early Toltec society. The Toltecs worshipped a pantheon of gods, with Quetzalcoatl being a key deity. Quetzalcoatl was revered as a creator god associated with knowledge, culture, and the arts. His presence was pervasive in early Toltec art and religious practices, symbolizing their commitment to intellectual and spiritual pursuits.

Toltec religious rituals included ceremonies, offerings, and sacrifices to honor the gods. These rituals were an integral part of Toltec life, and their temples and pyramids served as sacred spaces where these ceremonies took place.

Cultural Innovation and Interaction: Early Toltec achievements were not confined to their city of Tula. The Toltecs established a far-reaching trading network that facilitated the exchange of goods and ideas with neighboring cultures. This cultural interaction allowed for the diffusion of artistic styles, technologies, and knowledge.

The influence of the Toltecs extended beyond their immediate borders, with their artistic motifs and religious beliefs leaving a lasting impact on Mesoamerican civilization. Their legacy would continue to shape the art and culture of future Mesoamerican societies, including the Aztecs.

Agriculture and Economy: Agriculture was a crucial component of Toltec society. The fertile lands surrounding Tula provided the necessary resources for sustenance and economic development.

The Toltecs practiced advanced agricultural techniques, including terrace farming and irrigation systems, which allowed them to support a growing population.

Trade played a vital role in the Toltec economy. They engaged in long-distance trade networks, acquiring valuable resources such as obsidian, cacao, and precious metals. These trade connections contributed to the economic prosperity of the Toltec Empire.

Decline and Transformation: While the early Toltec period was marked by cultural and artistic achievements, it was also a time of political consolidation and expansion. However, like many great civilizations, the Toltec Empire eventually faced challenges and internal strife. Factors such as political instability, environmental stress, and conflicts with neighboring groups contributed to its decline.

By the 12th century CE, Tula had been abandoned, signaling the end of the early Toltec era. The decline of the Toltec Empire was accompanied by a period of upheaval, during which their cultural identity began to fragment. Some Toltec descendants migrated to other regions, such as the Yucatan Peninsula, where they contributed to the cultural development of the Maya civilization.

In summary, the early achievements of the Toltec civilization were characterized by artistic excellence, architectural innovation, and cultural interaction. The Toltecs' commitment to art, their reverence for Quetzalcoatl, and their advanced urban planning set them apart as a prominent Mesoamerican civilization. While their empire eventually declined, the early Toltec period laid the foundation for the cultural and artistic legacy that continued to influence subsequent Mesoamerican civilizations. The Toltecs remain an integral part of the rich tapestry of Mesoamerican history.

Toltec urban planning and architecture represent a remarkable chapter in the history of Mesoamerican civilization. During their peak in the 10th to 12th centuries CE, the Toltecs created cities and structures that showcased their architectural prowess and reflected their sophisticated understanding of urban design. These achievements left an enduring mark on the landscape and influenced subsequent Mesoamerican civilizations.

City Layout and Organization: The Toltecs established several important urban centers, with Tula being the most renowned. Tula's city layout was meticulously planned, reflecting both practicality and symbolic significance. The city was divided into various sectors, each serving distinct functions such as residential areas, ceremonial centers, and marketplaces.

Central to Toltec urban planning was the organization of public spaces, plazas, and ceremonial precincts. These areas served as focal points for religious rituals, social gatherings, and civic activities. The organization of public spaces also allowed for efficient movement within the city.

Monumental Pyramids and Temples: Tula's architectural marvels included monumental pyramids and temples, characterized by their grandeur and unique design elements. The Pyramid of Quetzalcoatl, also known as the Pyramid B, is one of the most iconic structures. It features four massive, intricately carved columns, each depicting the feathered serpent deity, Quetzalcoatl. These columns are a testament to the Toltecs' artistic and engineering prowess.

The Pyramid of the Sun, reminiscent of Teotihuacan's architecture, also stands as a prominent example of Toltec design. While not as large as its Teotihuacan counterpart, it showcases precise alignments with celestial events, highlighting the Toltecs' knowledge of astronomy and calendar systems.

Palaces and Residences: Toltec urban centers included palaces and residences for the ruling elite and the aristocracy. These structures often featured courtyards, open-air spaces, and intricate stone carvings. The Palace of Quetzalcoatl in Tula is a notable example, known for its detailed friezes and sculptural elements.

Residential areas in Toltec cities were designed to accommodate a growing population. Houses were typically made of adobe bricks and featured central courtyards. The arrangement of houses allowed for communal living while maintaining a degree of privacy for individual families.

Ball Courts: Toltec cities also featured ball courts, which played a significant role in Mesoamerican culture and ritual. The Great Ball Court of Tula, for instance, was an elongated space where the Mesoamerican ballgame, known as ullamaliztli, was played. The design of ball courts was precise, with specific dimensions and architectural elements that facilitated the ballgame's ceremonial and religious aspects.

Ceremonial Precincts: Ceremonial precincts in Toltec cities were carefully designed to accommodate religious rituals and ceremonies. Altars, shrines, and sculptures were placed within these precincts, serving as focal points for worship and offerings to the gods. The placement of these elements often aligned with celestial events, reinforcing the spiritual connection between the Toltecs and the cosmos.

Astronomical Alignments: Toltec architecture demonstrated a keen understanding of astronomy and the importance of celestial events in their culture. Buildings and structures were often aligned with specific solar and lunar events, such as equinoxes and solstices. These alignments not only reflected the Toltecs' astronomical knowledge but also played a role in their religious and calendrical practices.

In summary, Toltec urban planning and architecture exemplify the sophistication and ingenuity of this Mesoamerican civilization. The layout of their cities, the design of monumental structures, and the attention to detail in their architectural elements showcase the Toltecs' commitment to both functional and symbolic aspects of their built environment. These achievements continue to captivate modern scholars and visitors, serving as a testament to the enduring legacy of the Toltec civilization in Mesoamerican history.

Chapter 3: Toltec Artistry and Warfare (950 CE - 1100 CE)

Tula, often referred to as Tula Hidalgo to distinguish it from other places with the same name, stands as a prominent archaeological site and the heart of Toltec culture in Mesoamerica. During its zenith in the 10th to 12th centuries CE, Tula served as the political, cultural, and religious epicenter of the Toltec civilization, leaving a lasting legacy in the annals of Mesoamerican history.

Political Capital: Tula was not only the geographic capital of the Toltec Empire but also its political and administrative center. It served as the hub of Toltec governance, where leaders and rulers exercised their authority over the empire's territories. At its peak, the city was likely home to a ruling elite who directed the empire's policies, trade, and military campaigns.

Religious and Ceremonial Hub: Religion played a central role in Toltec society, and Tula was the epicenter of their religious and ceremonial activities. The city's layout featured numerous temples, pyramids, and sacred precincts dedicated to various deities. The most iconic of these is the Pyramid of Quetzalcoatl, also known as the Temple of the Feathered Serpent. This temple was dedicated to Quetzalcoatl, a key deity in the Toltec pantheon associated with knowledge, culture, and the arts.

The Great Ball Court of Tula, where the Mesoamerican ballgame was played, was a critical religious and ceremonial space. The game held deep religious significance and was often linked to creation myths and cosmic cycles. The precise design and alignments of the ball court reinforced its spiritual importance.

Cultural and Artistic Center: Tula was a vibrant center of culture and the arts during the Toltec era. The city's artisans created intricate stone carvings, sculptures, and ceramics that reflected their artistic excellence. The columns of the Pyramid of Quetzalcoatl are renowned for their detailed representations of the feathered serpent deity, showcasing the Toltecs' mastery of stone carving.

Tula's artistic achievements extended beyond sculpture to include pottery, metalwork, and mural painting. These artistic traditions influenced the styles of subsequent Mesoamerican civilizations and contributed to the region's cultural richness.

Trade and Commerce: Tula's strategic location allowed it to control key trade routes, making it a bustling center of commerce. The Toltecs engaged in long-distance trade networks, importing and exporting goods such as obsidian, cacao, textiles, and precious metals. The city's marketplaces bustled with activity, facilitating economic exchanges with neighboring regions.

Influence and Legacy: The influence of Tula extended far beyond its own borders. The city's cultural and artistic achievements had a profound impact on neighboring cultures, including the Aztecs and the Maya. Toltec artistic motifs, architectural styles, and religious beliefs left an enduring mark on Mesoamerican civilization.

Decline and Abandonment: Tula's prominence as the capital of the Toltec Empire eventually waned. Factors contributing to its decline include political instability, conflicts with neighboring groups, environmental stress, and internal strife. By the 12th century CE, Tula had been abandoned, marking the end of the Toltec era in the city.

In summary, Tula served as the beating heart of Toltec culture, embodying the civilization's political, religious, and cultural achievements. Its iconic structures, religious precincts, and artistic endeavors left an indelible imprint on the history of Mesoamerica. Tula's legacy as a cultural and artistic center continues to fascinate scholars and enthusiasts alike, illustrating the enduring significance of this ancient Toltec capital.

The Toltec civilization, known for its military prowess and strategic acumen, developed a range of weaponry and military strategies that played a crucial role in its expansion and dominance in Mesoamerica during its zenith in the 10th to 12th centuries CE. While Toltec warfare was marked by its formidable armies and advanced tactics, it was also intertwined with religious beliefs and ritualistic elements.

Weaponry:

Macuahuitl: The macuahuitl was a distinctive and deadly weapon used by the Toltecs. It was essentially a wooden club embedded with obsidian blades. These sharp-edged obsidian pieces, often compared to blades, could cause devastating injuries. Macuahuitls were prized for their ability to cut through flesh and bone with ease.

Spears: Toltec warriors commonly used spears as both throwing and thrusting weapons. These spears were typically made of wood and tipped with obsidian, bone, or copper. They provided the Toltec army with versatility in combat, allowing for both ranged attacks and close-quarter engagements.

Atlatl: The atlatl was a spear-throwing tool that augmented the range and force of projectile weapons. It allowed warriors to hurl darts or spears with greater speed and accuracy. The Toltecs employed the atlatl as a ranged weapon, making them formidable opponents in battles.

Shields: Shields were essential defensive equipment for Toltec warriors. These shields were often crafted from wood and featured intricate designs. They provided protection against projectiles and close combat attacks, enhancing the warriors' survivability on the battlefield.

Military Strategies:

Formation Tactics: Toltec armies employed organized formation tactics to maximize their effectiveness in battle. Formations included infantry, archers, and spear-throwers arranged in strategic patterns. These formations enabled coordinated attacks and defensive maneuvers.

Siege Warfare: The Toltecs were known for their ability to conduct successful sieges. They used both military strategy and psychological tactics to weaken and breach fortified enemy positions. Siege warfare played a crucial role in their territorial expansion.

Ritualistic Warfare: Toltec warfare was closely linked to religious beliefs and rituals. Captured enemies were often subjected to ritual sacrifices, reinforcing the Toltec view of war as a sacred undertaking. This ritualistic aspect added a psychological dimension to their military campaigns.

Alliances and Diplomacy: While the Toltecs were formidable in battle, they also understood the importance of diplomacy. They forged alliances with neighboring city-states, sometimes through marriage alliances, to strengthen their position and avoid unnecessary conflicts.

Control of Trade Routes: Control of key trade routes allowed the Toltecs to exert economic and political influence over neighboring regions. This control provided them with valuable resources and leverage in negotiations with other city-states.

Logistics and Supply Lines: Effective logistics and supply lines were crucial for the success of Toltec military campaigns. They had systems in place to ensure their armies were well-provisioned and maintained throughout their campaigns.

Fortifications: The Toltecs constructed fortifications around their cities and strategic locations to defend against external threats. These defensive structures included walls, watchtowers, and moats, making it challenging for invaders to breach their cities.

The Toltec military, with its advanced weaponry and strategic thinking, allowed the civilization to expand its influence and dominate regions of Mesoamerica. Their military legacy continued to impact subsequent Mesoamerican civilizations, including the Aztecs, who adopted and adapted many Toltec military practices and strategies.

The Toltecs, known for their martial prowess and strategic acumen, practiced the art of war with precision and purpose. Warfare held a significant place in Toltec society, often intertwined with religious beliefs and rituals. Here, we delve into the art of Toltec war, exploring their strategies, weaponry, and the ritualistic aspects of their military endeavors.

Strategies and Tactics:

Formations: Toltec armies employed well-organized formations that maximized their effectiveness on the battlefield. These formations included infantry, archers, and spear-throwers, each with specific roles. The arrangement of troops allowed for coordinated attacks and effective defense against enemy forces.

Ambushes: Toltec warriors were skilled in the art of surprise attacks and ambushes. They often used natural terrain features to conceal their forces and launch surprise assaults on unsuspecting enemies. This strategy capitalized on their knowledge of the local landscape.

Siege Warfare: Toltecs excelled in siege warfare, employing tactics to breach fortified enemy positions. They used various methods, including battering rams, siege towers, and psychological warfare to weaken the resolve of defenders. Successful sieges were crucial to their territorial expansion.

Psychological Warfare: Toltec warriors understood the psychological aspects of warfare. They aimed to instill fear and intimidation in their enemies through battle cries, war chants, and the display of macuahuitls embedded with menacing obsidian blades. The psychological impact of these tactics often worked in their favor.

Weaponry:

Macuahuitl: The macuahuitl was the iconic weapon of Toltec warfare. Crafted from wood and embedded with sharp obsidian blades, it was a formidable melee weapon. The macuahuitl's ability to inflict gruesome injuries made it a symbol of Toltec military might.

Spears and Atlatls: Toltec warriors wielded spears, both for thrusting and throwing, as well as atlatls. These weapons provided versatility in combat, allowing for ranged attacks and close-quarter engagements.

Shields: Shields were vital defensive equipment for Toltec warriors. These shields, often adorned with intricate designs, protected against enemy projectiles and melee attacks, enhancing the soldiers' survivability in battle.

Ritualistic Aspects:

Religious Significance: Toltec warfare was deeply intertwined with religious beliefs. It was viewed as a sacred undertaking, and battles were often preceded by elaborate ceremonies and offerings to the gods. Captured enemies were sometimes subjected to ritual sacrifices as part of these ceremonies.

Cosmic Connection: Toltecs believed that warfare was connected to cosmic cycles and the balance of the universe. Celestial events, such as eclipses or planetary alignments, were considered omens that influenced military campaigns. Successful battles were seen as acts in harmony with the cosmos.

Sacrificial Captives: Captured enemies played a pivotal role in Toltec rituals. They were often sacrificed to appease the gods and maintain cosmic balance. These sacrifices were conducted with elaborate ceremonies, often involving priests and rulers.

In summary, the art of Toltec war was a multifaceted endeavor that combined strategic thinking, advanced weaponry, and religious beliefs. Toltec warriors were skilled in various tactics, and their proficiency on the battlefield allowed the Toltec civilization to expand its influence in Mesoamerica. The ritualistic aspects of Toltec warfare added a spiritual dimension to their military endeavors, reinforcing their belief in the cosmic significance of conflict. The legacy of Toltec military strategies and traditions continued to influence subsequent Mesoamerican civilizations, leaving an enduring mark on the region's history.

Quetzalcoatl, often referred to as the Feathered Serpent deity, holds a significant and complex place in Mesoamerican mythology and religious belief systems. This revered deity was venerated by several civilizations in ancient Mexico, including the Olmecs, Maya, Teotihuacan, Toltecs, and Aztecs, each interpreting and incorporating the deity into their respective cultures and cosmologies. Here, we explore the multifaceted nature of Quetzalcoatl and its enduring significance in Mesoamerican history.

Attributes and Iconography:

Feathered Serpent: Quetzalcoatl's name is derived from the Nahuatl words "quetzalli," meaning "quetzal bird" (known for its vibrant iridescent feathers), and "coatl," meaning "serpent." As the Feathered Serpent, Quetzalcoatl is often depicted as a plumed serpent or a serpent with feathers, symbolizing the fusion of the earthbound serpent and the celestial bird.

Cultural Variations: While the core attributes of Quetzalcoatl remain consistent across Mesoamerican cultures, there are variations in how this deity is portrayed. In some cultures, Quetzalcoatl is associated with wind, rain, and agriculture, while in others, it embodies creativity, knowledge, and cultural enlightenment.

Color Symbolism: The vibrant colors associated with Quetzalcoatl, such as green and blue, represent life, rebirth, and growth. The quetzal bird's iridescent green and blue feathers are particularly significant, signifying the deity's connection to the natural world.

Roles and Attributes:

Creator God: Quetzalcoatl is often seen as one of the creator deities responsible for shaping the world and humanity. In this role, the deity is associated with cosmic order and the creation of the first humans.

God of Knowledge and Culture: Quetzalcoatl is revered as a deity of wisdom, arts, and culture. This aspect of the deity emphasizes the pursuit of knowledge, artistic expression, and intellectual achievement.

Wind and Weather God: Quetzalcoatl is also linked to weather patterns, particularly wind and rain. This association underscores the importance of agriculture and fertility in Mesoamerican societies, as these elements are essential for successful farming.

Symbol of Renewal and Rebirth: Quetzalcoatl's connection to the shedding of serpent skin symbolizes rebirth and renewal, aligning with the cycles of nature and the cosmos. This makes the deity integral to notions of cyclical time and cosmic balance.

Mythological Stories:

Quetzalcoatl and Tezcatlipoca: One of the most famous myths involving Quetzalcoatl revolves around a rivalry with Tezcatlipoca, the god of destiny and sorcery. This rivalry leads to Quetzalcoatl's self-imposed exile from Tula, an event that has been interpreted as symbolic of the Toltec civilization's decline.

Feathered Serpent as a Cultural Hero: Quetzalcoatl is also revered as a cultural hero who brought various gifts to humanity, including maize (corn) and the calendar. These contributions are seen as integral to the development of Mesoamerican civilization.

Legacy and Enduring Influence:

Quetzalcoatl's legacy endures through various means:

Continued Worship: Despite the Spanish conquest and the introduction of Christianity to Mesoamerica, veneration of Quetzalcoatl persisted in various forms. The syncretism between indigenous beliefs and Christianity often resulted in the blending of Quetzalcoatl with Christian saints.

Art and Architecture: Depictions of Quetzalcoatl are prevalent in Mesoamerican art, particularly in murals, sculptures, and temple architecture. The deity's image adorns numerous archaeological sites throughout the region.

Modern Cultural Representations: Quetzalcoatl continues to be an emblematic figure in contemporary Mexican culture and identity. The deity's image and symbolism are often celebrated in festivals, art, and literature, connecting modern Mexicans to their rich indigenous heritage.

In summary, Quetzalcoatl, the Feathered Serpent deity, stands as a symbol of the intricate interplay between nature, culture, and spirituality in Mesoamerican civilization. Its multifaceted attributes and enduring influence underscore the deity's profound significance in the history, art, and belief systems of the region.

The Toltecs, a prominent Mesoamerican civilization that thrived in central Mexico from roughly the 10th to the 12th century CE, had a complex system of religious beliefs and rituals that played a crucial role in their society. These beliefs and rituals were deeply intertwined with their daily lives, political structures, and cosmological views. Here, we explore the key aspects of Toltec religious beliefs and the rituals that defined their spiritual practices.

Cosmic Dualism:

Tezcatlipoca and Quetzalcoatl: The Toltecs, like many Mesoamerican civilizations, believed in cosmic dualism. They revered two primary deities, Tezcatlipoca and Quetzalcoatl, who represented opposing forces. Tezcatlipoca, the Smoking Mirror, was associated with sorcery, conflict, and the night. Quetzalcoatl, the Feathered Serpent, symbolized wisdom, culture, and the day. The interplay between these deities represented the balance and duality inherent in the cosmos.

Sacrifice and Offerings:

Human Sacrifice: Human sacrifice held a central place in Toltec religious rituals, as it was believed to appease the gods and maintain cosmic harmony. Captured enemies, slaves, and even volunteers were offered as sacrifices. These rituals often took place on top of pyramids or temples, emphasizing the connection between earth and heaven.

Animal Sacrifice: Apart from human sacrifice, animals like jaguars, eagles, and serpents were also sacrificed. These animals were chosen for their symbolic significance, representing various cosmic forces and deities.

Bloodletting Rituals: Bloodletting was a common practice among the elite in Toltec society. Nobles and rulers would pierce their ears, tongues, or genitalia to offer their own blood as a sacred offering to the gods.

Temple Complexes and Pyramids:

Pyramid Temples: Toltec cities, such as Tula, featured monumental pyramid temples at their centers. These pyramids served as sacred spaces for rituals and offerings to the gods. The Pyramid of Quetzalcoatl at Tula, adorned with carved stone serpents, is a famous example.

Altars: Altars on top of pyramids were the focal points of many religious ceremonies and sacrifices. They were meticulously constructed and often decorated with intricate carvings and sculptures.

Astrology and Cosmology:

Celestial Observations: The Toltecs, like other Mesoamerican cultures, closely observed celestial events such as eclipses, solstices, and equinoxes. These events were seen as omens and played a role in determining the timing of rituals and actions.

Calendar Systems: Toltecs utilized complex calendar systems, including the 260-day ritual calendar (tonalpohualli) and the 365-day solar calendar (xiuhpohualli). These calendars guided religious ceremonies and determined auspicious days for various activities.

Ceremonial Centers and Sacred Places:

Tollan (Tula): The city of Tula was the principal Toltec ceremonial center, featuring impressive pyramids, temples, and sacred plazas. It was believed to be a place of great spiritual power.

Other Sacred Sites: Toltecs also considered certain natural features, such as caves, mountains, and cenotes (natural sinkholes), as sacred places imbued with spiritual significance.

Syncretism and Legacy:

Influence on Aztec Religion: Toltec religious beliefs and practices significantly influenced subsequent Mesoamerican civilizations, including the Aztecs. Many aspects of Toltec religion, such as the worship of Quetzalcoatl, were incorporated into Aztec religious practices.

Enduring Traditions: Some Toltec religious traditions, including the veneration of specific deities and the use of calendars, continue to be observed by modern indigenous communities in Mexico.

In summary, Toltec religious beliefs and rituals were integral to their society, shaping their worldview, governance, and daily lives. The Toltecs' complex system of cosmic dualism, sacrifice, temple complexes, and celestial observations reflected their deep spiritual connection with the natural and supernatural worlds. These beliefs left an enduring legacy in Mesoamerican culture, influencing subsequent civilizations and continuing to be a part of modern indigenous traditions in Mexico.

Chapter 5: The Toltec Military Machine (1100 CE - 1200 CE)

The military organization of the Toltecs, a prominent Mesoamerican civilization that thrived from approximately the 10th to the 12th century CE, played a pivotal role in their society. The Toltecs were known for their military prowess and expansionist policies, and their military structure and strategies were essential to their success and influence in the region. Next, we will delve into the intricate details of Toltec military organization, shedding light on their army's composition, leadership, weaponry, and tactics.

Composition of the Toltec Army:
The Toltec military was a well-structured and organized force, comprising various components:

Soldiers (Tlamani): The backbone of the Toltec army consisted of skilled warriors known as Tlamani. These soldiers were typically drawn from the nobility and were trained from a young age in the arts of warfare. They were known for their discipline, combat skills, and loyalty to their commanders.

Auxiliary Troops: In addition to the Tlamani, the Toltec military included auxiliary troops who supported the core forces. These auxiliaries could come from conquered territories, allied city-states, or vassal states and provided additional manpower and resources.

Leadership and Hierarchy:
Toltec military leadership was structured hierarchically, with clear distinctions in roles and responsibilities:

Tlatoani: The supreme military leader and ruler of the Toltec state was known as the Tlatoani. This individual held ultimate authority over military matters, including the declaration of war and the appointment of high-ranking military officers.

Military Commanders (Tlacochcalcatl): Beneath the Tlatoani were military commanders known as Tlacochcalcatl. These individuals were responsible for overseeing the day-to-day operations of the army, including training, logistics, and tactics. They played a critical role in battle planning and execution.

Officers: Within the military hierarchy, there were various officer ranks, each responsible for specific units or divisions. These officers included captains (Tlacateccatl) and lieutenants (Tlacatecatl), who led smaller groups of soldiers.

Weaponry and Equipment:

The Toltec army was equipped with an array of weapons and gear tailored for Mesoamerican warfare:

Obsidian Blades: Obsidian blades, known as macuahuitl, were a signature weapon of the Toltecs. These were wooden clubs embedded with rows of razor-sharp obsidian blades, making them deadly in close combat.

Spears: Soldiers wielded spears made from wood or bone, often with obsidian or flint tips. These spears were effective for both thrusting and throwing.

Atlatl: The atlatl, a spear-throwing device, was used to launch spears with increased force and accuracy. It provided the Toltec army with a ranged weapon for attacking from a distance.

Shields: Soldiers used shields made of wood and leather to protect themselves from enemy projectiles and close-quarters combat. These shields were often decorated with intricate designs.

Armor: Some elite warriors and commanders wore armor made from animal hides or cotton padded with feathers. While not as extensive as European armor, it offered protection against certain weapons.

Military Tactics and Strategies:

The Toltec army employed various tactics and strategies to achieve success on the battlefield:

Ambushes: Ambushes were a common tactic used to surprise and disorient enemy forces. The Toltecs were skilled at concealing themselves in forests and using the element of surprise to their advantage.

Flanking Maneuvers: Flanking maneuvers involved attacking the enemy's vulnerable sides or rear, disrupting their formations and causing panic.

Siege Warfare: When facing fortified enemy cities, the Toltecs employed siege warfare techniques, including the use of siege towers, battering rams, and tunnels to breach city walls.

Psychological Warfare: Psychological warfare was often employed to demoralize and intimidate the enemy. This could involve the display of captured enemy heads or other gruesome tactics.

Logistics and Supply Lines:

Maintaining a well-supplied army was crucial for the Toltecs. They established supply lines and logistics networks to ensure their forces had access to food, water, and ammunition during campaigns. This involved the storage and transportation of provisions to support the army while on the move.

Legacy of Toltec Military Organization:

The Toltec military organization left a lasting legacy in Mesoamerican history. Their military strategies and tactics influenced subsequent civilizations, including the Aztecs, who adopted and adapted many aspects of Toltec warfare. The use of obsidian weaponry, military hierarchy, and battlefield tactics had a lasting impact on the region's military traditions.

In summary, the Toltecs were a formidable Mesoamerican civilization with a well-structured military organization. Their army, composed of skilled warriors and supported by auxiliary troops, was led by a hierarchical command structure. The Toltecs excelled in close combat and employed various tactics and strategies to achieve success on the battlefield. Their military legacy endured, influencing later Mesoamerican civilizations and contributing to the rich tapestry of ancient American warfare.

The Toltecs, a prominent Mesoamerican civilization that thrived from the 10th to the 12th century CE, were known for their remarkable expansionist policies and military conquests. Their territorial reach and influence extended across central Mexico and beyond, making them a dominant force in the region. Next, we will explore the Toltec expansion and conquests, shedding light on the strategies, motivations, and the far-reaching impact of their territorial ambitions.

Strategies of Expansion:

The expansion of the Toltec civilization was characterized by several key strategies and factors:

Military Prowess: The Toltecs were renowned for their formidable military capabilities. Their disciplined army, equipped with obsidian weapons and skilled in various combat tactics, was a significant driving force behind their expansion.

Alliances and Vassal States: The Toltecs established alliances and forged agreements with neighboring city-states and communities. In some cases, these allies became vassal states, paying tribute and providing military support in exchange for protection and support from the Toltecs.

Territorial Control: The Toltecs strategically occupied and controlled key regions and trade routes. Their capital city, Tula, served as a central hub for trade, culture, and governance, facilitating the administration of their expanding territories.

Economic Interests: The pursuit of economic resources, including control over fertile lands, valuable trade routes, and access to key resources like obsidian and jade, played a crucial role in their expansionist ambitions.

Conquests and Territories:

The Toltec expansion resulted in the acquisition of several significant territories and the establishment of influential city-states:

Chichen Itza: The Toltecs played a role in the founding of Chichen Itza, a prominent city in the Yucatan Peninsula. This city became a center of Toltec influence in the region and featured architectural and cultural elements associated with the Toltecs.

Xochicalco: The city of Xochicalco, located in modern-day Morelos, Mexico, was another key Toltec conquest. Xochicalco featured impressive pyramids and served as an important cultural and economic center.

Trade Routes: The Toltecs controlled vital trade routes that facilitated the exchange of goods, ideas, and culture throughout Mesoamerica. These trade routes extended to distant regions, enhancing their influence.

Cultural Influence:

The Toltecs' expansion went beyond territorial control; it also had a profound cultural impact:

Toltec Art and Architecture: The architectural and artistic styles of the Toltecs influenced the regions they conquered. Elements such as the use of carved stone, distinctive pyramids, and representations of deities left a lasting imprint on the cultures they encountered.

Religious Influence: The worship of Quetzalcoatl, the Feathered Serpent deity associated with the Toltecs, spread to regions under their control. Temples and rituals dedicated to Quetzalcoatl became common throughout Mesoamerica.

Writing and Glyphs: Toltec writing systems and glyphic representations were adopted and adapted by neighboring civilizations, contributing to the spread of written communication and record-keeping in the region.

Motivations for Expansion:

Several motivations drove Toltec expansion:

Resource Acquisition: The control of valuable resources such as fertile agricultural land, precious stones, and minerals provided economic benefits and sustained their growing civilization.

Political Influence: The expansion allowed the Toltecs to exert political influence over neighboring regions, creating a network of vassal states that paid tribute and acknowledged their authority.

Cultural Exchange: The Toltecs were also motivated by a desire to spread their culture, religion, and knowledge. This cultural exchange enriched the diverse mosaic of Mesoamerican civilizations.

Decline and Legacy:

The Toltec civilization eventually faced challenges, including internal strife and external pressures, leading to its decline in the 12th century CE. However, their legacy endured:

Influence on Successor Cultures: The Toltecs' cultural and architectural influence persisted in successor cultures such as the Aztecs and Maya. Elements of Toltec art, religion, and urban planning continued to shape Mesoamerican civilization.

Trade Networks: The trade networks established during Toltec expansion continued to thrive and fostered economic prosperity and cultural exchange in the region.

Historical Significance: The Toltec expansion remains a crucial chapter in the history of Mesoamerica. It exemplifies the complex interplay of political, economic, and cultural factors that shaped the region's civilizations.

In summary, Toltec expansion and conquests were marked by military prowess, strategic alliances, and the pursuit of economic and cultural interests. Their territorial reach and influence extended across central Mexico and contributed to the cultural tapestry of Mesoamerica. The Toltecs' legacy, seen in their art, architecture, religion, and trade networks, endured long after their civilization faced decline, leaving an indelible mark on the history of the region.

Chapter 6: Influence and Disintegration: The Toltecs Beyond Tula (1150 CE - 1200 CE)

The Toltecs, a prominent Mesoamerican civilization that thrived from the 10th to the 12th century CE, exerted a profound influence on neighboring civilizations in the region. Their impact extended across cultural, artistic, architectural, religious, and political domains, leaving an enduring legacy that shaped the course of Mesoamerican history. Next, we will explore the multifaceted influence of the Toltecs on their neighbors, shedding light on how their achievements and innovations reverberated throughout the region.

Cultural Exchange and Syncretism:

One of the most significant aspects of Toltec influence was the cultural exchange and syncretism that occurred with neighboring civilizations, including the Maya and the Aztecs. This exchange of ideas, practices, and beliefs enriched the tapestry of Mesoamerican culture:

Religious Syncretism: The worship of Quetzalcoatl, the Feathered Serpent deity associated with the Toltecs, spread to neighboring regions. In some cases, this syncretism resulted in the blending of indigenous deities with Toltec religious practices.

Artistic Styles: Toltec artistic styles, characterized by intricately carved stone sculptures and elaborate murals, influenced the artistic expressions of neighboring civilizations. Elements of Toltec art can be observed in the iconography and motifs of Maya and Aztec artworks.

Architectural Influence:

The Toltecs were renowned for their architectural achievements, which had a lasting impact on the architectural traditions of their neighbors:

Pyramids and Temples: Toltec-style pyramids and temples, featuring stepped platforms and staircases, influenced the architectural designs of subsequent Mesoamerican civilizations. Examples include the pyramids of Chichen Itza and Tenochtitlan.

Use of Carved Stone: The Toltecs' expertise in working with stone, particularly their use of intricately carved stone facades and sculptures, set a standard that influenced the construction and decoration of temples and palaces in neighboring cities.

Writing and Glyphs:

The Toltecs had a sophisticated system of writing and glyphic representation, which had a cascading effect on the development of written communication in the region:

Glyph Adoption: Neighboring civilizations adopted and adapted Toltec writing systems and glyphs, contributing to the spread of literacy and record-keeping. This influenced the development of writing among the Maya and Aztecs.

Record-Keeping: The use of glyphs for record-keeping, historical accounts, and religious texts became a common practice among Mesoamerican cultures. The preservation of historical records and codices owed much to Toltec precedents.

Urban Planning and Governance:

Toltec urban planning and governance practices served as models for neighboring civilizations:

City Layout: The layout of Toltec cities, with central plazas, temples, and ball courts, influenced the urban planning of cities like Tenochtitlan, the capital of the Aztec Empire.

Political Organization: The Toltecs' hierarchical political structure and administration left a blueprint for how neighboring city-states organized their governments and distributed power.

Trade Networks:

The Toltecs' control over vital trade routes contributed to economic prosperity and cultural exchange in the region:

Trade Routes: The extensive trade networks established by the Toltecs facilitated the exchange of goods, ideas, and culture throughout Mesoamerica. These networks continued to thrive and connect distant regions.

Economic Exchange: Economic exchange along these routes allowed for the circulation of valuable resources, including obsidian, jade, textiles, and agricultural products, enhancing the prosperity of neighboring civilizations.

Historical and Mythological Influence:

Toltec history and mythology also left a lasting mark on the narratives and legends of their neighbors:

Historical Accounts: Toltec historical accounts and legends, such as the migration of the Toltecs from Tula, became woven into the historical narratives of the Aztecs and Maya.

Mythological Figures: Toltec mythological figures, including Quetzalcoatl and Tlaloc, featured prominently in the pantheons of neighboring civilizations, often with adaptations and variations.

Legacy and Enduring Influence:

The influence of the Toltecs endured long after their civilization faced decline and collapse:

Artistic Continuity: Elements of Toltec art and iconography persisted in the artistic expressions of later civilizations, connecting the cultural threads of Mesoamerica through the ages.

Religious Continuity: Toltec religious practices and deities remained relevant in the spiritual beliefs of their successors, adding depth and complexity to Mesoamerican religion.

Historical Memory: The historical memory of the Toltecs as a powerful and influential civilization continued to shape the narratives and identities of subsequent Mesoamerican cultures.

In summary, the Toltecs' influence on neighboring civilizations in Mesoamerica was multifaceted and enduring. Their cultural exchange, architectural innovations, writing systems, urban planning, trade networks, and historical narratives left an indelible mark on the region's history. The legacy of the Toltecs can be seen not only in the tangible artifacts and structures but also in the cultural and spiritual fabric of Mesoamerican civilization, reminding us of the interconnectedness of ancient cultures in the Americas.

The Toltec civilization, which thrived from the 10th to the 12th century CE in Mesoamerica, was a dominant force in the region, known for its cultural achievements, military prowess, and territorial expansion. However, like all great civilizations, the Toltecs faced numerous challenges during their existence. These challenges, whether internal or external, contributed to the eventual decline of their power and influence. Next, we will explore the various challenges that the Toltecs encountered and how they impacted the civilization.

Internal Challenges:

Political Instability: One of the internal challenges the Toltecs faced was political instability. The Toltec state was not immune to power struggles and internal conflicts. Competition for leadership and control within the ruling elite could lead to fragmentation and weakening of central authority.

Resource Depletion: As the Toltec civilization expanded, the demand for resources grew. Over time, this could lead to resource depletion, particularly in regions under Toltec control. Depleted agricultural lands and resource scarcity could strain the economy and lead to social unrest.

Social Inequality: Inequalities in wealth and social status could create tensions within Toltec society. As with many ancient civilizations, a small elite class may have controlled a significant portion of resources and power, while the majority of the population faced economic and social disparities.

Environmental Factors: Environmental challenges, such as droughts, crop failures, or other natural disasters, could have had adverse effects on agriculture and food production. These challenges might have contributed to food shortages and population pressures.

External Challenges:

Conflict with Neighboring Civilizations: The Toltecs' territorial expansion often brought them into conflict with neighboring city-states and civilizations. Warfare, while a source of power and tribute, also posed risks. Protracted conflicts could drain resources and weaken the Toltec state.

Pressure from Nomadic Groups: The region surrounding the Toltec heartland was inhabited by various nomadic groups, some of which were hostile. These nomadic groups could raid Toltec settlements, disrupt trade routes, and create security challenges.

Trade and Economic Disruption: The Toltecs' control over trade networks made them vulnerable to disruptions in trade routes. Economic challenges, including trade interruptions or changing economic dynamics, could affect the stability of the Toltec state.

Rebellion of Vassal States: Vassal states, while providing tribute and military support to the Toltecs, were not always content with their status. Rebellion or resistance from vassal states could strain the Toltec's ability to maintain control over their territories.

Cultural and Religious Challenges:

Religious and Ideological Shifts: Cultural and religious shifts within the Toltec society or among their subjects could pose challenges. Changes in religious practices, beliefs, or ideological shifts might undermine traditional sources of authority.

Syncretism and Cultural Exchange: While cultural exchange enriched Mesoamerican civilizations, it also presented challenges to traditional identities. The blending of cultures and religious beliefs through syncretism could create cultural complexities and challenges.

Decline and Legacy:

The challenges faced by the Toltecs eventually contributed to the decline of their civilization. By the 12th century CE, the once-mighty Toltec state had collapsed, and their capital city of Tula was abandoned. While the exact reasons for their decline are still a subject of debate among historians, it is clear that a combination of internal and external factors played a role.

Despite their decline, the Toltecs left a lasting legacy in Mesoamerica. Their influence on neighboring civilizations, including the Aztecs and Maya, continued long after their fall. Elements of Toltec culture, art, religion, and urban planning endured and shaped the civilizations that succeeded them. The challenges they faced served as lessons for future Mesoamerican societies, contributing to the ever-evolving mosaic of the region's history.

In summary, the Toltec civilization, while powerful and influential, faced a range of challenges, both internal and external, that ultimately contributed to its decline. These challenges included political instability, resource depletion, conflicts with neighbors, environmental factors, and cultural shifts. Despite their fall, the Toltecs' legacy endured in the cultures of their successors, underscoring the complex interplay of factors that shape the rise and fall of civilizations in Mesoamerica and beyond.

Chapter 7: The Last Stand: The Decline and Legacy of the Toltec Empire (1200 CE and Beyond)

The Toltec civilization, known for its cultural achievements and military prowess, experienced a decline that marked the end of their dominance in Mesoamerica. This decline was influenced by a series of events and factors that gradually weakened the Toltec state. Next, we will explore the events leading to the Toltec decline and their significance.

1. Environmental Challenges:

Droughts and Agricultural Difficulties: Environmental factors, such as prolonged droughts and unpredictable weather patterns, affected agriculture. Crop failures and reduced food production put pressure on the Toltec society, leading to shortages and social unrest.

2. Political Instability:

Leadership Struggles: Internal political conflicts and power struggles among the Toltec elite weakened central authority. Rivalry for leadership and succession disputes could result in fragmentation and division within the ruling class.

3. External Conflicts:

Conflict with Chichimecs: The Toltecs faced ongoing conflicts with Chichimec nomadic groups in the region. These conflicts disrupted trade routes, threatened settlements, and diverted resources away from central governance.

4. Decline of Tula:

Abandonment of Tula: Tula, the Toltec capital, was abandoned around the 12th century CE. The reasons for its abandonment are debated among historians, but factors like resource depletion, political instability, and external threats likely contributed.

5. Migration and Exodus:

Toltec Migration Legends: Toltec migration legends suggest that a significant portion of the Toltec population migrated from Tula. These migrations may have been driven by a combination of factors, including conflicts and resource scarcity.

6. Rebellion of Vassal States:
Rebellious Vassals: Some vassal states under Toltec control rebelled against their overlords. These uprisings could have strained the Toltec's ability to maintain control over their territories.

7. Economic Disruption:
Trade Disruptions: Disruptions in trade networks and changing economic dynamics could have affected the Toltec state's prosperity. Economic challenges might have contributed to their decline.

8. Cultural Changes:
Religious and Cultural Shifts: Changes in religious practices, beliefs, and cultural shifts could have weakened traditional sources of authority and identity. Toltec culture and religious beliefs may have undergone transformations.

9. Impact on Successor Civilizations:
Legacy of the Toltecs: Despite their decline, the Toltecs left a lasting legacy in Mesoamerica. Elements of their culture, art, and religion persisted and influenced successor civilizations, including the Aztecs and Maya.

10. Historical Debate:
Debate Among Historians: The exact causes of the Toltec decline remain a subject of debate among historians. While some emphasize environmental factors, others point to political and social instability, external pressures, and migrations.

In summary, the decline of the Toltec civilization was a complex process influenced by a combination of internal and external factors. Environmental challenges, political instability, conflicts with neighboring groups, and migrations all played a role in the gradual weakening of the Toltec state. Despite their decline, the Toltecs' legacy continued to shape the cultures and societies of Mesoamerica, underscoring the enduring impact of their civilization.

The Toltec civilization, which thrived in Mesoamerica from roughly the 10th to the 12th century CE, left a profound and enduring legacy that continued to influence subsequent Mesoamerican cultures. While the Toltec civilization experienced a decline, its cultural, artistic, and religious contributions persisted and significantly impacted the civilizations that succeeded it, most notably the Aztecs and the Maya. Next, we will explore the legacy of the Toltec civilization.

1. Art and Architecture:

Influence on Aztec Architecture: Toltec architectural styles, characterized by pyramids and temples, influenced the architecture of the Aztec Empire. The Aztecs adopted Toltec designs and incorporated them into their own monumental structures.

2. Religion and Deities:

Quetzalcoatl Worship: The Toltecs' reverence for the feathered serpent deity Quetzalcoatl left a lasting mark on Mesoamerican religion. The cult of Quetzalcoatl continued among the Aztecs, who also integrated this deity into their pantheon.

3. Toltec Myths and Legends:

Transmission of Legends: Toltec myths and legends, including stories about the legendary ruler Ce Acatl Topiltzin Quetzalcoatl, were passed down to subsequent Mesoamerican cultures. These narratives enriched the mythologies of the Aztecs and Maya.

4. Artistic Traditions:

Toltec Artistry: Toltec artistic traditions, including pottery, sculpture, and mural painting, influenced the artistic expressions of the Aztecs. The Aztecs borrowed and adapted Toltec artistic styles and techniques.

5. Urban Planning and Infrastructure:

City Layout: The Toltec city of Tula featured well-planned urban infrastructure and layouts. Elements of Toltec urban planning influenced the design and organization of later Mesoamerican cities, particularly those of the Aztecs.

6. Warfare and Military Practices:

Military Strategies: The Toltecs' military strategies and tactics were adopted and adapted by subsequent Mesoamerican civilizations, such as the Aztecs. The Aztecs learned from the Toltecs' military prowess.

7. Influence on Maya Civilization:

Maya-Toltec Interactions: Interaction between the Toltecs and the Maya influenced Maya culture, particularly during the Postclassic period. Elements of Toltec art, religion, and symbolism can be observed in Maya sites like Chichen Itza.

8. Symbolism and Glyphs:

Toltec Symbolism: Toltec symbols and glyphs found in art and inscriptions contributed to the development of Mesoamerican writing systems. Elements of Toltec visual language can be seen in later Mesoamerican scripts.

9. Cultural Exchange and Syncretism:

Cultural Blending: The Toltecs engaged in cultural exchanges with neighboring civilizations. This exchange of ideas, beliefs, and practices led to cultural syncretism, enriching the cultural tapestry of Mesoamerica.

10. Historical Legacy: - Historical Record: The Toltec civilization left behind a historical record that has fascinated scholars and archaeologists. Studies of Toltec history and culture continue to shed light on Mesoamerican civilizations.

In summary, the Toltec civilization's legacy is an integral part of Mesoamerican history. While their political power declined, their cultural, artistic, and religious contributions endured and influenced subsequent civilizations, including the Aztecs and the Maya. The enduring impact of the Toltec civilization underscores the interconnectedness of Mesoamerican cultures and the importance of cultural transmission in shaping the region's rich history.

BOOK 6
AZTEC ASCENDANCY
FROM HUMBLE BEGINNINGS TO IMPERIAL MIGHT (1325 CE - 1521 CE)

BY A.J. KINGSTON

Chapter 1: The Founding of Tenochtitlan: Birth of the Aztec Empire (1325 CE - 1400 CE)

The Legend of the Eagle and the Serpent is a profound and symbolic tale deeply rooted in Mesoamerican mythology and history. This mythological narrative holds significant cultural and religious importance, as it reflects the complex beliefs and cosmology of indigenous peoples in the region, particularly the Aztecs and other Nahuatl-speaking groups.

At its core, the legend revolves around the struggle between two powerful forces: the eagle and the serpent. These two creatures are richly symbolic and represent contrasting aspects of Mesoamerican worldview and spirituality.

The eagle, often depicted with outstretched wings and fierce determination, represents the celestial realm and the sun. In Mesoamerican cultures, the sun was a central deity, associated with light, warmth, and life itself. It was believed that the sun god, Huitzilopochtli among the Aztecs, embarked on a daily journey across the sky, battling the forces of darkness and chaos.

On the other hand, the serpent symbolizes the underworld and the earth. The serpent's association with the earth reflects its connection to fertility and rebirth. In Mesoamerican cosmology, the earth was viewed as a living entity that required nourishment and care to sustain life and crops. Additionally, the serpent was linked to water, another essential element for agriculture and survival.

The legend unfolds as a cosmic battle between the eagle and the serpent, a reflection of the eternal struggle between light and darkness, life and death. This battle was believed to play out in the heavens and on earth, shaping the destiny of humanity.

One of the most iconic representations of this myth is found on the Mexican national emblem. The legend tells of the founding of Tenochtitlan, the ancient Aztec capital, in the 14th century. According to Aztec tradition, their god Huitzilopochtli guided them to establish their city at a location where they would witness a divine sign: an eagle perched on a cactus, devouring a serpent.

This symbol, known as the "Eagle on a Cactus," served as a divine directive for the Aztecs, signifying the chosen site for their great city. The legend reinforced their belief that they were destined for greatness and that their civilization was favored by the gods.

The symbolism of the eagle and the serpent extended beyond this founding myth. It was interwoven into various aspects of Aztec life, from religious ceremonies to the design of temples and artifacts. The eagle and serpent motif adorned temples and altars, emphasizing the connection between the celestial and earthly realms.

In addition to the Aztecs, the legend of the eagle and the serpent had variations in other Mesoamerican cultures, such as the Maya. In Maya cosmology, the eagle and the serpent also represented opposing forces in the natural world. They featured in stories, codices, and inscriptions, offering insights into Maya beliefs about creation and the cosmos.

The enduring significance of this legend is evident in its continued presence in Mexican and Mesoamerican culture today. The image of the eagle devouring the serpent remains a potent symbol of Mexican national identity, depicted on the Mexican flag and coins. It serves as a reminder of the rich cultural tapestry of Mesoamerica and the enduring legacy of its myths and beliefs.

Moreover, the legend has inspired artists, writers, and scholars, who have sought to explore its deeper meanings and cultural resonances. It invites contemplation on the duality of existence, the cyclical nature of life and death, and the eternal struggle between opposing forces in the natural world.

In summary, the Legend of the Eagle and the Serpent is a profound and enduring narrative in Mesoamerican mythology. It encapsulates the complex worldview and spiritual beliefs of indigenous peoples in the region, emphasizing the symbolic significance of the eagle as a celestial force and the serpent as an earthly one. This legend continues to be a source of inspiration and cultural pride in modern Mexico and serves as a testament to the enduring legacy of Mesoamerican heritage.

The early history of the Aztecs, also known as the Mexica, is a saga of resilience, migration, and conquest that eventually led to the establishment of one of the most formidable empires in Mesoamerican history. Their journey from humble beginnings to imperial might is a testament to their adaptability, determination, and capacity for transformation.

The story of the Aztecs begins with their mythical origin. According to Aztec legend, their god Huitzilopochtli guided them from their ancestral homeland of Aztlan to the Valley of Mexico, where they would establish their capital, Tenochtitlan. This migration, known as the "Wandering of the Aztecs," is a foundational element of Aztec identity and history. It is a tale of hardship and perseverance, as the Aztecs faced numerous challenges during their journey.

Arriving in the Valley of Mexico in the early 14th century, the Aztecs encountered a region already inhabited by other Mesoamerican peoples, including the Nahua-speaking inhabitants of Culhuacan and the dominant power of Tlatelolco. Initially, the Aztecs were considered a marginalized and subordinate group in this complex geopolitical landscape. They were forced to pay tribute and provide labor to their more powerful neighbors.

Despite their initial hardships, the Aztecs were far from passive victims. They were skilled farmers, using innovative agricultural techniques such as chinampas, or "floating gardens," to cultivate crops on the marshy shores of Lake Texcoco. These productive farming methods allowed them to sustain their growing population.

The Aztecs' ability to adapt and navigate complex political alliances played a crucial role in their early struggles. They formed alliances with other Nahua-speaking groups in the region, such as the city-state of Texcoco, which provided military and political support. Through these alliances, they gradually increased their influence and standing in the Valley of Mexico.

One of the most significant turning points in Aztec history was the rise of Moctezuma I (also spelled Montezuma), who became the Aztec ruler in the early 15th century. Moctezuma I expanded the Aztec empire through military conquest and diplomacy. He initiated campaigns to subdue neighboring city-states and exact tribute, further strengthening the Aztec economy and political power.

The Aztec Triple Alliance, formed between Tenochtitlan, Texcoco, and Tlacopan, marked a period of remarkable expansion and consolidation of power. The Triple Alliance engaged in extensive military campaigns, bringing numerous city-states under Aztec control. The tribute collected from these conquered regions enriched the Aztec capital and allowed for the construction of monumental temples and palaces.

One of the most iconic structures of the Aztec empire was the Templo Mayor, a massive temple complex in Tenochtitlan dedicated to the gods Huitzilopochtli and Tlaloc. The construction of such grandiose religious edifices reflected the Aztecs' commitment to their deities and their ambition to establish a powerful empire.

The Aztecs' religious beliefs and practices were deeply intertwined with their political and social life. They practiced human sacrifice as a means of appeasing their gods and ensuring the continued well-being of their empire. The Great Temple, with its dual shrines, served as the epicenter of these rituals, where captives were sacrificed to honor the gods.

The Aztecs' societal structure was hierarchical, with a ruler at the top, followed by nobles, priests, warriors, commoners, and slaves. This class-based society facilitated the organization of labor, construction projects, and the collection of tribute. It also allowed the Aztec rulers to maintain control over the empire.

Despite their military prowess and political achievements, the Aztecs faced internal and external challenges. These challenges included the strain of governing a vast and diverse empire, managing conquered territories, and dealing with the constant threat of rebellion.

Furthermore, the arrival of the Spanish conquistadors, led by Hernán Cortés, in 1519 would prove to be a cataclysmic event in Aztec history. The encounter between the Aztecs and the Spanish, who were technologically superior and had the support of various indigenous allies, would ultimately lead to the downfall of the Aztec empire.

In 1521, after a prolonged siege, Tenochtitlan fell to the Spanish conquistadors, marking the end of the Aztec empire. The conquest had devastating consequences for the Aztec people, as they were subjected to diseases, forced labor, and colonization under Spanish rule.

Despite their tragic end, the legacy of the early Aztecs endures. Their contributions to art, architecture, agriculture, and political organization continue to be studied and appreciated. The Aztecs' indomitable spirit, displayed in their ability to overcome early struggles and build a formidable empire, is a testament to the complexity and resilience of Mesoamerican civilizations.

Chapter 2: Tenochtitlan: The Magnificent Aztec Capital (1400 CE - 1450 CE)

The growth and urban development of the Aztec capital, Tenochtitlan, represent one of the most remarkable achievements in the history of Mesoamerican civilization. From its modest beginnings as a small island settlement in the heart of Lake Texcoco, Tenochtitlan evolved into a sprawling metropolis that rivaled the greatest cities of the Old World.

Tenochtitlan's location was both its greatest advantage and challenge. Situated on a series of small, interconnected islands in Lake Texcoco, the city had to contend with the limitations and opportunities presented by its watery surroundings. The Aztecs ingeniously adapted to this environment by creating artificial islands called chinampas, which functioned as highly productive agricultural plots.

Chinampas were constructed by dredging nutrient-rich mud from the lake bottom and using it to build up rectangular plots of fertile land. These plots were separated by canals, allowing for efficient irrigation and transportation. The chinampas played a pivotal role in sustaining the city's rapidly growing population by providing a consistent supply of maize, beans, squash, and other crops.

To navigate the city's extensive waterways, the Aztecs employed a sophisticated system of canoes and causeways. Canoes were used for transportation within the city and across the lake, making trade and communication between different city-states in the region possible. The causeways, elevated roadways made of soil and stone, connected the city to the mainland and allowed for the movement of people and goods.

Tenochtitlan's urban planning and architectural achievements were awe-inspiring. At its height, the city was adorned with grand temples, palaces, and public buildings that showcased the artistic and engineering prowess of the Aztecs. The most iconic of these structures was the Templo Mayor, a twin-temple complex dedicated to the gods Huitzilopochtli and Tlaloc.

The Templo Mayor was a monumental pyramid that reached a height of approximately 148 feet (45 meters). It consisted of two separate shrines, one for each deity, symbolizing the duality inherent in Aztec cosmology. The temples were adorned with intricate stone carvings, sculptures, and vibrant murals, all of which reflected the religious and mythological beliefs of the Aztec civilization.

The Aztecs were meticulous city planners, dividing Tenochtitlan into districts called calpulli, each with its own administrative and social structure. The city featured well-organized marketplaces, known as tianquiztli, where a vast array of goods, including food, textiles, pottery, and jewelry, were bought and sold. These markets were bustling centers of economic activity and cultural exchange.

The Aztecs also possessed a keen sense of aesthetics and urban design. Gardens, courtyards, and plazas were strategically integrated into the cityscape, providing green spaces for relaxation and recreation. The city's layout followed a grid pattern, with broad avenues and canals crisscrossing the urban center, facilitating both movement and drainage.

The population of Tenochtitlan was estimated to be between 200,000 and 300,000 people at its zenith, making it one of the largest cities in the world during the 15th century. This demographic diversity added to the city's vibrancy and cultural richness. People from different regions and backgrounds converged in Tenochtitlan, contributing to a cosmopolitan atmosphere.

The Aztecs' ability to manage and provide for such a large population was a testament to their advanced agricultural techniques and resource management. However, the rapid growth of the city also presented challenges in terms of infrastructure, sanitation, and public health.

As the city expanded, so did the demand for resources and tribute from the Aztec empire's subject territories. Conquered city-states were required to provide tribute in the form of goods, labor, and captives for sacrifice, which fueled the city's growth and development. The tribute system allowed the Aztecs to amass wealth and resources, which were funneled into the construction of grandiose temples and public works.

Despite its remarkable achievements, Tenochtitlan's fate was sealed with the arrival of the Spanish conquistadors, led by Hernán Cortés, in 1519. The subsequent siege and fall of the city in 1521 marked the end of Aztec civilization and the beginning of Spanish colonial rule.

The legacy of Tenochtitlan lives on in modern-day Mexico City, as the Spanish built their capital, Mexico City, atop the ruins of the Aztec metropolis. Today, archaeological excavations continue to reveal the grandeur and complexity of this once-mighty city, while also shedding light on the resilience and ingenuity of the Aztec people who created it.

The splendors of the Great City, also known as Tenochtitlan, were a testament to the remarkable achievements of the Aztec civilization during its zenith in the 15th century. Situated on a series of small islands in the heart of Lake Texcoco, Tenochtitlan was the capital of the Aztec empire and one of the largest and most impressive cities in the world at the time. Its grandeur lay in its urban planning, architecture, art, and cultural richness.

At the center of the city stood the Templo Mayor, a colossal twin-temple complex dedicated to the deities Huitzilopochtli, the god of war and the sun, and Tlaloc, the god of rain and fertility. The Templo Mayor, also known as the Great Temple, was the spiritual heart of Tenochtitlan and a symbol of the Aztec worldview. It embodied the dualities and cosmological beliefs that permeated Aztec religion and society.

The Templo Mayor's architecture was a marvel of engineering and symbolism. It consisted of two pyramidal structures, each with its own staircase leading to a temple at the summit. The eastern temple was dedicated to Huitzilopochtli, while the western temple honored Tlaloc. The significance of these deities was deeply ingrained in the Aztec culture, representing the opposing forces of war and rain, life and death.

The temples were constructed in the architectural style known as "talud-tablero," characterized by stepped terraces and vertical panels with elaborate sculptural reliefs. These reliefs depicted various mythological and ritualistic scenes, emphasizing the interconnectedness of the natural and supernatural realms. The Templo Mayor was not only a place of worship but also a canvas for the artistic expression of Aztec beliefs.

The Templo Mayor complex was adorned with numerous sculptures and offerings. Colossal stone statues, known as "chacmools," were placed at the base of the stairs, serving as receptacles for offerings and possibly as sacrificial altars. The chacmools were often depicted reclining on their backs, their heads turned to the side, and their chests exposed, suggesting their role in rituals involving offerings or sacrifices.

The Templo Mayor was not the only awe-inspiring structure in Tenochtitlan. The city's layout followed a grid pattern, with wide avenues and canals that intersected at various points. These canals served as both transportation routes and drainage systems, showcasing the Aztecs' engineering expertise in managing their unique island environment.

In addition to the Templo Mayor, Tenochtitlan featured other temples, pyramids, and palaces. One such structure was the Palace of Moctezuma II, the ruler of the Aztec empire during the Spanish conquest. This palace was a sprawling complex adorned with lavish decorations and murals, offering a glimpse into the opulence and sophistication of Aztec court life.

The city also boasted well-organized marketplaces known as "tianquiztli," where a vast array of goods was traded. These markets were vibrant centers of commerce and cultural exchange, attracting traders and visitors from across the region. Aztec artisans and craftsmen showcased their skills in producing exquisite textiles, pottery, jewelry, and other products.

One of the most impressive aspects of Tenochtitlan was its extensive system of chinampas, or "floating gardens." These artificial islands were created by dredging nutrient-rich mud from the lake bottom and piling it onto wooden frames, creating fertile plots for agriculture. The chinampas were a testament to the Aztecs' ingenuity in maximizing food production in a challenging environment.

Tenochtitlan's streets and public spaces were bustling with activity. People from diverse backgrounds and regions converged in the city, contributing to its cosmopolitan atmosphere. The Aztecs themselves hailed from various ethnic groups, reflecting the empire's complex mosaic of cultures and traditions.

The cultural richness of Tenochtitlan extended to its rituals, festivals, and ceremonies. The Aztecs celebrated a multitude of religious and calendrical events throughout the year, many of which were marked by colorful processions, music, dance, and offerings. These rituals reinforced the connections between the people, their deities, and the natural world.

The downfall of Tenochtitlan came with the arrival of the Spanish conquistadors, led by Hernán Cortés, in 1519. The city was subjected to a prolonged siege and ultimately fell to the Spanish forces in 1521. The conquest marked the end of the Aztec empire and the beginning of a new era in the Americas.

Despite the tragic end of Tenochtitlan, its legacy lives on. The ruins of the Templo Mayor and other structures provide valuable insights into the art, architecture, and beliefs of the Aztec civilization. The city's memory is preserved in the vibrant culture of modern-day Mexico City, which was built atop its ancient foundations.

In summary, the splendors of the Great City, Tenochtitlan, were a testament to the ingenuity, artistry, and cultural richness of the Aztec civilization. Its monumental structures, bustling markets, intricate rituals, and cosmopolitan atmosphere showcased the heights of Mesoamerican achievement. While the city's physical grandeur may have faded, its legacy endures as a testament to the resilience and creativity of the Aztec people.

Chapter 3: Aztec Religion and Cosmology (1350 CE - 1500 CE)

The Aztec civilization had a rich and complex pantheon of deities, reflecting their deep connection to the natural world, celestial bodies, and the cycles of life and death. These gods and goddesses played a central role in Aztec religion, culture, and daily life, influencing everything from agriculture to warfare, and they were honored through elaborate rituals and ceremonies.

At the heart of the Aztec pantheon was Huitzilopochtli, the god of war and the sun. He was considered the patron deity of the Aztecs and the protector of their city, Tenochtitlan. Huitzilopochtli was often depicted as a hummingbird or a warrior adorned with feathers and carrying a shield and spear. The Aztecs believed that the sun was a manifestation of this powerful deity, and they offered him human sacrifices to ensure the sun's continued journey across the sky.

Another prominent deity was Tlaloc, the god of rain and fertility. Tlaloc was vital to the agricultural success of the Aztecs, as he was responsible for providing the much-needed rainfall for their crops. He was often depicted with goggle-like eyes and fangs, representing the rainy clouds and the life-giving water. The Aztecs held regular ceremonies and offerings to appease Tlaloc and ensure a bountiful harvest.

Quetzalcoatl, the feathered serpent deity, was a complex figure in Aztec mythology. He was associated with creation, culture, and knowledge, and he played a significant role in the Aztec creation myth. Quetzalcoatl was often depicted as a serpent with vibrant feathers and was considered a benevolent god who brought civilization to humanity. However, his dual nature also included aspects of war and conflict, creating a complex character in Aztec belief.

Tezcatlipoca was another essential deity in the Aztec pantheon. He was the god of destiny, magic, and rulership, often represented as a jaguar or a mirror adorned with smoking obsidian. Tezcatlipoca was believed to control the fate of individuals and nations, and his influence extended to the Aztec rulers and their decisions. He was associated with both creation and destruction, symbolizing the duality of life.

Xipe Totec, the god of agriculture and renewal, held a unique place in Aztec rituals and ceremonies. He was often depicted wearing the flayed skin of a sacrificial victim, symbolizing the shedding of old growth to make way for new life. Xipe Totec was honored during the spring equinox, a time when nature awakened, and the renewal of the agricultural cycle was celebrated.

Coatlicue, the earth goddess and mother of the gods, was a central figure in Aztec cosmology. She was depicted as a woman with a skirt made of snakes, and her name meant "Serpent Skirt." Coatlicue was believed to give birth to the moon, stars, and the god Huitzilopochtli. She embodied the nurturing and destructive aspects of nature, reflecting the cyclical nature of life and death.

Chalchiuhtlicue, the goddess of water and rivers, played a crucial role in ensuring the availability of freshwater for the Aztec people. She was often represented wearing a skirt of blue-green feathers and carrying a water jar. Rituals dedicated to Chalchiuhtlicue were held to seek her favor and ensure an adequate water supply for agriculture and daily life.

Xochiquetzal, the goddess of beauty, love, and flowers, brought a softer and more artistic aspect to the Aztec pantheon. She was often depicted with vibrant flowers and was associated with fertility and the pleasures of life. Xochiquetzal was honored in ceremonies related to love and marriage, and her presence was invoked to bring harmony and beauty into the world.

In addition to these major deities, the Aztec pantheon included countless other gods and goddesses, each with specific domains and attributes. These deities were interconnected, reflecting the intricate web of beliefs and rituals that defined Aztec religion. The Aztecs believed in the constant interaction between the divine and human worlds, and their reverence for their pantheon of deities shaped every aspect of their culture, from art and architecture to agriculture and warfare.

Rituals, sacrifices, and offerings were integral aspects of Aztec religious and cultural life, serving as a means to appease their pantheon of deities, maintain cosmic order, and ensure the well-being of their society. These practices were central to the Aztec worldview and played a significant role in shaping their society and belief system.

Rituals:

Aztec rituals were intricate and highly organized events conducted by priests and other religious specialists. They were performed on a daily, monthly, and annual basis, aligning with the Aztec calendar and celestial events. These rituals ranged from simple household ceremonies to large-scale public events held in temples and plazas.

One of the most crucial rituals was the daily offering of copal incense, where fragrant resin was burned to purify the air and honor the gods. Households conducted this ritual each day, creating a constant connection between individuals and the divine.

Sacrifices:

Sacrifices held a central place in Aztec religious practice, with various forms of offerings made to the gods. The most well-known form was human sacrifice, which was seen as a way to nourish the gods and maintain the cosmic balance. Captives from warfare were often chosen as sacrificial victims, and their deaths were viewed as a sacred duty.

The Templo Mayor in Tenochtitlan was the epicenter of Aztec sacrifices. It had two shrines—one dedicated to Huitzilopochtli, the god of war, and the other to Tlaloc, the god of rain. Human sacrifices took place on these pyramidal structures, with victims ritually slaughtered and their hearts offered to the gods. The sacrificial act was believed to ensure the continuity of the sun's movement across the sky and maintain the world's order.

Animal sacrifices were also common, with specific animals offered to specific deities. For example, eagles and jaguars were often sacrificed to Huitzilopochtli, while turkeys were sacrificed to Xipe Totec, the god of agriculture and renewal. These offerings served both religious and practical purposes, as meat was consumed as part of communal feasts following the sacrifices.

Offerings:

In addition to living beings, the Aztecs made a wide range of offerings to their gods. These offerings included food, textiles, jewelry, pottery, and other valuable items. Offerings were often placed on altars or in specially designated areas within temples. The choice of offerings was tailored to the deity being honored and the specific ritual being performed.

Maize (corn) held particular significance in Aztec culture and was a common offering in agricultural rituals. Maize was seen as a divine gift and a symbol of life and sustenance. Cacao beans, used to make a bitter chocolate drink, were also offered and consumed during sacred ceremonies.

The Aztecs believed that their offerings created a reciprocal relationship with the gods. By giving generously, they hoped to receive blessings, protection, and prosperity in return. The act of offering was a way to maintain harmony between the human and divine realms.

Calendar-Based Rituals:

The Aztec calendar played a crucial role in determining when specific rituals and ceremonies were conducted. They had two main calendars—the 260-day ritual calendar, known as the Tonalpohualli, and the 365-day solar calendar, known as the Xiuhpohualli. Together, these calendars guided the timing of various religious observances and festivals.

One of the most significant calendar-based rituals was the New Fire Ceremony (Toxcatl), held once every 52 years. This grand event marked the end of a 52-year cycle and was a time of purification and renewal. The Aztecs believed that the world could potentially end if the gods were not appeased through this ceremony. A victim, chosen for their beauty and purity, was sacrificed to ensure the continuation of the cosmic order.

Festivals and Celebrations:

The Aztecs celebrated a wide range of festivals and ceremonies throughout the year. These events were often dedicated to specific deities and were marked by colorful processions, music, dance, and feasting. Some festivals honored agricultural deities to ensure a successful harvest, while others celebrated celestial events or historical anniversaries.

The Feast of Huitzilopochtli, known as Panquetzaliztli, was an important celebration in honor of the god of war. It featured a reenactment of Huitzilopochtli's birth and the construction of a special reed effigy adorned with offerings.

The Tlacaxipehualiztli festival paid tribute to Xipe Totec and involved gladiatorial combat and the wearing of the flayed skin of sacrificial victims to symbolize renewal and rebirth.

In summary, rituals, sacrifices, and offerings were foundational elements of Aztec religious and cultural life. They served as a means to maintain a connection with the gods, seek their favor, and ensure the well-being of the Aztec civilization. These practices were deeply ingrained in the Aztec worldview and contributed to the complex tapestry of their society, where the divine and the earthly were intricately intertwined.

Chapter 4: The Aztec Triple Alliance: Expansion and Conquest (1428 CE - 1492 CE)

The formation of the Triple Alliance was a pivotal event in the history of the Aztec civilization, marking a strategic and political alliance between three powerful city-states: Tenochtitlan, Texcoco, and Tlacopan. This alliance not only laid the foundation for the Aztec Empire but also had far-reaching implications for the Mesoamerican region as a whole. The formation of this alliance was the culmination of intricate political maneuvering, military prowess, and a shared vision of regional dominance.

Background and Context:

Before the establishment of the Triple Alliance, the region of Mesoamerica was characterized by a patchwork of city-states, each vying for dominance and often engaging in conflicts with one another. Among these city-states, Tenochtitlan, Texcoco, and Tlacopan emerged as major players in the late 14th and early 15th centuries.

Tenochtitlan: Tenochtitlan, founded in 1325 on an island in Lake Texcoco, rapidly grew in power and influence. It was the capital of the Mexica (or Aztec) people, and their warrior elite, known as the Mexica, were expanding their territory through military conquests.

Texcoco: Texcoco, situated to the northeast of Tenochtitlan, was a highly cultured city-state known for its intellectual achievements, including the development of a sophisticated writing system. Its ruler, Nezahualcoyotl, was a key figure in the formation of the Triple Alliance.

Tlacopan: Tlacopan, located to the west of Tenochtitlan, was a smaller city-state but played a critical role in the alliance. Its ruler, Totoquihuatzin, was a close ally of the Mexica.

The Political Landscape:

At the time, the region was characterized by shifting alliances, rivalries, and conflicts. The Mexica, under the leadership of their ruler Itzcoatl and his adviser Tlacaelel, sought to expand their influence and gain control over neighboring city-states.

The Role of Tlacaelel: Tlacaelel, the chief adviser to Itzcoatl and later Montezuma I, was a key architect of the Triple Alliance. He advocated for a more centralized and aggressive approach to expanding Mexica power. He also promoted the idea that the Mexica were destined to rule over other city-states, framing it as a divine mandate.

Alliance Formation:

The Triple Alliance took shape gradually, with a series of events and strategic decisions contributing to its establishment.

Conquest of Texcoco: In 1418, the Mexica launched a successful military campaign against Texcoco, led by Itzcoatl and Tlacaelel. This conquest brought Texcoco under Mexica control, but instead of imposing direct rule, the Mexica established a puppet ruler, Nezahualcoyotl, who was sympathetic to their cause.

Tlacopan's Involvement: Tlacopan, under the rule of Totoquihuatzin, joined forces with Tenochtitlan and Texcoco in a military campaign against the city-state of Azcapotzalco in 1428. This campaign, known as the Battle of Azcapotzalco, was a pivotal moment. The three city-states defeated Azcapotzalco and established a joint ruling council, effectively forming the Triple Alliance.

Shared Vision: The formation of the alliance was not just about military conquest; it also reflected a shared vision of regional dominance. The rulers of Tenochtitlan, Texcoco, and Tlacopan recognized that by working together, they could strengthen their positions, consolidate their power, and exert control over neighboring city-states.

Structure of the Triple Alliance:

The Triple Alliance was governed by a complex set of arrangements. Each city-state retained its autonomy, but they came together for matters of mutual interest, particularly military campaigns and tribute collection.

Tribute System: The conquered city-states were required to pay tribute to the Triple Alliance, which included goods, resources, and even human sacrifices. Tribute was collected systematically and redistributed among the members of the alliance.

Leadership and Decision-Making: The leadership of the alliance was rotational, with each member taking turns to hold the position of "Huey Tlatoani," or Great Speaker. This system ensured that power was shared among the three city-states.

Conquests and Expansion:

With the Triple Alliance in place, the Mexica-led coalition embarked on a series of military campaigns to expand their territory and influence. These campaigns extended as far south as present-day Guatemala and involved the subjugation of numerous city-states.

Cultural Exchange: The alliance also facilitated cultural exchange among the member city-states. Texcoco's cultural contributions, including poetry and philosophy, influenced the Mexica and enriched their civilization. Similarly, Tlacopan played a role in the spread of cultural practices within the alliance.

The Aztec military campaigns represent a significant chapter in the history of Mesoamerica, characterized by the expansionist ambitions of the Mexica civilization, which was centered in the city of Tenochtitlan. These campaigns, carried out with remarkable strategy and ferocity, allowed the Aztecs to extend their influence and dominance over a vast region of present-day Mexico and beyond.

Early Aztec Military Structure:

Before delving into specific campaigns, it's essential to understand the organization and structure of the Aztec military. The Aztec military was a highly disciplined and organized force, with a clear hierarchy and specialized units.

Leadership: At the helm of the military was the supreme ruler of the Aztec Empire, known as the Huey Tlatoani. Beneath the Huey Tlatoani were military commanders and officers, responsible for planning and executing campaigns.

Warriors: The backbone of the Aztec military consisted of the eagle and jaguar warriors, elite warrior societies known for their combat prowess and bravery. These warriors underwent rigorous training from a young age, and their status was a source of pride.

Auxiliary Troops: In addition to the eagle and jaguar warriors, the Aztec army included conscripted commoners, archers, and specialized units like slingers and spear-throwers.

Campaigns of Expansion:

The Aztec campaigns of expansion can be divided into several key phases, each marked by specific conquests and territorial gains.

Conquest of Nearby City-States: The Aztecs began their expansionist endeavors by subjugating nearby city-states and tribes. One of the earliest conquests was that of the city-state of Texcoco, which was brought under Aztec control in the late 14th century. This marked the beginning of the Triple Alliance, a strategic alliance between Tenochtitlan, Texcoco, and Tlacopan, which played a crucial role in subsequent campaigns.

Xochimilco and Tepanecs: The Aztecs continued to expand their territory by conquering the city-state of Xochimilco and the Tepanec confederacy. These conquests extended Aztec influence over the Valley of Mexico and solidified their control over key trade routes and resources.

Southern Conquests: With the southern expeditions, the Aztecs ventured into more distant territories. They conquered the region of Morelos and extended their control southward, eventually reaching the present-day state of Guerrero. These campaigns allowed the Aztecs to secure access to valuable resources such as cotton and cacao.

Expansion to the Gulf Coast: The Aztec Empire's expansion was not limited to the central highlands. They embarked on campaigns to the Gulf Coast, subjugating regions like Tuxpan and Veracruz. The capture of coastal regions facilitated maritime trade and allowed the Aztecs to import luxury goods from distant lands.

Conquests Beyond Borders: The zenith of Aztec expansionism came with campaigns that extended beyond their borders. In the early 15th century, Aztec forces, under the leadership of Itzcoatl and Montezuma I, reached as far south as Guatemala, conquering city-states like Coatzacoalcos and Soconusco. These campaigns not only brought additional tributary states under Aztec control but also allowed them to access coveted goods like cacao and quetzal feathers.

Tribute and Alliance Building: The Aztec campaigns were not solely about conquest. They were also aimed at collecting tribute from the subjugated regions. Tribute included various goods, resources, and even human sacrifices, which played a central role in Aztec religious rituals. The Aztecs skillfully used a combination of military force and diplomacy to establish tributary relationships and alliances with neighboring city-states.

Challenges and Resistance:

While the Aztec military was successful in many of its campaigns, it faced resistance from various quarters. Some city-states, like Tlaxcala, put up fierce resistance and remained independent of Aztec rule. Additionally, the expansion brought the Aztecs into contact with other Mesoamerican civilizations, leading to conflicts and rivalries.

The Fall of the Aztec Empire:

The story of the Aztec military campaigns ultimately culminated in the arrival of Spanish conquistadors led by Hernán Cortés in 1519. The clash between the advanced weaponry and tactics of the Spaniards and the indigenous forces, coupled with the devastating impact of European diseases, led to the fall of the Aztec Empire in 1521.

Legacy of Aztec Military Campaigns:

The legacy of the Aztec military campaigns is complex and multifaceted. While the Aztecs are often remembered for their expansionism and militarism, they also made significant contributions to the cultural and intellectual heritage of Mesoamerica. Their empire, which emerged from these campaigns, was characterized by a rich and complex society with sophisticated art, architecture, and religious practices. Today, the Aztec civilization is a testament to the complexities of history, where military conquests were interwoven with cultural achievements and enduring legacies.

Chapter 5: Everyday Life in the Aztec Empire (1450 CE - 1520 CE)

The Aztec social structure was a complex and hierarchical system that played a crucial role in shaping the society of the Aztec Empire. At the top of this structure was the emperor, known as the Huey Tlatoani, who held absolute power and authority over the empire. Below the emperor were various social classes and groups, each with its own roles, responsibilities, and privileges.

The Emperor (Huey Tlatoani): At the pinnacle of Aztec society was the emperor, who served as both the political and religious leader of the empire. The emperor was believed to be the intermediary between the gods and the people and was responsible for overseeing all aspects of governance, including the military, justice, and tribute collection.

The Noble Class (Pipiltin): Below the emperor, the noble class, known as the pipiltin, held significant power and privilege. This class was composed of the highest-ranking nobles and their families, who often held important administrative positions within the empire. They were entitled to wear distinctive clothing, live in luxurious homes, and receive tribute from commoners.

Commoners (Macehualtin): The majority of the Aztec population belonged to the commoner class, known as the macehualtin. This class was further divided into several categories based on occupation and wealth. Commoners included farmers, artisans, traders, and laborers. While they had various rights and responsibilities, they also paid tribute to the nobility and the state.

Slaves (Tlacotin): At the lowest rung of Aztec society were the slaves, known as tlacotin. Slavery was common in Aztec society, and individuals could become slaves as a result of war, debt, or as punishment for certain crimes. Slaves performed various labor-intensive tasks, including agricultural work, construction, and household chores.

Priesthood (Tlamacazqueh): The priesthood played a central role in Aztec society, as religion was deeply integrated into daily life. Priests held significant authority and were responsible for conducting religious ceremonies, making offerings to the gods, and interpreting omens and signs. They also played a role in educating the nobility and commoners about religious beliefs and rituals.

Warriors: The Aztec warrior class consisted of elite warriors who belonged to specialized warrior societies, such as the eagle and jaguar warriors. These warriors were highly respected and often received honors, land grants, and tribute from conquered territories. Their primary duty was to defend the empire and expand its borders through military campaigns.

Merchants (Pochteca): Merchants, known as pochteca, formed a unique social group in Aztec society. They were responsible for long-distance trade and played a crucial role in connecting the Aztec Empire with other Mesoamerican cultures. Pochteca had their own organization and were skilled negotiators and diplomats.

Women: While men held most of the prominent roles in Aztec society, women also played essential roles in the family and community. Women were responsible for tasks such as weaving, cooking, and childcare. Noblewomen had more privileges and could own property, but their roles were still largely defined by traditional gender roles.

Children and Education: Aztec children received education primarily at home, where they learned practical skills, moral values, and the customs of their society from their parents. Noble children had access to more formal education, often provided by priests or specialized tutors. Education focused on history, religion, and practical skills.

Social Mobility: While the Aztec social structure was generally rigid, there were some opportunities for social mobility. Exceptional commoners or warriors could earn noble status through acts of bravery in battle or significant contributions to society. Additionally, some individuals from conquered regions could rise in status over time.

The Aztec social structure was intricately tied to the empire's religious and political systems. It played a vital role in maintaining social order and ensuring the smooth functioning of

Aztec society. While the noble class and the emperor held significant power, the commoners, priests, and warriors all played essential roles in the empire's prosperity and expansion. This complex social structure contributed to the rich tapestry of Aztec civilization, which remains a source of fascination and study in the present day.

Agriculture and the economy were the backbone of the Aztec civilization, providing the necessary sustenance and resources to support the empire's population and complex society. The Aztecs developed sophisticated agricultural practices and a thriving economic system that allowed their civilization to flourish.

Agriculture: Aztec agriculture was highly advanced and adaptable to the diverse landscapes of their empire, which ranged from highland plateaus to lowland tropical areas. They employed various agricultural techniques to maximize crop yields and ensure food security.

1. Chinampas: One of the most innovative agricultural techniques employed by the Aztecs was the use of chinampas, artificial farming plots created on the shallow waters of Lake Texcoco and other water bodies. These rectangular plots were constructed by dredging nutrient-rich mud from the lake bottom and building them into raised beds, separated by canals. Chinampas were incredibly fertile, allowing for the cultivation of a variety of crops such as maize, beans, squash, and chili peppers.

2. Terracing: In the mountainous regions of the Aztec empire, terracing was employed to create flat agricultural surfaces on steep slopes. These stepped platforms allowed for the cultivation of crops like maize and agave.

3. Crop Diversity: The Aztecs cultivated a wide range of crops, with maize (corn) being the most essential staple. Maize formed the basis of their diet and was used to make tortillas, tamales, and other foods. Other important crops included beans, squash, amaranth, chia, and tomatoes. The cultivation of a variety of crops helped ensure a balanced diet and reduced the risk of food shortages.

4. Crop Rotation: To maintain soil fertility, the Aztecs practiced crop rotation, alternating between different crops in the same fields to prevent soil depletion.

Economy: The Aztec economy was a complex and diversified system that included various forms of economic activity, trade networks, and tribute collection.

1. Tribute System: A significant part of the Aztec economy was the tribute system. Conquered regions and city-states were required to pay tribute in the form of goods, labor, or military service to the Aztec capital, Tenochtitlan. Tribute was collected regularly and helped sustain the empire.

2. Trade: The Aztecs engaged in both local and long-distance trade, facilitated by a network of specialized merchants known as pochteca. These merchants traveled to distant regions to exchange Aztec goods, such as textiles, obsidian, and luxury items, for goods not available in the Aztec heartland, including cacao, feathers, and precious stones. Trade routes connected the Aztec Empire with other Mesoamerican cultures, allowing for the exchange of valuable commodities.

3. Currency: While the Aztecs did not have a standardized currency like modern coins, they used various forms of currency, including cacao beans and small cotton fabric squares called quachtli. These items were used in trade and as a means of exchange.

4. Markets: Local and regional markets were vital hubs of economic activity in Aztec society. These markets offered a wide range of goods, including food, textiles, pottery, and tools. They also served as places for social interaction and cultural exchange.

5. Craftsmanship: The Aztec economy benefited from skilled artisans who produced a variety of goods, including pottery, jewelry, textiles, and sculptures. Many of these items were used in trade or as tribute to the empire.

6. Agriculture and Tribute: Agriculture played a significant role in the Aztec economy, as it was the primary source of sustenance for the population. Tribute collected from subject regions contributed to the wealth of the empire and supported the ruling elite.

7. Labor: Labor was another essential aspect of the Aztec economy. Commoners and slaves provided the labor force necessary for farming, construction, and various economic activities. The tribute system often included the provision of labor as a form of payment.

8. Wealth Disparities: While the Aztec economy allowed for wealth disparities between social classes, it also promoted social cohesion and stability by ensuring the distribution of goods and resources to the population at large.

In summary, Aztec agriculture and the economy were closely intertwined and fundamental to the civilization's success. Their innovative agricultural techniques, extensive trade networks, tribute system, and diverse economic activities contributed to the empire's prosperity and allowed it to support a complex society with a vast population. The Aztecs' ability to manage and harness their economic resources played a pivotal role in the rise and sustenance of their civilization in ancient Mesoamerica.

Chapter 6: Montezuma and the Arrival of the Spanish (1519 CE)

Montezuma II, also known as Moctezuma Xocoyotzin, was one of the most prominent and complex figures in the history of the Aztec Empire. He reigned as the ninth emperor of the Aztecs, overseeing a period of both grandeur and turmoil during his rule. Montezuma's reign is marked by significant events, including encounters with Spanish conquistadors and the ultimate downfall of the Aztec Empire.

Early Life and Rise to Power: Montezuma was born around 1466, the son of Axayacatl, a previous Aztec ruler, and a noblewoman. He belonged to the noble class of pipiltin and received a comprehensive education that included training in military strategy, religious customs, and governance. His upbringing and education prepared him for a future role as emperor.

In 1502, Montezuma ascended to the throne as emperor of the Aztecs, following the death of his uncle Ahuitzotl. His rule began during a time of relative peace and prosperity for the empire, which had expanded its territories and influence throughout Mesoamerica.

Montezuma's Rule and Achievements: During Montezuma's reign, the Aztec Empire reached its zenith in terms of territorial expansion, military power, and cultural achievements. His rule saw the construction of magnificent temples and buildings in the imperial capital, Tenochtitlan, including the famous Templo Mayor. The empire's tribute system, which required subject regions to provide goods and resources to the capital, flourished under Montezuma's leadership, contributing to the empire's wealth.

Montezuma's reign was also characterized by his dedication to the Aztec religious system. He took on the role of high priest, overseeing important religious ceremonies and rituals, including human sacrifices, which were believed to appease the gods and ensure the empire's prosperity. His religious devotion was integral to the social and political fabric of Aztec society.

Encounters with Spanish Conquistadors: One of the most significant events during Montezuma's reign was the arrival of Spanish conquistadors led by Hernán Cortés in 1519. Initially, Montezuma believed that Cortés might be the god Quetzalcoatl, returning as prophesied. This belief, combined with the Aztec tradition of hospitality to guests, led Montezuma to receive Cortés and his men in a cautious yet accommodating manner.

Over time, however, it became clear that the Spanish were not divine but mortal and that their motives included conquest and the pursuit of riches. Tensions escalated, leading to a captivity of Montezuma by the Spanish in an attempt to control the empire. During his captivity, Montezuma's rule was effectively undermined as the Spanish sought to exert their influence over the Aztec nobility and population.

The Downfall of the Aztec Empire: The situation in Tenochtitlan grew increasingly unstable, with both Aztec nobles and commoners becoming discontented with Montezuma's leadership, viewing him as weak for cooperating with the Spanish. Meanwhile, outside the city, resistance to Spanish rule was growing among other indigenous groups who opposed the conquistadors.

In 1520, a series of events, including the killing of Montezuma by the Spanish or his own people (the exact circumstances remain debated by historians), further escalated tensions. His death marked a turning point in the conflict between the Aztecs and the Spanish. Montezuma's successor, Cuitláhuac, led a fierce resistance against the conquistadors, resulting in a period of intense conflict known as the "Noche Triste" (Sad Night), when the Spanish were driven out of Tenochtitlan.

However, the Spanish, reinforced and equipped with indigenous allies, returned to lay siege to the city. In 1521, after months of battle, Tenochtitlan fell to the Spanish forces, marking the end of the Aztec Empire.

Legacy and Historical Interpretations: Montezuma II's legacy is a subject of ongoing historical debate. Some view him as a wise and capable ruler who was caught in a difficult and complex situation when the Spanish arrived. Others see him as a leader who initially underestimated the threat posed by the conquistadors and whose actions may have contributed to the downfall of the Aztec Empire. Regardless of these debates, Montezuma's reign and his encounters with the Spanish conquistadors remain a pivotal moment in history, representing the collision of two worlds and cultures that would have profound and lasting consequences for Mesoamerica and the Americas as a whole. Montezuma's life and reign continue to be a subject of fascination and exploration in the study of pre-Columbian history.

Hernán Cortés, a Spanish conquistador, led one of the most audacious and consequential expeditions in world history when he embarked on his journey to the New World in the early 16th century. His actions would ultimately result in the downfall of the powerful Aztec Empire and the reshaping of the Americas. Cortés's expedition was marked by ambition, determination, conflict, diplomacy, and cultural exchange.

Cortés was born in 1485 in Medellín, Spain, into a family of lesser nobility. He received a good education and later studied law at the University of Salamanca. However, he abandoned his legal career to seek fortune and adventure in the newly discovered lands of the Americas, setting sail for the Caribbean in 1504.

In 1519, Cortés landed on the coast of what is now Mexico with a small expeditionary force. His primary objective was to explore and establish a presence in the region, following reports of a rich and advanced civilization. Cortés had heard of the Aztecs, and he was driven by a desire for conquest, wealth, and glory.

The first challenge Cortés faced was securing the loyalty of his own men, who were initially divided in their loyalty between him and the appointed governor of Cuba, Diego Velázquez. To prevent his men from deserting, Cortés took bold and risky measures, such as scuttling his own ships to eliminate the option of retreat and emphasizing the potential rewards of the expedition.

Cortés also utilized diplomacy and alliance-building as essential tools of his conquest. He forged alliances with various indigenous groups who were discontented with Aztec rule, capitalizing on existing rivalries and resentments. One of the most important alliances he established was with the Tlaxcala, a powerful city-state that had resisted Aztec dominance. Through alliances, Cortés gained essential allies, warriors, and crucial knowledge about the Aztec Empire.

The encounter between Cortés and the Aztec ruler, Montezuma II, is a pivotal moment in history. Initially, Montezuma welcomed Cortés and his men, believing that Cortés might be a deity or the return of the god Quetzalcoatl, as foretold in Aztec prophecy. This belief, combined with the Aztec tradition of hospitality to guests, led Montezuma to receive Cortés and his men in a cautious yet accommodating manner.

Over time, however, it became clear that the Spanish were not divine beings but mortal invaders. Tensions escalated, and Cortés took Montezuma captive in an attempt to control the Aztec empire. Montezuma's captivity weakened his authority among his people and added to the growing unrest in Tenochtitlan, the Aztec capital.

The conflict between the Spanish and the Aztecs intensified, leading to a series of battles and skirmishes. The Spanish faced significant challenges, including unfamiliar terrain, diseases that devastated both indigenous populations and their own forces, and resource limitations. Despite these challenges, Cortés and his men pressed forward.

In 1521, after months of siege and warfare, Tenochtitlan fell to the Spanish forces. The city was plundered, and Montezuma was killed during the tumultuous events of the conquest. The fall of Tenochtitlan marked the end of the Aztec Empire, and Cortés claimed the region in the name of Spain, naming it New Spain.

Cortés's expedition had far-reaching consequences beyond the conquest of the Aztec Empire. It opened the door for Spanish colonization and exploration throughout the Americas, leading to the exploration of vast territories, the establishment of new settlements, and the spread of European culture, religion, and language.

The Spanish conquest also had profound impacts on indigenous societies, leading to changes in their political, social, and religious systems, as well as the introduction of new diseases and technologies. The fusion of European and indigenous cultures gave rise to a new mestizo identity and a rich blend of traditions, art, and cuisine that continue to shape the Americas today.

Hernán Cortés himself became a symbol of both Spanish heroism and imperial ambition. His legacy remains a topic of historical debate, with some viewing him as a ruthless conquistador responsible for the destruction of indigenous civilizations, while others see him as a visionary explorer who played a pivotal role in shaping the course of history.

In the centuries that followed, the story of Cortés and the Spanish expedition became a symbol of European exploration and colonization, leaving an indelible mark on the history of the Americas and the world.

Chapter 7: The Fall of the Aztec Empire: Conquest and Aftermath (1519 CE - 1521 CE)

The Siege of Tenochtitlan is one of the most significant events in the history of the Americas, marking the climax of the Spanish conquest of the Aztec Empire and the ultimate downfall of the once-mighty Aztec capital. This epic siege, which lasted from May 22, 1521, to August 13, 1521, was a protracted and grueling battle that changed the course of history.

The siege began when Hernán Cortés and his Spanish expeditionary force, along with their indigenous allies, laid siege to Tenochtitlan, the capital of the Aztec Empire. This city, situated on an island in Lake Texcoco, was a marvel of pre-Columbian urban planning and architecture, with grand temples, causeways, and canals crisscrossing the cityscape.

The decision to lay siege to Tenochtitlan was not taken lightly by Cortés. It followed months of skirmishes, diplomatic maneuvering, and strategic planning. The Spanish had initially been welcomed by the Aztec ruler, Montezuma II, who believed Cortés might be a deity or the return of the god Quetzalcoatl. However, relations soured as the Spanish asserted control and Montezuma was taken captive. The Aztecs, resentful of Spanish domination and inspired by the prophecies of their own doom, eventually revolted.

Cortés and his men found themselves besieged within the city, trapped by an Aztec force that greatly outnumbered them. The Spanish, who were already at a disadvantage due to unfamiliar terrain, disease, and resource limitations, now faced the daunting task of breaking the siege or enduring it until reinforcements arrived.

The siege took a heavy toll on both sides. The Spanish and their indigenous allies were subjected to relentless Aztec attacks, often launching deadly raids under the cover of darkness. Meanwhile, the Aztecs endured a prolonged blockade that strained their resources and caused suffering among the civilian population.

Cortés and his men faced numerous challenges during the siege, including the need to secure a reliable source of fresh water, which was vital for their survival. They also constructed brigantines, small sailing vessels, which provided them with a means to control Lake Texcoco and cut off the city's food supplies. Despite the hardships, Cortés and his men persisted, launching a series of assaults on the city's causeways and bridges. These battles were brutal and costly, with both sides suffering heavy casualties. The Spanish used their superior weaponry, including cannons and muskets, to devastating effect, while the Aztecs fought fiercely to defend their home.

One of the pivotal moments of the siege occurred when Cortés decided to attack the heart of Tenochtitlan, the Templo Mayor, a massive pyramid that served as the center of Aztec religious life. This attack, known as the "Noche Triste" or "Sad Night," took place on the night of July 1, 1520. The Spanish succeeded in capturing the temple briefly but were ultimately forced to retreat, suffering significant losses in the process.

Despite this setback, Cortés and his men continued to tighten their grip on the city, blockading it from all sides. The Aztecs, weakened by famine and disease, were running out of options. In a desperate bid to break the siege, they elected a new ruler, Cuauhtémoc, who rallied his forces for a final stand.

The decisive moment of the siege came in early August 1521, when the Spanish launched a final assault on the city. Fierce fighting ensued, but the Spanish gradually gained the upper hand. Cuauhtémoc was captured, and Tenochtitlan fell to the conquistadors.

The fall of Tenochtitlan marked the end of the Aztec Empire and the beginning of Spanish colonial rule in Mexico. The city was plundered, its temples were dismantled, and a new Spanish city, Mexico City, was built on its ruins. The indigenous population endured further hardships under Spanish rule, including forced labor, religious conversion, and the introduction of European diseases.

The Siege of Tenochtitlan had profound and far-reaching consequences. It symbolized the clash of civilizations between the Old World and the New, and it marked the beginning of a new era in the Americas. It also left a lasting legacy on the landscape, culture, and identity of modern-day Mexico, where the memory of the siege continues to be a potent symbol of resilience and resistance.

In summary, the Siege of Tenochtitlan was a momentous event that forever altered the course of history in the Americas. It was a brutal and protracted struggle that tested the resolve and resourcefulness of both the Spanish conquistadors and the Aztec defenders. Ultimately, it was a turning point that reshaped the destiny of an entire continent.

The destruction of the Great City, referring to the magnificent Aztec capital of Tenochtitlan, was a pivotal event in the history of Mesoamerica. It marked the end of the Aztec Empire and the beginning of Spanish colonial rule in the region. The story of the city's destruction is a tale of conquest, conflict, and the clash of two vastly different worlds.

Tenochtitlan, situated on an island in Lake Texcoco, was one of the most remarkable cities of its time. It was characterized by its grand architecture, intricate canal system, and bustling markets. The city's Templo Mayor, a massive pyramid complex, stood as a symbol of Aztec religious and political power. With its impressive causeways and vibrant neighborhoods, Tenochtitlan was a thriving metropolis.

The destruction of Tenochtitlan was set in motion when the Spanish conquistador Hernán Cortés and his expedition arrived in Mesoamerica in 1519. Initially welcomed by the Aztec ruler Montezuma II, Cortés and his men soon revealed their true intentions: to conquer and claim the wealth of the Aztec Empire for Spain. Montezuma's attempt to appease the Spanish with gifts and hospitality ultimately failed, leading to tensions and hostilities.

The turning point came when Cortés, seeking to consolidate his control, took Montezuma hostage within his own palace. This act enraged the Aztec people, who viewed their ruler's captivity as a sign of weakness. The city erupted in violence, with Aztec warriors and commoners uniting to resist the Spanish intrusion.

The situation escalated further when Cortés and his men were forced to leave Tenochtitlan temporarily to deal with a Spanish expedition sent to arrest them. During their absence, a brutal massacre known as the "Noche Triste" (Sad Night) occurred on June 30, 1520. Spanish forces, besieged within the city, attempted to flee but were ambushed by the Aztecs. Many Spanish soldiers were killed, and their looted treasures sank into the canals.

Despite the setback of the Noche Triste, Cortés and his men were determined to return and conquer Tenochtitlan. They regrouped, gathered more indigenous allies who were hostile to the Aztecs, and, crucially, acquired the means to build brigantines, small sailing vessels that allowed them to control Lake Texcoco and isolate the city.

The final assault on Tenochtitlan began in earnest in May 1521. The Spanish and their allies launched a multi-pronged attack, targeting the city's causeways and bridges. These battles were fierce and costly, with both sides suffering heavy casualties. The Spanish, armed with superior weaponry such as cannons and muskets, used their military advantage to devastating effect.

One of the most critical moments of the siege occurred when the Spanish, led by Cortés, launched a determined attack on the Templo Mayor, the heart of Aztec religious life. This was a symbolically significant target, and its capture sent shockwaves through the city. The Aztec warrior Cuauhtémoc, who had become the new ruler, fought valiantly to defend the temple but was ultimately captured.

As the Spanish tightened their grip on Tenochtitlan, the city's fate was sealed. The Aztec defenders, weakened by famine, disease, and relentless combat, could no longer resist the siege. On August 13, 1521, after nearly three months of brutal fighting, the Great City fell to the Spanish.

The fall of Tenochtitlan marked a turning point in history. It symbolized the conquest of the Aztec Empire by the Spanish and the beginning of Spanish colonial rule in Mexico. The city was plundered, its temples were dismantled, and a new Spanish city, Mexico City, was constructed atop its ruins.

The destruction of Tenochtitlan had profound and lasting consequences. It reshaped the cultural and social fabric of the region, as indigenous peoples were subjected to Spanish colonialism and forced conversion to Christianity. The legacy of this conquest, including the blending of indigenous and European cultures, continues to shape Mexico's identity today.

In summary, the destruction of the Great City of Tenochtitlan was a momentous event that altered the course of history in Mesoamerica. It marked the end of the Aztec Empire, the fall of a majestic civilization, and the rise of Spanish dominance in the region. The memory of this event continues to resonate as a symbol of conquest, conflict, and the enduring legacy of the Aztec people.

The legacy of the Aztec conquest, which culminated in the fall of the Aztec Empire and the rise of Spanish colonial rule in Mesoamerica, is a complex and multifaceted one that has had a profound and lasting impact on the history and culture of Mexico and the broader Americas. This legacy can be explored through several key themes and aspects that continue to shape the region to this day.

One of the most significant legacies of the Aztec conquest is the enduring influence of indigenous cultures in Mexico. While the Spanish colonization imposed new institutions, religions, and languages on the indigenous peoples of Mesoamerica, it did not entirely erase their traditions and beliefs. Instead, a process of syncretism occurred, where indigenous and European elements merged and evolved. This blending of cultures is evident in many aspects of Mexican society, including language, religion, art, and cuisine.

One of the most striking examples of this cultural fusion is the melding of indigenous and Catholic religious practices. The Spanish brought Catholicism to the region and built churches on the foundations of former Aztec temples. However, many indigenous communities integrated their pre-Hispanic beliefs with Christian rituals, resulting in unique syncretic forms of worship. The most famous example is the cult of the Virgin of Guadalupe, whose appearance to the indigenous man Juan Diego is seen as a bridge between the old and new faiths. This fusion of religious practices remains a vibrant and integral part of Mexican culture, exemplifying the resilience of indigenous traditions.

Language is another area where the legacy of the Aztec conquest is evident. The Spanish imposed their language on the indigenous population, leading to the gradual decline of many indigenous languages. However, Nahuatl, the language of the Aztecs, survived and is still spoken by over a million people in Mexico today. It has left an indelible mark on Mexican Spanish, with countless loanwords and linguistic influences. Additionally, many indigenous communities throughout Mexico maintain their languages, preserving the linguistic diversity of the region.

The Aztec conquest also left a profound impact on land and resource distribution in Mexico. The Spanish Crown granted vast landholdings, known as encomiendas, to conquistadors and settlers. This system allowed for the exploitation of indigenous labor and resources, leading to the concentration of wealth in the hands of a few. Over time, this unequal distribution of land and resources contributed to social and economic disparities that continue to affect Mexico today.

The introduction of new crops and agricultural practices by the Spanish had a transformative effect on the Mexican landscape and diet. European crops such as wheat, rice, and sugarcane were introduced, alongside livestock such as cattle, pigs, and horses. Conversely, indigenous crops like maize, beans, and chili peppers became staples in Europe and other parts of the world. This exchange of agricultural knowledge, known as the Columbian Exchange, had a profound impact on global food systems and remains a central part of Mexican cuisine.

The legacy of the Aztec conquest is also visible in Mexico's political and administrative structures. The Spanish colonial system established a hierarchical and centralized form of government, which has endured in various forms throughout Mexican history. The modern Mexican state is characterized by a strong presidency and a federal system of government, both of which have their roots in the colonial period.

The Aztec conquest also left an indelible mark on Mexico's physical landscape. The Spanish dismantled and repurposed many indigenous temples and structures to build churches and colonial cities. The historic center of Mexico City, for example, was constructed on the ruins of Tenochtitlan. Today, archaeological excavations and preservation efforts continue to uncover and showcase the rich history buried beneath modern Mexican cities.

Another enduring legacy of the Aztec conquest is the profound impact it had on indigenous demographics and identity. The devastation caused by diseases introduced by the Spanish, such as smallpox, had a catastrophic effect on indigenous populations. Millions of indigenous people died as a result, leading to a demographic collapse. Despite this tragic loss, many indigenous communities persevered, adapting to new circumstances and preserving their cultural heritage. Today, indigenous communities in Mexico are working to revitalize their languages, traditions, and ways of life, reaffirming their resilience in the face of centuries of adversity.

In summary, the legacy of the Aztec conquest is a complex and multifaceted one that continues to shape Mexico and the broader Americas. It is a legacy of cultural fusion, linguistic diversity, economic disparities, and enduring indigenous resilience. While the conquest brought profound changes to the region, it also laid the foundation for the rich tapestry of Mexican culture and history that we see today. It is a testament to the resilience of indigenous peoples and their ability to adapt, endure, and continue to thrive in the face of adversity.

Conclusion

In the pages of "Ancient Mexican History: Olmec, Maya, Teotihuacan, Zapotec, Toltec, & Aztec Civilizations," we have embarked on a captivating journey through the annals of time, delving into the enigmatic past of Mexico's ancient peoples. Across six meticulously researched and vividly detailed volumes, we have explored the rise and fall of remarkable civilizations that once flourished in this dynamic and diverse region.

In "Book 1 - The Enigma of the Olmec," we unraveled the mysteries surrounding Mexico's ancient founders, the Olmec. We delved deep into their art, their monumental sculptures, and their cultural contributions that laid the foundation for Mesoamerican greatness.

"Book 2 - Maya Mastery" transported us to a flourishing civilization that spanned millennia. We uncovered the secrets of the Maya, from their advanced city-states to their celestial observations and intricate hieroglyphics that continue to puzzle and amaze.

"Book 3 - Teotihuacan: City of the Gods" immersed us in the awe-inspiring world of Teotihuacan, with its monumental pyramids, intricate murals, and mysterious decline that has captivated scholars and explorers for centuries.

"Book 4 - Zapotec Resilience" took us on a journey through the rugged landscapes of ancient Oaxaca. We explored Zapotec innovation, their writing system, and their enduring legacy in the heart of Mexico's diverse cultural tapestry.

In "Book 5 - Toltec Warriors," we witnessed the rise and fall of an empire renowned for its military prowess and religious significance. We delved into the world of Quetzalcoatl, the feathered serpent deity, and the Toltec's lasting impact on Mesoamerican history.

Finally, "Book 6 - Aztec Ascendancy" transported us to the heart of the Aztec Empire, from its humble beginnings on a lake to its imperial might that dominated Central Mexico. We followed the conquests of Montezuma and the arrival of the Spanish, which marked a turning point in the region's history.

Throughout this epic journey, we have marveled at the intricate artistry, architecture, and cultural exchanges that defined these civilizations. We've explored their intricate societies, religious practices, and daily lives, gaining a deep appreciation for the rich tapestry of Mesoamerican history.

As we conclude this exploration of ancient Mexican history, we are left with a profound understanding of the enduring legacies these civilizations have left behind. Their contributions to art, science, language, and spirituality continue to shape the vibrant cultures of modern Mexico and the broader world.

In this bundle, we have uncovered the mysteries, triumphs, and challenges of Mexico's ancient past, and in doing so, we've paid homage to the civilizations that forged the foundations of a rich and diverse nation. The echoes of the Olmec, Maya, Teotihuacan, Zapotec, Toltec, and Aztec civilizations still resonate in the present, reminding us of the enduring power of history to inform and inspire our collective future.

About A. J. Kingston

A. J. Kingston is a writer, historian, and lover of all things historical. Born and raised in a small town in the United States, A. J. developed a deep appreciation for the past from an early age. She studied history at the university, earning her degree with honors, and went on to write a series of acclaimed books about different periods and topics in history.

A. J.'s writing is characterized by its clarity, evocative language, and meticulous research. She has a particular talent for bringing the lives of ordinary people in the past to life, drawing on diaries, letters, and other documents to create rich and nuanced portraits of people from all walks of life. Her work has been praised for its deep empathy, its attention to detail, and its ability to make history come alive for readers.

In addition to her writing, A. J. is a sought-after speaker and commentator on historical topics. She has given talks and presentations at universities, museums, and other venues, sharing her passion for history with audiences around the world. Her ability to connect with people and make history relevant to their lives has earned her a devoted following and a reputation as one of the most engaging and insightful historical writers of her generation.

A. J.'s writing has been recognized with numerous awards and honors. She lives in California with her family, and continues to write and speak on historical topics.

Printed in the USA
CPSIA information can be obtained
at www.ICGtesting.com
LVHW020554011123
762694LV00001B/70